Women's Uncommon Prayers

Our Lives Revealed, Nurtured, Celebrated

Editors
Elizabeth Rankin Geitz
Marjorie A. Burke
Ann Smith

Associate Editors
Debra Q. Bennett
Kathryn McCormick
Tracy J. Sukraw

MOREHOUSE PUBLISHING
Harrisburg, Pennsylvania

Morehouse Publishing
4775 Linglestown Road
Harrisburg, PA 17112

Morehouse Publishing is an imprint of Church Publishing Incorporated.

Unless otherwise noted, the Scripture quotations contained herein are from the New Revised Standard Version Bible, copyright © 1989 by the Division of Christian Education of the National Council of Churches of Christ in the U. S. A. Used by permission. All rights reserved.

Passages marked BCP are from *The Book of Common Prayer*, 1979.

"Proper 27" on page 321 is used by permission of Edward B. Marks Music Company.

"Maria Sacerdota—Mary, Protopriest of the New Covenant" on page 287, also known as "Before Jesus," first appeared in Life Prayers, edited by Elizabeth Roberts and Elias Amidon, published 1996 by HarperSanFransisco.

The opening sentences and portions of the final prayer of "Rite for Pregnancy Loss or Stillbirth" on page 348ff. are from *A New Zealand Prayer Book—He Karakia Mihinare o Aotearoa* and are used with permission.

"Liturgy for Divorce" on page 352 is excerpted from *Prayers of Our Hearts: In Word and Action* by Vienna Cobb Anderson. Copyright 1991. All rights reserved. Used with permission of The Crossroad Publishing Company, New York.

The publisher wishes to express gratitude to the copyright holders who have granted permission to include their material in this book. Every effort has been made to trace the owners of existing copyright material; apology is made for any copyright inadvertently omitted.

Printed in the United States of America

Cover design by Trude Brummer

Library of Congress Cataloging-in-Publication Data

Women's uncommon prayers: our lives revealed, nurtured, celebrated / editors, Elizabeth R. Geitz, Marjorie A. Burke, Ann Smith; associate editors, Debra Q. Bennett, Kathryn McCormick, Tracy J. Sukraw.
    p. cm.
  ISBN-13: 978-0-8192-1864-3
    1. Women—Prayer-books and devotions—English. I. Geitz, Elizabeth Rankin. II. Burke, Marjorie A. III. Smith, Ann, 1942–

BV283.W6 W68 2000
242'.843—dc21
    00-029226

Spirit of Christ, visit us and draw out our exquisite female essence, that we may exude the strength of tenderness, the power of humility, the mercy of redemptive suffering, and the joy of unearned grace. So girded for life in this inequitable yet exhilarating world, may we reflect your essence, through which we are sustained and empowered to be your loving, gracious, wounded hands that embrace and then propel toward greatness the formed, human, breathing dust of your creation. Come, Holy Spirit, come. Amen.

—*The Rt. Reverend Barbara C. Harris*

Council of Women's Ministries

Started in 1983, the Council's purpose is to bring together leaders of the women in the Episcopal Church, to increase the effectiveness of women's ministries, to support the different gifts, value, and ministries of women, and to advance the roles of women in the mission of the Church.

Anglican Women's Indigenous Network
Anglican Women's Network
Appalachian People Service Organization
Black Ministries
Church Periodical Club
Committee on the Status of Women
Compass Rose Society
Conference on Religious Life
Episcopal Asiamerica Ministries Women's Convocation
Episcopal Church Women
Episcopal Communicators
Episcopal Family Network
Episcopal Society for Ministry on Aging
Episcopal Women's Caucus
Episcopal Women's Foundation
Episcopal Women's History Project
Episcopal Young Adult Network
Girl's Friendly Society
Hispanic Ministries
Integrity
National Altar Guild Association
National Network of Episcopal Clergy Association
National Network of Lay Professionals
North American Association for the Diaconate
Parish Health Ministry, Parish Nursing
The Order of the Daughters of the King
United Thank Offering
Women in Mission and Ministry
Women in Seminaries
Women with Disabilities
Worker Sisters of the Holy Spirit

Contents

Preface

Now you are the body of Christ and individually members of it.
—1 Corinthians 12:27

On a cold January morning in 1999, the Council of Women's Ministries gathered at the Episcopal Church Center in New York. In the midst of planning for the future and praying for guidance, a compelling vision emerged: a vision of Episcopal women speaking authentically with one another and with the church at large; a vision of women sharing the richness and diversity of their spirituality; a vision of women uniting in the midst of that diversity, modeling wholeness and health to the church.

Since that sacred moment, our vision has been shaped and reshaped by the prophetic imagination of women throughout our church: women of different races and cultures, women as young as eleven and as old as eighty-nine, women who address God as "Mother" and those who would never dream of doing so, women from all four orders of ministry—bishops, priests, deacons, and laity.

With the publication of *Women's Uncommon Prayers: Our Lives Revealed, Nurtured, Celebrated,* our vision has now become a reality. It is a book we hope you will turn to again and again when you need the reflection, insight, and company of women; when you need support in realizing that you are not alone in your struggles; when you feel overcome with sorrow or filled with joy.

Working on this book has been one of the most exciting yet humbling experiences of our lives, reaffirming for us the incredible and unending gift of God's grace. How blessed we feel to have been invited into that sacred and holy space that dwells within each of us where we can be open and vulnerable to ourselves, to one another, and to God.

We have cried and laughed our way through the reading and rereading of over fifteen hundred prayers and poems—wishing we could reach out and give a hug, a smile, or a word of reassurance to each author. How we wish we could meet every woman who offered herself through personal sharing! How deeply we appreciate everyone who submitted material. By far, the most difficult aspect of the project was the selection process. We sincerely thank everyone who submitted prayers.

We owe a tremendous debt of gratitude to the associate editors who contributed significant amounts of time and effort to this project: Debra Q. Bennett, Kathryn McCormick, and Tracy J. Sukraw. As professional editors, their experience and expertise made this massive project more manageable.

We also wish to thank the field coordinators who collected material: Pam Boyette, Daughters of the King; Rebecca Crummey, Young Adult Network; Jenney Ladefoged, Episcopal Church Women; Ana MacDonald, Diocese of

West Texas; and Gertrude Murchison, United Thank Offering. Many women were reached through their networks.

Our Corporate Prayers section would be far less than it is without the wisdom and input of the Reverend Dr. Clayton L. Morris, Liturgical Officer of the Episcopal Church and the Reverend Sister Jean Campbell, O.S.H., member of the Standing Commission on Liturgy and Music. Their additional editing of this section added significantly to the integrity of the work.

Last, but certainly not least, we would like to thank the President of The Morehouse Group, Kenneth Quigley, who immediately grasped our vision for the book, helped us expand it, and supported us every step of the way. We also wish to thank the Publisher and Editorial Director of Morehouse Publishing, Mark Fretz, for his insightful suggestions.

As the project developed, the Council of Women's Ministries became aware of the need for a common mission to unite us further. Together, we decided to focus on violence against women and children. As part of that decision, we are dedicating the profits from *Women's Uncommon Prayers* to the Episcopal Women's Foundation* for ministries to women and children who are victims of violence. This two-fold purpose of the book is central to our understanding of what it means to be the Body of Christ in the world today.

Yes, as St. Paul so poignantly writes, we "are the body of Christ and individually members of it." He also states, "If one member suffers, all suffer together with it; if one member is honored, all rejoice together with it" (1 Corinthians 12:26–27). As we suffer and rejoice together through the pages of this book, let us hold within our hearts the vision of our individuality affirmed and strengthened in the oneness of the Body of Christ. May we keep this vision ever before us as we continue to minister as the Body of Christ in our world today.

In Christ,

The Reverend Elizabeth Rankin Geitz
Ms. Marjorie A. Burke
Ms. Ann Smith

For more information, log onto www.dfms.org\women. Additional contributions may be sent to: Episcopal Women's Foundation, c/o Barbara Chiodo, 2324 Buena Vista Ave., Belmont, CA 94002.

About the Editors

Editors

Elizabeth Rankin Geitz is an Episcopal priest and the author of *Soul Satisfaction: Drawing Strength from Our Biblical Mothers and Sisters, Gender and the Nicene Creed,* and *Entertaining Angels: Hospitality Programs for the Caring Church.* She lives in Summit, New Jersey, with her husband and two children.

Marjorie A. Burke is the chair of the Committee on the Status of Women for the Episcopal Church and a frequent contributor to the *Journal of Women's Ministries.* She is a former national president of the Episcopal Church Women and lives in Lexington, Massachusetts, with her husband.

Ann Smith has served as the director of Women in Mission and Ministry of the Episcopal Church for the last seventeen years, providing resources, leadership development, communication, events, and advocacy for women. She is the co-author of *Stories from the Circle* and *WomenPrints,* which brings alive the United Nations Platform for Action Document for women.

Associate Editors

Debra Q. Bennett is the senior editor at Rubin Ehrenthal Healthworld New York. She resides in Jamaica, New York, and has edited such periodicals as *Linkage Magazine* and *In Season Out of Season: A Collection of Sermons by the Reverend Canon Harold T. Lewis.* She is an avid collector of clowns.

Kathryn McCormick, a former newspaper editor, is associate director of the Office of News and Information of the Episcopal Church. She lives in Brooklyn, New York, and is a member of the Church of the Holy Apostles in Manhattan.

Tracy J. Sukraw is a professional writer and the editor of *The Episcopal Times,* the newspaper of the Diocese of Massachusetts. In addition to church communications, she writes for a reference series on young adult literature. She lives in Cambridge, Massachusetts.

The editors wish to honor contributors to Women's Uncommon Prayers *who are "firsts" in the Episcopal Church: the Rt. Reverend Barbara C. Harris is the first woman to be a bishop in the Anglican Communion; the Rt. Reverend*

Mary Adelia R. McLeod is the first woman to be a diocesan bishop in the United States; the Rt. Reverend Geralyn Wolf was the first woman to be a dean of a cathedral before being elected bishop; the Very Reverend Martha J. Horne is the first woman to be the dean and president of an Episcopal seminary, Virginia Theological Seminary; the Reverend Dr. Alla Renée Bozarth, the Reverend Dr. Alison M. Cheek, the Reverend Dr. Suzanne Hiatt, the Reverend Dr. Carter Heyward, and the Reverend Canon Nancy Wittig are among the first women ordained to the priesthood in the Episcopal Church; Dr. Pamela P. Chinnis is the first woman to be the President of the House of Deputies; and Ms. Terese A. Parsons is the first woman and first layperson to be the Stewardship Officer of the Episcopal Church.

A Beginning Prayer

Loving, Creative God,
Guide our prayers
At the altar of this book
That authors and readers
United by Your Spirit
May find you within
yet beyond the words.
May we be found by You
and know comfort in times of trouble
compassion in times of despair
celebration in times of joy
healing in times of suffering
direction in times of confusion
and gratitude in times of grace.
May we claim and cherish
the feminine elements in our lives,
and in Your Divine Being,
in whose image we are created
and in whose name we pray. Amen.

—*Ms. Pat Peterson*

Identity

I Am a Woman

One

I am a woman
born of God
I am a woman
born of love

I am caring and competent
vulnerable and powerful
seeking wholeness
physically, emotionally, and spiritually

I am a woman
reaching out to others
making a difference in myself
my family
community
church
and the world

I am empowering myself
to empower others

I am struggling to accept my anger
and use it to gain strength, confidence,
courage, and intimacy with others

I am a woman
who sees the interconnectedness of all human beings
who values the unique gifts of all

I am a woman who leads and follows
who accepts responsibility for myself
and the choices I make

Yes, I am a woman
who sees each day as a new beginning
a chance to grow in self, love, and service

I am a woman
born of God
I am a woman
born of love
And I can be
All that I am

—*Ms. Katherine Tyler Scott*

These words express the deep beliefs that remembering the source of everything and claiming our wholeness are foundational to being effective in the work of transformation—our own and that of others.

Two

I AM A WOMAN
called immigrant
a foreigner with an accent
those are the things
people see

I AM A WOMAN
a child of God, a daughter, a sister,
a mother, a lover, a friend,
I am a shaker, a reformer

I AM A WOMAN
I am a nurturer, this is my nature
I am
more than what you see
a survivor, a fighter, and
a dreamer

I AM A WOMAN
I am the other
I am the one who hopes
I am the complement
the missing piece of what you know

I AM A WOMAN
a *mujerista**
unless you see me beyond
the obvious

you will never see
the woman that I really am

I AM A WOMAN

—*The Reverend Yamily Bass Choate*

* *A* mujerista *is a Hispanic woman.*

Three

Choir 1 On a hot summer's day
      when minds fly every which way but good
      Clanmother comes on a cool, gentle breeze
      calling us to come together
      She carries the pain of yesterday
      the celebration for today
      and the wisdom for tomorrow

All   Clanmother, teach us to dance

Choir 2 When leaves dance to the ground
      and Mother Earth begins to nod
      Clanmother opens her shawl
      to take us all inside
      We share her warmth but
      then she sends us on to gather
      the corn, beans, squash
      the sun, the moon and even stars
      for our journey into winter's time
      she guides us, holds us
      holds, guides

All   Clanmother, teach us to speak

Choir 1 When snow drifts to our Mother
      blanketing the colors of the world
      Clanmother sleeps in our dreams
      Resting, looking inside
      looking for good to grasp
      sharing the stories of before
      dreaming for today
      honoring the Seventh Generation*

All	Clanmother, teach us our ways
Choir 1	When the snow begins to drip away and sap begins her run Clanmother comes to awaken us from winter's rest She speaks softly in tune with the refreshing rain sets our mind in motion to claim another season for our walk in balance
All	Clanmother, dance with us
Choir 2	Clanmother has come full circle They all join hands to hold us in place Clanmother is about remembering the ancestors the people of present the Seventh Generation Wherever they go whatever they do
All	Clanmother carries strength and wisdom to help us live on

—*Ms. Ginny Doctor*

* *When the Iroquois arrived upon Mother Earth for their visit, the Creator gave them a set of instructions, rules for living. One of these rules is that when making decisions, leaders are to consider what kind of impact decisions will have upon the "Seventh Generation" not yet born.*

Women of Haiti

What happens to women
who have no fuel
nothing to burn

who live on treeless slopes
barren to the sky
who walk in sun
and sleep in moon
unpatterned
dreaming of branches

—*Ms. Lucy Germany*

Psalm 2

Blessed is she
who touches mystery,

who is not caught and held
only by what she knows.

How can she know the ways of the sun
if she does not know the ways of the moon?

Sunflowers need not count their seeds,
nor bees reveal the secrets of their hives.

She goes in peace
who listens well.

The planet turns
on one long, perfect tone,

and Woman's song
echoes the planet's turning.

She is secure in Love
which is the other Name.

Blessed is she
who learns the mysteries.

—*Ms. Caryl A. Porter*

For Making Me a Woman

For making me a woman
in what still so often
seems a man's world,
I thank you.
Because you taught me by example
that power is your gift,
and not my possession.

For giving me a body
though it sometimes fails me
and is not all I wish it was
or rather, a good deal more
than I wish it was,
I thank you.
Because you taught me
that I am much more
than my body
and yet my body is
your holy temple.

For calling me to be
more than I believe I can be,
and less
than I sometimes pretend I am,
I thank you.
Because you taught me
that being is more than doing,
that who I am
and whose I am
are more important than
what I do
or what I have.

For all that you are
Creator,
Redeemer,
Sanctifier,
Great "I Am,"
I bless you
as you have so greatly blessed me.

—*Ms. Marty Conner*

Passover Remembered

Pack nothing.
Bring only
your determination
to serve and
your willingness
to be free.

Don't wait for the bread to rise.
Take nourishment for the journey,
but eat standing, be ready
to move at a moment's notice.

Do not hesitate to leave
your old ways behind—
fear, silence, submission.

Only surrender to the need
of the time—to love
justice and walk humbly
with your God.

Do not take time
to explain to the neighbors.
Tell only a few trusted
friends and family members.

Then begin quickly,
before you have time
to sink back into
the old slavery.

Set out in the dark.
I will send fire
to warm and encourage you.
I will be with you in the fire
and I will be with you in the cloud.

You will learn to eat new food
and find refuge in new places.
I will give you dreams in the desert
to guide you safely home to that
place
you have not yet seen.

The stories you tell
one another around your fires
in the dark will make you
strong and wise.

Outsiders will attack you,
and some who follow you,
and at times you will weary
and turn on each other
from fear and fatigue and
blind forgetfulness.

You have been preparing
for this for hundreds of years.
I am sending you into the
wilderness
to make a way and learn my ways
more deeply.

Those who fight you will teach you.
Those who fear you will strengthen
you.
Those who follow you may forget
you.
Only be faithful.
This alone matters.

Some of you will die in the desert,
for the way is longer than anyone
imagined.
Some of you will give birth.

Some will join other tribes
along the way, and some
will simply stop and create
new families in a welcoming oasis.

Some of you will be so changed
by weather and wanderings
that even your closest friends
will have to learn your features
as though for the first time.
Some of you will not change at all.

Some will be abandoned
by your dearest loves
and misunderstood by those
who have known you since birth
and feel abandoned by you.

Some will find new friendship
in unlikely faces, and old friends
as faithful and true
as the pillar of God's flame.

Wear protection.
Your flesh will be torn
as you make a path
with your bodies
through sharp tangles.
Wear protection.

Others who follow may deride
or forget the fools who first bled
where thorns once were, carrying
    them
away in their own flesh.

Such urgency as you now bear
may embarrass your children
who will know little of these times.

Sing songs as you go,
and hold close together.
You may at times grow
confused and lose your way.

Continue to call each other
by the names I've given you,

to help remember who you are.
You will get where you are going
by remembering who you are.

Touch each other and keep telling
    the stories
of old bondage and of how
    I delivered you.

Tell your children lest they forget
and fall into danger—remind them
even they were not born in
    freedom,
but under a bondage which they no
longer remember, which is still
with them, if unseen.

Or they were born
in the open desert
where no signposts are.

Make maps as you go,
remembering the way back
from before you were born.

So long ago you fell
into slavery, slipped
into it unaware,
out of hunger and need.

You left your famished country
for freedom and food in a new
    land,
but you fell unconscious and
    passive,
and slavery overtook you as you fell
asleep in the ease of your life.

You no longer told stories
of home to remember
who you were.

Do not let your children sleep
through the journey's hardship.
Keep them awake and walking
on their own feet so that you both
remain strong and on course.

So you will be only
the first of many waves
of deliverance on these
desert seas.

It is the first of many
beginnings—your Paschaltide.

Remain true to this mystery.

Pass on the whole story.
I spared you all
by calling you forth
from your chains.

Do not go back.

I am with you now
and I am waiting for you.

—*The Reverend Dr. Alla Renée Bozarth*

*This prayer was read at the Twenty-fifth Anniversary of the Ordination of Women
to the Priesthood in the Episcopal Church.*

Called to Common Mission

Gracious God, we give you thanks for the possibilities for common mission
you place before us as Lutheran and Episcopal women. As Ruth and Naomi
reached across their cultural divide to love and care for one another, may we
embrace one another in sisterly solidarity. In our towns, cities, rural areas, and
campuses, may we enliven our communities as we join together to work and
witness in your name.

As women, we know that there is always too much work to be done, too little
time to do it, and too few people to get it done. We know that pride and
posturing often get in the way of coming together in your service. We know
that mission often gets more talk than action. But, we also know that joy
and power can be found in the companionship and creation into which you
invite us.

As our churches affirm that you call us to common mission, may we, as
Episcopal and Lutheran women, untie that which binds us and dismantle
that which divides us. By your grace, may we gather these ropes and rails that
limit our lives and communities and weave them into your new creation. May

we, through our prayers and plans and programs, pursue the possibilities you set before us in our call to common mission. Amen.

—The Reverend Jane Soyster Gould and The Reverend Constance F. Parvey

Jane and Constance are the Episcopal and Lutheran chaplains at MIT, respectively.

Dancers of Spirit

I am them,
they are me,
together, we are.

Sisters journeying
separate, yet together,
joined by the spirit
transported in time and space.

Sisters discovering
movements from impulses
of feelings embedded
deep within that
transcend the moment.
Simple gestures, seeking shapes,
transformed into wordless prayer.

—Ms. Marjorie A. Burke

Nurture

Women who have lived on the Love of God
Through many seasons,
Are as sisters to blooming gardens
Around the world.

Warmed by grace and peace,
They grow in times of sorrow,
Absorbing comfort
In God's presence.

Reaching long roots
Into never-failing sustenance,
They lift bright blossoms
As witnesses to faith.

—*The Reverend Alison Carpenter Lucas*

Water Women

We do not want
to rock the boat,
you say, mistaking
our new poise
for something safe.

We smile secretly
at each other,
sharing the reality
that for some time
we have not been
in the boat.

We jumped
or were pushed
or fell
and some leaped
overboard.

Our bodies form
a freedom fleet,
our dolphin grace
is power.

We learn and teach
and as we go
each woman sings;
each woman's hands
are water wings.

Some of us have become
mermaids or Amazon whales
and are swimming for our lives.

Some of us do not know how to swim.
We walk on water.

—*The Reverend Dr. Alla Renée Bozarth*

A Woman's Special Gifts of Leadership

God of Elizabeth, Sarah, and Rebecca; God the Divine Mother
and Father of the wholeness of my being; I give you thanks for the
gift of being a woman. In your name I celebrate the special qualities that you have given: the gift of connectedness, the gift of
empathy, the gift of compassion, the gift of nurturing, the gift of
insight, the gifts of flexibility and multiplicity. Guide me, gracious
God, that I may claim the unique strengths of these gifts and use
them to your glory in the world. Give me the wisdom to honor
these attributes within myself that they may be used freely, fully,
and always in your name. Amen.

—*Dr. Kay Collier-Slone*

Cell Phones and Paychecks

Cell phone on my shoulder
Raging traffic in my face,
The clock moving toward some hour
When I must be in place
Why should I
Let this mind ransomed to "now"
Feed only on such urgencies?

Reflecting, I fall gently into a time
When women taught God to their young,
Sarah Patton Boyle fought for women's rights,
The Emery sisters spread the gospel,
Florence Li Tim Oi shared China's pain,
And countless women changed history
Setting to right old wrongs,
Believing, praying, teaching from the midst of pain.

With a sense of the right
They led and others followed
And here we are today
With our cell phones and paychecks.

O God, give us the sense not to forget
The women who made us possible.
Give us time to revisit time,
To know as friends and heroes
Those women whose names struck fire
Who started us on marches still unfinished.

God, give us time. Let us remember.

—*Ms. Lucy Germany*

This poem was inspired by the work of the Episcopal Women's History Project.

Ecclesiasticus 44:1–18
(A Woman's Version)

Let us now sing the praises of famous women,
The heroes of our feminine faith history
Through whom God our Mother established her renown
And revealed her majesty in each succeeding age.
Some held sway over patriarchy
And made themselves a name by their exploits.
Others were sage counselors
Who spoke out with prophetic power.   ,
Some led women by their counsels
And by their knowledge of the power of sisterhood;
Out of their fund of wisdom they gave instruction.
Some were composers of music or writers of poetry.
Others were endowed with humility and strength,
Living peacefully in their homes.
All these won fame in their own generation
And were the pride of their times.
Some there are who have left a name behind them
To be commemorated in herstory.

There are others, though, who seem unremembered.
Let them not be dead, as though they had never existed,
As though they had never been born
Or left children to succeed them.
We are their children.
They are our foremothers and we honor them now.
Women unknown, called to be priests
While the Church called only men.
Women unheralded, called to celebrate the sacraments
While the communicants refused to receive.
Women unheard, called to preach
While the world called them names.
Women unrecognized, called to read inclusive Scriptures
While the "righteous" ridiculed their words.
These women, our foremothers, are women of loyalty
Whose good deeds should never be forgotten.
Their prosperity of spirit will be handed down to their descendants,
And their inheritance of courage to future generations of women.
Thanks to them their daughters are free—
The whole race of their descendants.
Their line will endure for all time,
And their fame will never be blotted out.

May their names live forever.
Nations will recount their wisdom,
And God's people will sing their praises.

—*Ms. Melanie Lamb Robinson*

The Many Faces of Rachel

I am Rachel, shepherdess, lover, despairing one, hopeful one.
Many have read my story over the ages,
    but few have searched me out.
They have squeezed me into small boxes.
    I have been viewed simply as
        daughter, wife, mother.
    I have been portrayed as extremes,
        the prayerful one, the cunning one,
        the feminine wife, the conflictive sister.

Worse than those who have boxed me up are those who simply overlook me.
  I was overlooked when I was so alive,
      the intense sun kissing the dark skin around my dancing
      eyes.
  I was only a stepping stone to the birth of the Twelve Tribes.

  I was overlooked when I was on death's door,
      breathing my last word as I strained, screamed, and
      sweated in childbirth.
  The Twelve were established; I was no longer needed.

But I'd like to tell you who I am.

To some degree, I encompass all the boxes into which I have
been put. But I am also more.

Some may have told you that I am weak.
  But they don't recognize me as I am. I am strong, both inside
      and out.

  I am a runner. I love the outdoors.
      You've not lived life until you have run barefoot on the
      green hills in springtime.
  I am a shepherdess. I'm a good leader and healer.
      When I yearned for a child, I found solace in leading my
      flocks and caring for the lambs who had no mothers.
  I am powerful. I have taken control over my life as an adult.
      I am a loving equal to my husband,
      and even my father could not keep his grip on me.

I live in centuries past, yet you might find me not unlike yourself.

Like you, I
    am Alive
    will die someday
    have strong moments
    have weak moments.

Like you, I
    love God at times
    cry out to God at times
    love others
    cry out against others.

I live in centuries past, yet you might find me not unlike yourself;
   only the descriptive names have changed.

In your generation, others would say to me:
   You come from a dysfunctional family.
   Your father is a liar and abuses others.
   Your mother has no voice.
   You have fertility problems.
   You question your faith in the One God.
   You have been poor . . . and you have been rich.

But the strangest thing happened some time ago . . .
   I had a vision of what my name will come to mean.

I will become known as Mother Rachel.
   I will become known as Mother of a Nation.
   I will become known as the One who Weeps.
   I will become known as the One on whom the Shechinah,
   The Spirit of God rests.
   I will become known as the Comforter of Women.

So what do I, Rachel, tell you?

If you are sad, weep for yourselves, but not for me.
   I will join you in Paradise.
Be strong.
   I will run beside you on the hills, beaches, or mountains
   wherever you may be.
Live life in all its glory. Pray. Work. Love others. Be passionate.
   I could do no less.
Worship God and enjoy God's creation.
   I will sing with you in praise and petition.

No more shall you and I weep in exile.
   Join with our sisters and run on the green, green grass.
   And the Spirit of God will come upon us.

—*The Reverend Rachel Endicott*

Jephthah's Daughter

Two months I walked the narrow hills,
bewailing my virginity;
two months I walked within the heart of fire,
until all pain bled out of me.
Now I return, leached cold as bone,
and I am prophet, I am seer.
    The heart is larger than the world.

Now I return through icy silences;
my father's eyes accuse—why did I not
do the expected thing, follow the mountain roads
to other lands? Why should I keep
a promise that I never made? I find
a woman's honor is a strange, spare thing.
    The heart is larger than the world.

If I could speak, my people, I would cry: Behold!
In this cocoon of air and burning light
we darkly move, all unaware,
into transfiguration. All our flesh
is broken, all our blood is mute:
the singer does not make the song.
    The heart is larger than the world.

—The Reverend Anne McConney

The Unnamed Woman

I thought I was a lamp
burning and shining
but I was a footlight

I knew when time came
to walk into the crowded room—
air thick with ideas

Men's ideas, buzzing
purposeful as flies on
their errands: redistribution

of goods, for instance,
purity or duty or dominion
abstract, impractical

I put
my bare foot on the cool
tile floor and entered

and the sun caught
in my hair a moment
glinted

What I could, I did, sat
beside Jesus, massaged his poor
cold feet
firmly, with purpose
My hands, my fingers were made
for this
all intent, all focus—
one work of love, assuage
or comfort
heel, ball, arch
between the toes, finding at last
that point
of relief, release
of some ancient wound or grief
stored
for a lifetime
He sighed, in gratitude, I like
to think
What I could
I did, not everything, but nothing
is everything—
enough

—*The Reverend Anne C. Fowler*

Daily Life

Morning Prayers

A Morning Collect

Gracious God, as our prayers rise
To greet you, gather us who are
Scattered into your realm of Justice
And of Love.

—*Fredrica Harris Thompsett, Ph.D.*

Shalom: A Prayer from Many Spiritual Sources to Begin and End the Day

Let me be at peace within myself.
Let me accept that I am profoundly loved and
need never be afraid.
Let me be aware of the Source of Being that is common to us all
and to all living creatures.
Let me be filled with the presence of the Great Compassion
toward myself and toward
all living beings.
Let me always be an instrument of my own liberation and
not of my own oppression.
Let me see the face of Jesus in others.
Let me be the face of Jesus for others.
Let me be at peace within myself. Amen.

—*The Reverend Canon Elizabeth Kaeton*

Good Morning, Holy Spirit

Good morning, Holy Spirit.
I need you this day.
Fill me with your presence
And guide me on my way.

Good morning, Holy Spirit.
I need you this day.
Fill my mind, my soul, my thinking,
And guide me as I pray.

Precious Holy Spirit,
I need you every day.
Surround me with your Being
And in my heart, please stay.

—*Mrs. Jacqueline Russel*

Today

Let me live today.
Let me be open to the miracle of this day.
Let me breathe the best of today.
Let me not miss the heart of today.
Let me find the gift of today,
hidden like a jewel in rubble of care, duty, and detail.

Let me pause to hear
the steady beat of the heart of God—
hoping, aching, sorrowing, expectant, patient,
despairing heart of God.

Listen, listen.
Do you hear it?
Ever so faint but steady, steady,
rhythmic organ, strong muscle,
thumping, beating, pumping, sustaining, encompassing,
wildly dancing heart of God.

Let me live this day, aware, open, listening, breathing, alive.

—*The Reverend Virginia Going*

Morning Prayer for the New Millennium

Thank you, Creator,
Giver of Life,
for allowing me to be

alive this day
as a human creature,
so young a species
with so much to learn!
    Let it unfold,
    I say.
    Practice
    the discipline
    of non-intrusion
    and non-control.
    Be grace-full.

    Let the quiet
    beauty of a life
    reveal itself
    in a place free
    of judgment.

    Make a soul covenant
    with Life—for all
    that is wild and free,
    bless it, love it
    and let it be.

—*The Reverend Dr. Alla Renée Bozarth*

A Lorica for Beginning Work

In my being, the Father of light,
In my seeing, the Mother of sight,
Christ in my hearing.
Christ in my speaking.
In my nakedness, in my strength,
Spirit covering my length
And breadth and all around.
Wash me with warm water,
Root me in deep ground.

–*Ms. Elizabeth Forbes*

Prayer at the Beginning of a One-Day Retreat

O God of my heart and understanding, be alive in me this day. Nourish me and challenge me. Show me how to ask and how to receive from you. Be in me, with me, beside me, around me. Open my heart to a way that will support your purpose for my life. Amen.

—*Ms. Trudy James*

Morning Song

O LORD, in the morning you hear my voice;
in the morning I plead my case to you, and watch.
—Psalm 5:3

In the new light
of each day's questions,
I am never prepared.
Today, again, I have nothing
to offer but a handful
of old prayers, worn down
by the relentless abrasion
of doubt, and a fragment
of dream that plays on in my head
only half remembered. Still,
the doves coo and circle
through the pines
as they do when I pass
each morning. Their sorrow
is so nearly human, it rings
sweet with regret. By dusk,
the trees will bow down and I, too, will
make my appeal, will find
again your mercy,
your solace.

—*Ms. Elizabeth Drescher*

September Morning

The early sun cast its filmy, slanting rays
Upon the trees along my way to work this morning,
Lighting leaves both green and gold,
Even the one, dry, brown, and curled,
That blew down on my windshield and then
Skittered off, just like a living thing.

I drove by trees, and creek and school,
By houses sleeping still in shade
By children, as they stood awaiting
The yellow bus to take them to their class.

Another day begins in light and fog
With rays that speak of higher love,
God's bounty cast with careless grace
Across the land again.

—The Reverend Karen E. Gough

Prayers for Daily Living

Just a Person

For the first time in my life, I felt at peace—a kind of peace I never had experienced before. I was visiting an island in the southern Caribbean populated primarily by people of African, Indian, Spanish, and Dutch descent. When I went to the beach, entered stores and restaurants, or boarded public transportation, I felt like a person—just a person, not a black person.

Black, brown, white, and yellow people were sitting, eating, walking, riding, and conversing, in what seemed to be harmony—people whose physical characteristics embodied a blend of traits from different ethnic groups. What a glorious composite of God's creation. What exhilaration, what freedom I felt. What an epiphany!

Why do such feelings elude me each and every day of my life here in the United States? Having grown up in the segregated South, painful memories of daily life are part of my history. I remember going to the beach where a partition separated white bathers from black bathers. I recall being required to drink from water fountains marked "for coloreds only" and to use bathrooms labeled "for colored women." I remember being required to ride on the back of the bus, not being allowed to eat in restaurants, and being allowed to shop in department stores that had food counters from which I could not eat.

And are things really so different today? The United States has had approximately one hundred eight Supreme Court justices: one hundred four white males, two white females, and two black males—one of whom I believe is apathetic about black and minority interests. In 1999, a black Marine near San Diego was beaten and stomped unmercifully while being called racial epithets, resulting in his being paralyzed for life. In Texas, a black man was dragged to his death behind a pickup truck, simply because he was black. In New York, a black man was fired at forty times and shot approximately nineteen times by police without cause. In addition, the Ku Klux Klan was given a permit to march in New York.

The United States was formed with the signing of the Declaration of Independence, which states: "We hold these truths to be self-evident, that all men are created equal, that they are endowed by their Creator with certain unalienable Rights, that among these are Life, Liberty and the pursuit of Happiness." Yet, blacks were not given these rights.

I will never understand how our founding fathers could write such a powerful document declaring and yet denying these same rights to a segment of society whom they deemed as property. At one point, for apportionment purposes, slaves were considered human beings and were counted as three-fifths of a person. I will never understand how this legally-sanctioned inhumanity could have occurred. Yet when legal racism ended, systemic institutional racism took its place. In the United States, I am still not just a person; I am a black person. O God, will it ever be different? Will I ever be able to live in the greatest country in the world as just a person?

My daily prayer:
O God of infinite justice, my fervent prayer is to live in a world in which all human beings are valued, and another human being does not determine my worth. I pray for a world in which the color of

my skin does not determine my access to privileges or denial of my rights. O God, you know that I struggle daily to prove my worth. Let me not fall into hopelessness. Help me hold on to the belief that one day people will embrace cultural differences and respect all people as created in your glorious image; in the name of Jesus Christ, in whose body we are all one. Amen.

—*Ms. Cordell J. Trotman*

We See a Gardener

Risen Lord,
so often encountered,
so seldom recognized,
you meet us in the gardens of our hearts,
on the lonely roads of our lives,
our empty beaches, and greet us.
But in our blindness,
we mistake you for someone else.
Through our tears, we see a gardener;
in our weariness and wariness, a stranger.
But you call us back to ourselves.
Forgive us our hard-heartedness,
our lack of understanding.
Open our eyes and our ears to you,
wherever you are found,
and give us grace to love you with abandon,
to throw ourselves into your service,
as Mary threw herself at your feet,
as Peter threw himself into the sea.
Amen.

—*Ms. Jennifer Heckart*

Topsy-Turvy

You've taken my neat-as-a-pin
all categorized
compartmentalized
down-to-the-split-second schedule
and turned it all topsy-turvy—again!

Are you trying to tell me something?
What are you trying to tell me?

You've been doing that a lot lately, you know;
turning my world, my life, upside-downside.
Oh—you know.

You're not going to tell me now, are you?

—*Ms. Patricia B. Clark*

Dishwashing Blessing

Lord, bless to me my sink. As it fills during the day with dirty dishes, each one is a memory of family meals shared. There are cereal dishes from our quick breakfasts, lunch fixings, pots and pans from my husband's dinner forays. The endless parade of glasses and cups across the counter (more in the summer) reminds me of how our natural and spiritual thirsts are quenched. The eating utensils pile up—knives for cutting, spoons for stirring, forks—still-primitive tools of nourishment.

I come before my sink, usually with reluctance, but as it fills with hot water and suds it is transformed into an altar upon which I place the sins and hurts of the day. As I carefully wash the delicate china, my mind gently nurses the day's injuries and disappointments. Some of my actions and words need to be scoured like greasy pots and pans. As I scrub the dishes, the "dirt" from the day starts to wash away. As I rinse and dry them, the sink is drained and dirty water swirls away. The dishes are clean and I, somehow, am refreshed—more peaceful and settled than when I started the task.

Bless to me, O Lord, my sink.

—*Mrs. L. Ruth Douglas*

Prayer for Support

Jesus reach for me.
Spirit strengthen me.
God catch me.

—*Mrs. Phoebe W. Griswold*

Serenity

Just give me some time in my garden,
There all my troubles to free,
For when I am there in my garden,
I am ever so near, Lord, to thee.

I can see all the wonders of living
As the rich soil I sift through my hand;
And I watch as the seeds become blossoms;
Then bear their fruits from the land.

Just give me some time in my garden.
Let me glory in it all alone.
For when I am there in my garden,
I am calm deep within and at home.

—*Mrs. Ruth Brooks Silver*

On Reflection: Ten Things I've Learned in the Garden

1. From the hedge roses: When you remove the deadwood, the new growth can dance.
2. From the chives who jumped the fence: Weed carefully so that you don't pull that which you didn't know you had planted.
3. From the geraniums saved from last year: What appears to be dead may have life if it's fed.
4. From the wrens: Young birds play; so should young people.
5. From the compost pile: Garbage, properly treated, becomes food.
6. From the lemon mint along the garden shed: Communicate—when someone else mows, they don't know where you have planted.
7. From the hostas: God can work miracles in the darkness.
8. From the lilacs: The sweet smell of success is short-lived.
9. From the lamb's ears: It is possible to have too much of a good thing.
10. From my heart: If Adam and Eve belonged in a garden, don't we?

—*Mrs. Janet Hitchcock*

Popovers

Except I be filled with thy spirit, I am like a popover that never pops: flat and tasteless.

Except I be filled with thy love, I am like a biscuit that never rises: flat and indigestible.

Except I be filled with thy grace, I am like a root beer that has been left unstoppered: flat and insipid.

—*The Reverend Virginia C. Thomas*

Benedicite *Around the Block*

Out the door

In the parking lot a nun is reading the Office in her car;
    she reads Psalms from a little black book to a woman with
    the palsy whose grey head wobbles in time.

The noisy dirty city sparrows are singing tuneless frantic songs
    in the little ratty city sidewalk cherry trees.

turn right

A man in a brown suit and a cowboy hat is running;
    he careens around the corner.
    He wears a secret smile like a pregnant virgin.

A woman with hair the color of flame is smoking a cigarette.
    She is leaning on an idling bus with a suitcase at her feet.
    Joan of Arc, listening to the voices or to the crackle of fire.

turn right

At the crossroads, the light changes
    and a whistle like a single sparrow note blows for the blind
    so we can safely change direction.

A lawyer with a face like Gregory Peck as Atticus Finch
    strides with the light over the street of his city
    and his silk tie blows wild over his left shoulder.

A straight-backed woman with black hair
    in a short perfect black dress trips along on black very high
    heels, crossing over as fast as ever she can.

A small dark boy carries on his little shoulder a battered duffel
    bag the size of the world,
    a tiny image of Atlas moving heavy while the light turns
    yellow and the whistle stops.

Leftover morning papers waste in blue boxes on the corners,
    no gospel in them at all.

   turn right

Empty storefronts: leftover bits of trash on the floors behind their
    dirty windows
A contest advertised on a lightpost: What shall we name the New
    Mall?
Rotting houses with rotting porches, scraps of plastic toys in the
    grassless side yards
Tumbling thin-sticked wood fire escapes
littered with bottles in boxes and cans in bags
Shabby cheap clothes drying in the rain
A broken shopping cart twisted on the cracked sidewalk

   return

The nun is still reading the Divine Office to the crooked old
    lady, to God, for the city,
and together we chirp a *Benedicite* in counterpoint.
    We croak out our tuneless praise and blame
    to the shimmering Creator hanging in our midst.

—*The Reverend Mary F. C. Pratt*

Red Flowers

For some years now, I have planted one large pot with dark purple petunias, especially for their lovely smell. The pot usually sits between two chairs on a small concrete patio at the back of the house. Often morning or evening, for the morning and evening dews intensify that odor, I sit there contentedly inhaling their perfume. To my horror one year, I found that one petunia in a box of purple petunias I had planted came out *red!* Making a later trip to the greenhouse, I saw a packet of much nicer purple petunias, so I brought them home only to find after several days that *another red* flower had crept into that repotted collection.

At this point, I felt a bit frustrated. But as I sat there contemplating the intruders, I thought to myself, why not? When did you ever come to expect complete perfection in nature or in life? I've come to view that persistent red interloper as a little joke, a bit of comic relief, a reminder of all those people and incidents in life that don't fit the mold. It reminds me to take joy in the less-than-perfect. Actually, am I not also one of God's imperfections?

Let us pray:
O God, Creator of all that is perfect and imperfect in our lives and in the often imperfect world around us, help us to see those things in ourselves that are less than perfect and make us find perfection in our service to you. We ask this in the name of your Son, the perfect sacrifice. Amen.

—*Mrs. Winifred M. Hoppert*

Holder of My Fears

Blessed be thou, Jesus Christ,
holder of my fears.

They tremble like small birds in your hands,
desperately struggling to get free.

Am I losing my sight? Will my child be safe?
Can I do my job? Will I be loved?
Am I good enough? There's no time!

You hold each securely in warm, strong hands.
You stroke them tenderly until they relax.
They fall asleep in the nest of your embrace.

And when all my fears are calmed,
you hold only me.
Beloved be thou, Jesus Christ.
Beloved!

—Ms. Carol K. Everson

Just for Me, Just for Today

Each day I want to be with you, Lord.
I wait patiently for you to be near.
I shut out the "goings on" in my head, at least I try.
I so want to be with you, to hear
what special things you have to say—
just for me, just for today.

We sit on the bridge, just you and I,
and often watch as the stream flows by.
With our feet dangling and swinging,
I allow the stream to take my thoughts, to wash them away,
to clear my head to hear what you have to say—
just for me, just for today.

This is our special time together—we share
what's happened yesterday, what's planned for today,
how much we love, how much we care.
Ideas flow, love reaches below.
Thank you, Father, for giving me this time every day—
just for me, just for today.

—Mrs. Joy H. Tway

Send a Spark

Lord, when things go wrong
You sometimes give us clues.

Life has gone wrong today.

Please send a spark into my mind
the way sunlight sometimes
strikes a single leaf
or brightens one figure
in a stained-glass window.

I know you're here
for I've heard your whisper
in creeks and waterfalls.

I'm listening.
Even a hint will do.

—*Ms. Mary Ann Coleman*

Missed Miseries!

When we are busy bemoaning some dreadful hardship that has befallen us, it would be a help to write down all those other dreadful hardships—the ones we lie awake dreading, the ones that never happened. Then, as we ready this long, long list of all the nasty things that never happened, we might praise and thank you, Lord, for these blessings and ask you to forgive us. For we trust our lives into your hands and then snatch them back again, to lie awake as we dread the next hardship that may never come.

—*The Reverend Virginia C. Thomas*

A Blessing Prayer for Frustration

Bless this distracting frustration, O Lord,
as it must be a powerful source of growth for me.
I cannot pray it away (although I have tried)
as it is obviously
part of your plan.

So with wisdom and spiritual poise,
let me embrace this blessed frustration,
trusting in your divine intentions,

your omniscient ways, and even at times,
your sense of humor.

In the name of your Son, my Savior,
Jesus Christ.
Amen.

—*Mrs. Cynthia Horvath Garbutt*

The Bully

I have never liked round-abouts,
those playground torture platforms
that spin around and around
while children cling to the bars
to keep from flying off.

There is always one bully
who makes it go faster and faster,
who laughs while others scream or sicken,
who loves the speed,
who loves the power.

My world is a round-about
spinning faster and faster
while I sicken with vertigo and fear.
I fight the force that pushes me
farther and farther from the center,
where my true self rests,
where God is.

I call to Mother Jesus—"Amma!
Make the tyrant stop!"
She looks at me with love and says,
"You must tell him *yourself.*"

"Bully! My Mother says to stop!"

He steps back from where he has been
accelerating the bars as they pass.
He looks at me, his eyes

challenging my courage,
questioning my Mother's power.

As the round-about slows,
his blurry form becomes distinct.
In growing peace,
with mounting courage,
I look at him,
and I see
that he is me.

—*Ms. Carol K. Everson*

Today I Can Only Be

Today I can only be . . .
    a broken cup,
    a cracked vase.
I know my need,
    for I am needy.
Too tired to acknowledge
    my thirst,
Still I know it's there.
Come, Holy Spirit, and
    fill this shattered vessel
with your life, love,
    and energy
That I may do your will.
Today I can only be.

—*Mrs. Gretchen Olheiser*

After months of chronic fatigue, I wrote this prayer when I had no energy to move myself into a "better" spiritual state.

The Three Most Sacred

I give unto the Father most Glorious, the fears and tears of days
    gone by;
by crying to thee this day and always,
I will live in hope and not in doubt.

I give unto the Son most Lowly, the sins of which I'm most
        ashamed:
by looking on thee this day and always,
I will not look down, but up and out.

I give unto the Spirit most Holy, the hopes and dreams of years
        to come:
by trusting in thee this day and always,
I will live on, and I will sing out.

I give unto thyself today my heart, my will, my total self:
by calling on thee this day and always,
I will go out, and I will come back.

I give unto the Three most Sacred my life down here and up above:
by hoping in thee this day and always,
I will sleep in peace and not in fear.

—*Dr. Jane Richardson Jensen*

God's Time

God's time,
that comes to mind
when
I am impatient,
        waiting for something I want to happen.

I pray, ". . . in God's time."
then
I tap my fingers.
I want to move; I want it to happen
        now!

God's time,
I guess I'm learning, little by little.
Why does it take so long?
        A lifetime!

Amen.

—*The Reverend Patricia Daniels Pierce*

Night Prayers

Night Prayer

As I meditate on you in the night,
My soul thirsts for you, my flesh faints for you.
I bend the knee of my heart and pray for light.

A candle flickers dimly in the darkness,
And grotesque shadows beat against my brain
As I meditate on you in the night.

Lost is the rainbow's vivid promise,
Here amid the murky predawn gloom.
I bend the knee of my heart and pray for light.

My stubborn will needs bending like the bow,
Like my knees on this cold floor,
As I meditate on you in the night.

Where is my openness to grace, to Noah's
Covenant, Abraham's promise, Jesus' redemption?
I bend the knee of my heart and pray for light.

As slivers of dawn gently touch the sky,
So touch my soul and ease my aching heart.
I meditate on you in the night.
And bend the knee of my heart to pray for light.

—*Mrs. Mary Lee Wile*

Another Day

Thank you Lord for another day
Where I have
Lost some but gained much more
Where I have
Forsaken some but fulfilled more
Thank you Lord for another day
Where I have prospered

—*Ms. Amelia Ann Friedman*

Guidance

God of Life

God of life,
> Surge through every cell of my being.
From my core through all that I am,
> to all the world that surrounds me.
Through my fears,
> My unknowings,
> My dreams,
> My detachments.
Let me know myself, and simply be.
And from that point, let me reach out to all my complexities,
> gently,
> lovingly.
I Am.
> In the great "I AM."

—*Ms. Donna J. Maebori*

A Dieter's Prayer

Heavenly Father, at the first twinge of hunger
Let me turn to you first for fulfillment.
Fill me with your love.
Fill me with your truth.
Fill me with your compassion.
Fill me with your wisdom.
Fill me with your peace.
Fill me with your joy.
Help me to preserve this holy temple you have given me.
Help me to honor my body with healthy choices.
Help me to control my cravings and to discern my true hunger.
Do I seek nourishment for my body or sustenance for my soul?
Let me seek you first, knowing everything else will be given to me.

—*Ms. Glenna Mahoney*

I have been struggling with a few unwanted pounds. I tried dieting and exercise but wasn't making much progress. Then I had this idea to turn to God each and every time I thought I was hungry. In most cases, by the time I go through the prayer I'm no longer hungry! When I am still hungry after the prayer, I can eat knowing I'm really eating for the right reason.

Angels

Angels.
Doesn't that word just send flurries of tears and feather sparks
    down your back?
And you feel your soul trying to slip out your eyes.
It slides down your cheek
And when you reach up to capture it
You realize it has liquefied.
Angels.
It brings to mind a celestial being with the heart of a child,
The mind of a Roman,
The hair and face from that girl in the magazine you read
    before bed.
Angels.
Embodiment of our hopes,
And ideals,
And prayers.
But what if angels have scars down their legs?
What if angels are bald, and have only one eye?
What if they're sitting outside of that old store
With pain glimmering in their eyes, dirt in their appearance,
And a filthy hand reaching up toward yours?
But if they're from God,
Why would that matter?
So God, Heavenly Father,
Open my heart,
My mind,
My soul.
To all your Creation.
Grant me peace with myself
That I might find peace with others,
And cherish their beauty
In all ways possible.

—Ms. Mary Cate Chapman

Teach Us, Lord

Lord, teach us to see thee
    not just in stained glass
    but in stained lives;
    not in Gothic arches,
    but in arthritic fingers.
Lord, teach us to hear thee
    not just in hymns of praise,
    but in sneers of disdain.
Lord, let us know thee and love thee
    in all things as thou lovest us—
For thou lovest
    the self-seeking as well as the unselfish;
    the vindictive as well as the kind,
    the sinners as well as the saints.
Thou lovest even me, Lord.

—*The Reverend Virginia C. Thomas*

A Prayer for Wholeness

Lord, I have become too busy:
    too busy for you,
    too busy for me,
    too busy for those who need me.
Gather the fragments of my scattered self.
Help me to discern what is important and what is expendable.
It is so difficult, this business of giving—of being all for you.
I am overwhelmed by its enormity and lose sight of its utter simplicity.
Show me how to let go—to give up control—
    that you might draw and bend and mold and carry,
Lord, in your goodness and incomprehensible love for me,
    That I may be now and ever one in you,
    Gather the fragments of my scattered self.

—*Ms. Patricia B. Clark*

Come Close to the Door

The wind is a tempest in the peach trees.
The sun warms the skin on my face.
But coldness creeps close to my heart
When I think I have to live so far from you.
The birds chirp: "Come close to the Door.
Open it! God's there waiting to resurrect you!"
I am speechless.
This is love beyond reason!

—The Reverend Elyn MacInnis

Here in Beijing the pollution is overwhelming, and I rarely get out of it into the countryside. But one day in spring two years ago, when it was still cold, I visited a peach orchard and listened to the birds.

Questioning

Earthquakes, Lord—
how about earthquakes?
How about fire and flood?
How about crime—the ways
innocent people suffer and die?

I'm sending my confusion up to you.
Are there some things you just can't change
because of the way the world is now
and because of the laws you set in place
when the earth was new?

Whatever the answer is,
I remember the pain
Jesus suffered for us
And I love you.

—Ms. Mary Ann Coleman

From a collection I wrote as a result of my experiences as a caseworker in the welfare department, and as a teacher and mother.

A Young Woman's Prayer

Dear Lord,

Please grant me strength in dealing with my problems. Help me to be a more caring daughter, sister, and friend. Please be there to help me live up to the expectations I set for myself, and to not be pressured into realizing the expectations set for me by others. Help me so that my words can lead others to you in times of need. Finally, please help ease the suffering, as it comes, of myself and others. Amen.

—Ms. Catherine A. Poetker

A Light in the Darkness

Dear God, merciful Lord, I come to you as your humble daughter in need of your wisdom, your goodness, your love, your light. I want to thank you, my dear God, for your love. I know that you want the very best for me. Now help me, my dear Lord, to be a light for my family, friends, neighbors, and colleagues, and even for those I do not know. They may be carrying a heavy burden; they may not be able to find their way. It is my prayer that I may be the light in their path. I want them to know that I can help them carry a burden that feels too heavy. You want me to help, Lord. You want me to be a friend, and I know that you will give me the strength and the love they need. Work through me, Lord, and I know that with your help I can be a light in the darkness! Amen.

—Ms. Betty Torres

Reawakening in January
(an opening prayer for vestry meetings)

Our Great and Caring God—creator, preserver, comforter. White beauty feathers out from every brown twig and blade. Yet in the cold deadness of winter, many of us are hibernating, untouched by the beauty, waiting for the warm aliveness of spring.

Whenever our hours of self-absorption come, may our spirits rise to the recreative freshness of uniting with you. May we seek your glory in loving and serving one another. May we will to put forth the effort it takes to understand our parish partners.

Through worshiping and working together, may we come to know our God and our neighbors more profoundly. In Christ's Name. Amen.

—Miss Afton Bitton

He's There

When I feel I cannot go any farther,
He picks me up and tells me he knows.
When I feel I cannot sink any lower,
He pulls me out and tells me he sees.
When I feel that the pain can't hurt any worse,
He takes it away and shows me he cares.
When I feel that I cannot open my heart,
He reaches in and shows me he can.
When I think that my life can't get any harder,
I turn to him.
He's always there.

—Ms. Katie Nicole Aquino

My First Personal Psalm

In the cool of an autumn morning, I feel your presence, O Lord.
I feel your presence in the wind.
With the wind I am touched by your love.
In all of the seasons of my life, you are with me.
As a frightened child, I felt you holding my hand.
You held my hand through sickness and storms.
Though the night was dark, you were with me.
When no one seemed to care, you were with me.

When, in fear of death, I called on my friends and all my friends
had given until their own wells were dry,
your waters quenched my thirst.
Your waters, the wellspring of my life, cooled the fires of my anxiety.
They buoyed me up, O Lord, and gave me strength.
Your strength is ever present.
When I call in the darkness of the night, I hear your voice;
    it comforts me.
When I call in the morning, the first anxieties of the day
    rushing on me,
You are there.
Your peace and calm envelop me.
Envelop me, O Lord, and let me praise you.
Let me lift my heart and my hands to the Lord who is always
    with me.
Let me lift up my heart and hand to the One I love.

—*Ms. Susan Herport Methvin*

Psalm 1: It Is Not Enough, Lord

It is not enough, Lord;
it does not suffice.
Your eye, O Lord, is on the sparrow;
you will not ever let a sparrow fall.
Does the sparrow know?
Can she take wing with security,
or sit safely in her nest?
Are you just a God of safety nets, O Lord?
Or does your breath beneath her wings
lift her through currents of the air,
support her as she soars and swoops alike?
Is the soaring and the swooping all the same to you?
Are the rising and the falling both alike?
Does it matter if the tide is in or out,
or if the lungs are void or full of air?
To you, eternal, changeless,
Encompasser of constant motion
    in ultimate stillness,

there may be no difference:
no safety in repose,
no terror in the drop.
But it matters to the sparrow, Lord.
The sparrow knows the difference.

—*Ms. Terri Jones*

I spent most of one recent winter and spring angry at God for the emotional isolation of my childhood, saying, in effect, "I know you were there! Would it have killed you to communicate a little more directly? Thank you for survival: couldn't there have been some tangible sign, some word of comfort and care?" This psalm is a railing psalm at a God of Old Testament detachment. It dawned on me some months after I wrote it that Christ is the word and the promise that we're never alone. But that level of theologizing was beyond my miserable eight-year-old self.

Lord, Help Me to Hold in My Heart

Lord, help me to hold in my heart
The sun and the rain
The kernel of thought
To grow my own sweet corn.

—*Ms. Lucy Germany*

Letting Go

Somehow a word, a thought, a memory
    crosses my heart
    and leaves a bruise.

The pain it causes is sometimes deep and
Lingers to color all my days.
Who can ease this pain that binds me?
I can—
By letting go.

—*Ms. Joan L. Huff*

Barbara's Prayer

May I seek and find the sacred within me, reaching beyond panic, worry, anger, and fear to my part of the eternal. May the Holy Spirit dissolve my pain, selfishness, and vanity so that I may cheerfully accept success and failure equally, be grateful for the life I have been given and able to share what I have with others. Help me to understand that it is not through something outside of myself, but in recognizing the consequences of my own choices and my own exercise of faith that I will find the refreshment, strength, and other qualities I need if I am to be useful. Help me remember that it is not in striving against events, but in accepting what comes, even disappointments and sorrows, in the spirit of Christ and the Cross, that I will find peace and fulfillment. Amen.

—*Ms. Barbara A. Monsor*

Believe in Destiny

Finding your way,
discovering your purpose,
the spark of delight
becomes a roaring fire
of passion for destiny.
Believe in destiny.
There is always a purpose.
Know that now;
understand it
when it happens.
Your time will come,
they say.
You will know your purpose,
we're told.
It is true,
if you believe.
Believe,
destiny is God's will.
Believe,
God has a purpose for you.
And when you discover it,
you grow closer to hugging Jesus in the end.

—*Ms. Holly J. Wyman*

I Believe That Goodness

Dearest One,
I believe that goodness is the driving motion of it all,
That we can participate in and with that goodness,
That at the heart of goodness is the love of all life.
Lead us to see, participate in, and cooperate with that goodness.
Help us to complete goodness' joy and our own.
By doing that, we enter into your presence.

—Mrs. Phoebe W. Griswold

Prayer for Protection

Lord, guard us, your children, wherever we wander,
Release us from pressures we cannot withstand,
Lift us high when we falter or founder,
Place our feet on rocks and not on sand.
Give us your hand as we walk through the darkness,
Strengthen our souls with bright hope from above,
Keep joy in our hearts against all the world's starkness,
And fill all our emptinesses with your love.
Amen.

—Ms. Miranda K. Smith

I Pray for Faith

Dear Lord,
I pray that you will give me the strength
to face the trials of the coming day.
As the needs of my children arise
and I am called upon to help them,
I pray for strength.
As I strive to meet the demands of my aging parents,
to help them work through the decisions that must be made,
and to care for them with the same love that they shared with me,
I pray for compassion.

As I work to keep up my home,
to make it a place that my family will enjoy,
and that I can be proud of,
I pray for patience.
As I try to keep up with my own studies,
to read and study your word,
and to expand on my general knowledge,
I pray for understanding.
As I face the concerns of the world around me
and endeavor to keep up with all sides to issues,
as I try to find solutions to the injustices that I see,
I pray for guidance.

Dear Lord,
I face so many issues throughout my days,
sometimes I feel so torn.
I look to you for so many things.
Please guide my path,
that I may have the wisdom and skills to do my best.
Most of all
I pray for faith.
Amen.

—*Mrs. Suzanne Chiles Buchan*

A Prayer for Guidance

O God, here I am, a single entity, bearing the cares of many on my shoulders.
Help me to continue to be a source of light for them by your spirit.
Keep me from being weary.
Help me to continue to remember that your grace is sufficient.
Continue to light my path
And
Help me in all things not to rely on my own insight but to trust in you with all my heart, for you will direct my path.

—*Ms. Debra Q. Bennett*

Wild Geese at Night

I stepped into the darkness
from the bright, blind world
of men and hours.
The sound leaped down to me
echoing
from the frozen blazing stars.

My heart broke open
and Joy lifted me
to calling moonlit wing
as I, too, drove through the icy night
to the only possible destination.

—Thayer W. Beach, Ph.D.

Walking the Labyrinth

Walking the labyrinth
Thinking of the frustrating turns in women's lives
How empowering to find Christ at the center
where Mother Spirit leads us
As we yield to the path, the mind slows and quiets
The voice of the heart can be heard
Telling us how to be prophetic change makers
If we keep on walking through confusion
Speaking our truth
We enter the dwelling place of peace.

—The Reverend Diane Brelsford

I was walking the eight-hundred-year-old labyrinth in Chartres Cathedral and had a powerful sense of energy moving around me as I stood in the center of it. As I entered the labyrinth I prayed for discernment about a course of action. I felt I received guidance about which path to take. This was a blessing for me and hopefully will be to others who walk a labyrinth.

Re-nerving

Work out your own salvation with fear and trembling;
for it is God who is at work in you, enabling you both
to will and to work for his good pleasure.
—Philippians 2:13

When a woman listens to her own inner Wisdom and acts in accordance with her inner integrity, it is often with fear and trembling, for it may challenge cultural assumptions and disturb the status quo, bringing fierce hostility down upon her. I have a very vivid memory of watching a televised gathering in a Catholic church in Washington, D.C., for the first visit of the Pope in the 1970s. A number of church dignitaries were delivering welcoming messages, among them Sister Teresa Kane.

Unexpectedly, Sister Teresa deviated from her prepared text and in a modulated and persuasive way made an eloquent plea for consideration of the status of women in the Catholic Church. It was a riveting moment as camera close-ups showed the face and body language of an angry Pontiff leaning over and staring at the floor.

I had been having my own public struggles with the Episcopal Church, and I could sense the "fear and trembling" under Sister Teresa's calm demeanor and knew what courage was called for to take such an action. I was deeply moved. It made me feel proud to be a woman, and a surge of energy ran through me, re-nerving me to continue speaking my own truth in my own context.

—The Reverend Dr. Alison M. Cheek

Transitions

With God's Help

With God's help, I shall not fear change.

Some changes will cause great pain; others will bring joy.
Some will pass by barely noticed; others will alter the deepest
parts of my being. I will bring about many changes myself;
but changes I experience will also be brought about by others
around me, and I will be the tool God uses to change
others' lives.

With God's help, I shall accept that change will happen every day,
for I am not alone.

God shares the changes with me. God rejoices with me and
comforts me through the difficult days. As the quiet, solid
center that gives me something to cling to, God is the constant
in my quicksilver existence.

With God's help, I shall embrace it all.

Therefore, I shall not fear change. I shall trust that I can face
all the changes, welcome them all, and be stronger after they
have done their work on me.

I can do all this, with God's help.

—*Ms. Ethel Crawford*

Transitions

The diesel engine rumbles,
    idling aimlessly outside my door,
    telling the world
And especially my neighborhood
    of my Transition.

Strange burly men
    invade our home.
Wrapping treasured memories in layers
    of protective paper preparing them for Transition.

The boxes on shoulders march out the door,
    stripping our beloved house of all its home-ness,
    returning it to its anonymity.

No longer home—
    We have none today.
    We are in Transition.

I am tear-misted, chest-tightened.
> I cannot swallow a future
> on some other cul-de-sac.
I'm leaving all the familiars.
> Engines pull me farther, farther away.

AT&T, Sprint, MCI,
> Even e-mail.
They aren't face-to-face, skin-to-skin.
They're not the same as dreams and sorrows
> shared over iced tea while children's voices echo from our yard.
They're not the same as all the ordinary pleasures
> that have marked my days here.

My head knows the Transitions mean
> *Change, Opportunity, Growth, New Promise.*
And isn't that what life is all about?

But why, Lord?
Why does my heart ache so?

—*The Reverend Diane Moore*

A Prayer for Transition
(inspired by many search committees)

Ever-present God,
You call us on a journey to a place we do not know.
We are not where we started.
We have not reached our destination.
We are not sure where we are or who we are.
This is not a comfortable place.
Be among us, we pray.
Calm our fears, save us from discouragement,
And help us to stay on course.
Open our hearts to your guidance so that our journey to this
Unknown place continues as a journey of trust.
Amen.

—*The Reverend Canon Kristi Philip*

Reclaiming Revolution

Revolution is a fearsome word. It's not a word most can comfortably embrace. Perhaps that is because it conjures up images of something being destroyed, of violent acts, of chaos or anarchy. These are frightening to contemplate because it seems immoral to destroy something unless it is part of creating something better, more purposeful, more caring, and inclusive. It's terrifying to think of an exchange of power in which a new group will be the candidate for diminishment.

Perhaps we could think of revolution as evolution with an "r." To do so recognizes that change is a process and that we are, or can be, actively involved in what form it takes.

—*Ms. Katherine Tyler Scott*

Women at Work

The Interview

"Where have you been for the last twelve years?"
"Taking care of my children."
"What do you want to do?"
"Whatever I have to," I think to myself.

I feel myself starting to squirm.
I try to smile and tell her, "I can learn."
Now I don't know which way to turn.

She asks me again,
"Where have you been?"
"Taking care of my children."

She's so young; I'm so old.
"Keep your head up," I'm told.
"Just don't let them know."

O God, please give me strength.
Jesus, don't let her see me cry.
I want to run behind my family and hide.

And she asks me, again and again,
"Where have you been?"
"Taking care of my children."

"We will call you soon," they always say.
Tomorrow's interview will be better, I pray.

—Ms. Susan D'Antonio

Deacon in the Stock Market World

Gracious God, hear my prayer as I prepare to enter the workplace. Help me to be a faithful servant this day, responding to each opportunity you send me. Help me to sit among those who see the almighty dollar as their god, to bring your word to all that use unethical procedures or are tempted to do so, and to be a calming presence in an up or a down market.

Compassionate God, I pray for those who cannot be kind to their coworkers; help them find the path of kindness. Help especially those who have short tempers and use foul language that they may reach a higher level of communication. Help me to be flexible when the atmosphere begins to sour and to bring it back to serenity.

Empowering God, I thank you for my workplace, for the many opportunities to serve you there, and for calling me to an order of servanthood with my brother, Jesus. Hear my prayer for all your people both here in the market world and beyond the parameters in which I work. Help this deacon to be a beacon! Amen.

—The Reverend Rose Marie Martino

It's a Girl!

Day 1

"Can you tell if it's a girl or a boy?" the officer said, with fear.
In the background everyone could hear
The screams of pain both physical and not.
"That's my sister," a voice from the back seat said. "I love her a lot."

The accident scene was filled with lights and smoke.
The car was a tangled wreck.
Wiggling my fingers down her back
I found the remains of her bra strap.
Only then could I reply to my partner,
"It's a girl!"

Day 2

"Has anyone seen our daughter Lauren?
Do you know where she might be?"
The officer next to Mom and Dad looked straight at me.
"You know she's near," the officer said.
So we searched through the night,
Each minute filling with dread.
"I know where she is; I saw it in a dream."
And I knew the suspect was lying,
For he was purely mean.
When he led us to Lauren,
Her hair was matted with blood,
But her face was serene.
She was safe in God's arms.
"It's a girl!"

Day 3

"You'd better hurry up, Sarge," I heard the officer say,
But I was trying to go faster anyway.
Momma looked scared and Daddy not so sure,
But I knew exactly what to do, as I stepped through the door.
Suddenly the tiny head appeared.
The umbilical cord was wrapped tight
But a quick move released it
And a new life was brought into the world.
"It's a girl!"

—*Lieutenant Amy Myzie*

Eternal Questions

A radio plays its 5:30 A.M. tune.
I'm up, flip a switch,
and begin a brisk walk going nowhere.
Then pull it together, and I'm off.

The edge is gone, yet the job remains.
In-basket full to overflowing,
the day is done before I get a grip.
It's job security.

Home after dark,
I never seem to see the sun.
It's all so busy.
I drop exhausted into bed.

Another day,
no time to look at
the Big Questions.
There are so many "important" things to see.

—*Ms. Rietta Bennett*

A Prayer for Hospital and Hospice Caregivers

O "God unseen yet ever near," help us to make evident your near-ness to those with whom we minister. Empower us to make our caring for others a true reflection of our love for you. When we reach forth our hands to touch, let our fingers transmit your gen-tleness and healing love. When we part our lips to speak, let our words convey the constancy of your knowing. When we open our hearts to embrace, may the arms of your love reach through us to cradle the helpless, to strengthen the feeble, to caress the hurting, to celebrate all life as beginning and ending in you. Amen.

—*The Reverend Canon Jean Parker Vail*

This prayer was originally offered on St. Alexius Day at Alexian Brothers Medical Center in Elk Grove, Illinois, where I had done a residency in advanced clinical pastoral education.

Prayer of a Seamstress

Blessed are you,
O Lord, King of the Universe,

Who has given us skills and materials
to clothe ourselves and others
with warmth, comfort, and beauty.

As we spread whole cloth
and measure and cut and sew,
As we let hems down or up,
As we take seams in or out,

Let this be a holy reminder
that not one of God's children
can outgrow or wear out
the enfolding love of
God, our Creator.

Amen.

—Mrs. Ann C. Case

My mother sewed, my daughter has a college degree in costume design, and I'm now gathering sewing tools for my granddaughter.

Prayer of San Pasqual
(patron saint of cooks and kitchens)

O Loving and Nurturing God,
When we were starving in the desert,
You blessed us with manna,
That we would not perish from hunger.
Make of my hands an instrument
of your sustaining love.
Help me to so prepare this food that
all who partake will be
blessed twice by your bounty.

Keep all who work in this kitchen
free from hurt, anger, or carelessness.
Help us always to remember that even
in the midst of joy, sorrow, crisis, and despair,
people still must be fed and cared for.
Grant that what is prepared here
brings strength and health.
Nourish all who eat here with your love,
And give us all grateful hearts for daily bread.

Grant us joy in our daily cycle of work,
and keep us mindful of the
necessity for laughter, play, and rest.
Keep us from self-pity, reminding us always
of your command, "Feed my sheep."
Fill us with your Spirit,
that we always will remember
from whence come our joy and our salvation.

—*Ms. Katie Sherrod*

*Written on the occasion of the opening of my husband's restaurant/
art gallery.*

Prayer for a Teacher's First Day of School

God the Father and Mother of all,
Bless this first day of school.
Give patience, understanding, and hope to all teachers and
students in this journey of learning in a new school year.
Calm the butterflies in stomachs
and secure us in your care and love; be with us this day and forever.
Amen.

—*Ms. Bonnie L. Turner*

In twenty-four years of teaching, I still get excited about school.

A Night Worker's Prayer for Forgiveness

Lord, please forgive the person who woke me up. Calm my anger at him and all others who forget—or don't care—that my sleep time is while they are awake. Give me a quiet and forgiving heart. If it is possible, let me sleep again. If not, let me wake with peace and charity. Amen.

—*Ms. Anne L. Haehl*

Sunday Night Tub Cleaning

Lord, how is it that I find you
    even in cleaning the bathtub?

I sling my body over its side,
    such an awkward position.
And then I realize that simultaneously
    I am on my knees.

Down into this cavern—one hand bracing
    and the other scrubbing.
We create strange postures in our lives
    lived before you.

I look around and know that I do not
    plunge myself *inside* other things to clean them!

There is simple delight in transforming
    the scum into bubbles.
I do this part.

And then the flow of water carries away my effort
    and reveals the wondrous shine of porcelain.

It is merely me on the sides of this tub:
    my dirt that I try to wash away.
How odd the effort to send my many layers
    down the drain.
How disgusted I become with my scum
    when I see it.

Yet you stand ready, Loving God, to release
    me from this burden.
You come with the mighty rush of Living Waters
    to complete the task.
Or you appear in the quiet trickle.

Your water as *beginning* to make the lather,
    your water as *cleansing* to make me sparkle
    in your light's reflection.

Fresh and new this clean vessel,
    restoring waters,
Ready to provide the warmth and calm
    of a late-night bubble bath—
A gift of grace—
    to take me into rest and the morrow.

—*The Reverend Mary Anne Akin*

I lead a weekly study/support group for women in the workplace. This reflection on Sunday night chores before another week begins was my contribution to prayers written by the group.

Abuse

Lament for a Broken Child

Help me O God
I don't know how to give voice
    to this pain
the brooding ache in my heart

My little child spirit
    broken like a wild horse
a wild alive person cut down
    something cut out
    and in its place
    terror
fear locked in the bone

Like Sarafina she vowed
    to be very very good and careful
and watchful and ashamed
    cowed pretending acting
    hidden sick lying
sick at heart, sick at life
    deeply deeply depressed
    alone
rage all shriveled up
    and contorted
into secret episodes of self-torture

Hear me O God
    She came home broken
That is why I am weeping inside
    for that little girl who was
    taken to Hell
    and left to walk home
alone

—*Ms. Barbara Hughes*

The House of Secrets

Like a vise the heavy roof grips
the tall house and squeezes
out its light and life.
Stone eyebrows over narrow windows
and airless rooms frown at passersby.
Lies slide into shadowed corners
of high-ceiling rooms. Dusty cobwebs
trap secrets next to dead flies and moths.
In the dark, nightmares wake the children,
monsters advancing through black corridors
and locked doors into their rooms.

The children go forth each morning,
concealing bruises, hiding terror
behind smiling mouths and cold eyes.
In the dusk of late afternoon
the children return and hide in their rooms,
cowering under beds, in the closets.

They shiver in shame remembering
their sins—a bike left in the driveway,
crumbs on the floor.
Then, the father's long arm snatching, shaking,
before they sit down to dinner
and he asks the blessing.

—*Ms. Gloria Masterson Richardson*

Playing with Dolls

A rag doll thrown against the wall
falls into a heap, its clothes in
disarray.

Somewhere a child sobs,
takes short breaths, and
sighs too deep for words.

Hands pick up the doll and
spin it around, throwing
it again.

Somewhere
a puppy whimpers.

I look down from the ceiling and
watch the man play with his
anger.

The man is my father.
The rag doll is me.

Why, Daddy, why?

—*The Reverend Canon Gwendolyn-Jane Romeril*

Knowing

God so loved the world that
    he gave his only begotten Genesis,
Exodus, Leviticus shall come rejoicing,
    bringing in the sheaves.
Grandmother taught me important things when I was six.

Later, the omnipotent,
    ever-present and loving father taught
Me in ways that made my body burn,
    breaking sacred boundaries,
My bleeding soul left longing.
I feel so clean, I remember saying
    as I came up out of the baptismal waters.
It was Columbus Day, and like Columbus
    I didn't know the horizon I gazed upon.

Decades later the view on the horizon
    comes clear and I see God
Like father a child molester.
    God like father abandons the faithful.
Rage comes keening,
    and in low, animal-like grunts
Primitive objections to instinctively felt chaos.
    Just where the hell were you when
Father was molesting me?

I want to know.

Out of the dark silence
    Comes God's wordless answer.
Kneeling by the bed, face buried in heaven's
    Crazy quilt, God is crying. Pain flowing out
In tears mixes with my blood on the sheets.
    Original freedom, unrepented, tears God's soul.

Often still, when I let God in,
    I feel the silent consent of incest.
But each time I find the courage to say yes.
    Each time, another drop of blood soaks in, and
I am nearer to knowing that
    God so loves the world.

—Ms. Elizabeth Forbes

Rebirth

Dear Heavenly Father, I ask that you place your healing hand on my precious *husband* and all others who have lost their childhood because of abuse. May they find the loving, caring Father in you that they never had in their earthly *fathers*. Through your Holy Spirit, may the child in them be reborn and nurtured in a new life with Christ Jesus, in whose name we pray. Amen.

—*Ms. Kathryn S. Ford*

The word child *could be substituted for the word* husband, *and the word* elders *could be substituted for the word* fathers *to adapt this prayer for personal needs.*

Women's Words in the Night

We are the hands that rock the cradle.
But what if our hands are battered and bloody?
tremble from coercion?
abandon the cradle?

We are the voices that sing the lullaby.
But what if our voices are faint?
shriek with rage?
are silenced?

We are the eyes that behold hope.
But what if our eyes are closed?
glazed with pain?
ignore the vision?

We are the hearts that burst with reconciliation.
But what if our hearts embrace forgiveness?
flower with justice?
redeem the violence?

—*Ms. Margaret J. Faulk*

Back to the Garden

Everyone is celebrating.
Everyone is gay.
But I withdraw on every night
and with my visions, pray.

I go into my garden
Away from all the cheers.
I go into my garden
And gaze into my fears.

I go into my garden.
I wander down the past.
Beyond the flowers, I still can see
the cloud the future casts.

I go into my garden
Alone as it must be.
I spend many hours in this place.
It's called Gethsemane.

—*Ms. Tessie Ann Adams*

Faith

Amazing what a couple of beers can do—

I have watched as you have:
    Pushed and shoved our kids:
I will lift up mine eyes unto the hills; From whence cometh my help?
    Wrestled one down to the floor, drawing blood;
My help cometh even from the Lord, Who hath made heaven and earth.

I have listened as you have:
    Called them degrading names,
He will not suffer thy foot to be moved, and He that keepeth thee will not sleep.
    While giving me the silent treatment.
The Lord himself is thy keeper, the Lord is thy defense upon thy right hand.

I have staggered under the weight as you have:
    Declined to help with housework or yard care,
So that the sun shall not burn thee by day, nor the moon by night.
    Cooking, transportation, or childcare.
The Lord shall preserve thee from all evil; Yea, it is even He that
shall keep thy soul.

I am crushed as you have:
    Discounted me as a mother,
The Lord shall preserve my going out
    Rejected me as a friend,
And my coming in
    Turned away from me as a lover
From this time forth for evermore.

Amen.

—*The Reverend Ophelia G. Laughlin*

To Mother: Reflections Following Her Suicide

How could you, propped up in your four-poster bed?
I've spent months reflecting on that.
Jigsaw puzzle images pop into mind,
Each one precariously but perfectly in place, held together
    with patriarchal glue.

Was it the talent unspent or the dreams not pursued
From energies focused on home?
Car pools, bake sales, luncheons, and shopping,
You knew well the '50s-woman's place.

"Depressed?" asked your doctor.
"Sure, honey, don't worry. Take these. You'll feel much
    better then.
Addictive? Not Valium; take one each day.
Just don't call me. You're one of too many."

Was it the nest vacated, your purpose dissipated
After each of your chicks flew away
Their own nests to establish, their own lives to live
Leaving a vacuous twenty-four-hour day?

Or was it the incest attempt or the physical abuse suffered
    so long ago?
"Don't tell now. We're church folk.
What would they think?
Bury your feelings, even the memory, and smile."

So you smiled and took pills and smiled and took more pills
Just like they told you you should.
Spiraling downward ever deeper, gaining momentum, hurling,
    lurching,
Toward the black nothingness of a barrel pointed inward.

"She was sick, not well, very depressed," they mused,
Filled with patriarchal aplomb.
"No one's to blame, that's for sure, that we know.
She just couldn't cope, poor soul."

They destroyed your soul; how could you?

—Ms. Jeanette Moffatt

I Was Born to Be . . .

I was born to be
an evening primrose.
I was destined to
blossom into
a poet
a writer
a musician
an artist
a teacher and
healer
but my family
wrapped itself tightly
around my tender fragile petals
binding and restraining me
until the light of morning
draws near
and I have never blossomed.
O God, be with me, as I try to bloom.

—Anonymous

Candle Prayer
(for Roxanne)

O God of Love,

Look kindly upon the flame that is my soul.
Though it glows like a tiny sapphire,
Barely visible in the dark,
It contains the life of light.
It is precious to me,
For in this infant flame I know you dwell;
And as you choose to dwell in me,
So also must I be precious in your sight.
In your patience, Lord, never allow this flame,
    however small, to be extinguished.
Let me nurture it in stillness,
Giving it ample room to breathe;
And grant *me* patience as I watch and feel it grow,
Slowly, imperceptibly,
Into the Light of Life.

Amen.

—*Ms. Wendy Lyons*

From Jerusalem to Jericho: A Retelling of the Good Samaritan for Battered Women

"A woman who was much abused by her wealthy husband left Jerusalem and headed toward Jericho to seek shelter among kinswomen," Jesus told the crowd. "And as she was going, her wounds caused such pain that she sat down beside the road and wept.

"Now by chance a priest was going down that road, and noting her fine garments, he stopped to ask the cause of her distress. When she told him that her husband had beaten her near to death, the priest drew back and counseled her to return to her husband and be a better wife. Then he crossed the road and continued on his journey.

"So likewise a judge, when he came to the place, stopped to question the woman, and learning the cause of her agony he, too, counseled that her duty was to her husband and that she should return at once to Jerusalem. When she refused, he, too, crossed the road and continued on his journey.

"But a Samaritan, as he journeyed, came to where the woman lay beside the road, and when he heard her story, he had compassion, and he bound up her wounds and set her on his own beast and brought her to an inn where he found women to care for her, saying, 'There are those who seek her life to destroy it, and no one must know that she is here. When she is well enough to travel, see that she has safe passage to Jericho. And whatever more you spend, I will repay you when I come back.'

"Which of these three, do you think, proved neighbor to the woman?"

And the lawyer said, "Should not the woman have returned to her husband? You preach words of forgiveness. Should she not have forgiven her husband, obeyed the law, and returned home? Weren't the priest and judge the better neighbors? The Samaritan assisted the woman in her disobedience."

And Jesus said, "Woe to you who pervert justice and allow injury to the innocent! You fools! Did not God make woman and man both in the Divine image? Is not a woman's body a temple of God? I say to you, whoever injures anyone, woman, man, or child, injures the Divine image and is held accountable before God."

And the women in the crowd spoke to one another, "Here is one who understands; truly this must be the Holy One of God."

—*Mrs. Mary Lee Wile*

At a Vigil for Domestic Violence

Dear God our Creator,
We gather today because we care
about those affected by domestic violence:
women, children, and men.

We remember those who have lost their
lives to this malfunction of our society.
We pray that their souls are now at rest.

We remember children living in homes of domestic violence.
Deliver and protect them from further harm.

We pray for perpetrators,
that they may seek help.
Help them to relinquish their need to exert power and control.

We remember current victims
whose lives are filled with fear and uncertainty.
Those who are trapped in the psychological cycle
of violence and abuse,
hope and false love.
We ask that you give them a new vision.
Guide them with your wisdom to make sound choices
that will lead to new life.

We pray that religious leaders will
end Scripture abuse
so that they may no longer contribute to the
oppression of women.

We give thanks to those who
dedicate their lives to providing
education, shelter, and support.

Finally, O gracious God,
be present with us,
restore peace and hope
that we may persevere with your Holy Spirit.
In faith we pray,
Amen.

—*The Reverend Angela F. Shepherd*

Reflections at Marketplace

I went to see the memorial
to Holocaust victims the other day
I walked reverently through
making no noise
thinking of those poor dead souls
who suffered, unrescued, and died

There was an inscription
saying to pause and reflect
pause and reflect
"on the consequences of a world
in which there is no freedom
a world in which basic human rights
are not protected . . .
where . . . discrimination and victimization
are tolerated"

I reflected
and then returned to the shelter
where they bolted me in.
O Lord, turn these reflections' tears
to prayers

—*Ms. Tessie Ann Adams*

Prayer to Our Sheltering God

O God, our comforter in hard times, often have we called to you
in pain and you have answered our pleas. Here we sit this night,
guardians of a shelter where women lie sleeping, briefly safe from
the battering and bitterness of a world that does not protect
them. They look to us to knit together their shattered hopes,
dreams, and lives. But, you, O God, are the tailor, the binder of
wounds, and the great healer. Help us to be conduits for your
love, to reveal you to them, and in seeing their joy, to know you
more deeply. In the name of him who fully opened himself to all
in need, Jesus Christ, your Son. Amen.

—*Ms. Jayne Oasin*

A Meditation for a Displaced Homemaker

Displaced but not forgotten. In faith I carry on.
Jesus, dear shepherd of his sheep, to whom my heart belongs.
Thank you, dear Lord Jesus, for a most holy dwelling place.

One of joy, peace, and quiet confidence for those who seek
   your face.
Created in God's image, I know to whom I belong.
Abandoned I will never be. In faith I'll carry on.

—*Ms. Naomi Vitelli*

For Peace after Sexual Assault

Loving God, I know that you hold me in the palm of your hand.
I know it is so.
But *why*, O Lord, *why*?
I rage at this sin against me, at this defilement of my body,
this assault on my peace of mind.

I mourn my lost serenity, security, confidence;
I mourn the loss of my ease and open nature.
I hate what his assault has done to me.
I feel that my body and soul may never be the same.
What has been forced upon me may not be forgotten.

But send your healing upon me like cool rain.
Soothe my spirit with the balm of your tender love.
Help me to feel secure again, as safe as ever within the shelter
   of the Lord.

Let my anger not turn inward to self-loathing,
but outward for action and purpose: to help others like me,
to bring hope to those whose faith is not so strong.
Help me, with your grace,
to move beyond *victim*, to call myself *survivor* instead.

May you forgive this man's offense against me,
and grant me the peace and serenity
of a mind and body made whole again.

Amen.

—*Ms. Julia Park Rodrigues*

Insight

"Now I lay me down to sleep
I pray the Lord . . ."
that one night
I might sleep
the whole time through.

I came to your sanctuary
seeking solace from the Beloved
and instead received
more pain from your ordained.

I wandered the storms of the
desert trying to reclaim that
which was lost in the presence
of your ministers.

I looked for answers outside
the Faith, but nothing outside
would suffice.
I knew the answer must come from
inside the life of Jesus Christ.

So I returned to bow once more
to the knowing love of Jesus Christ
who is my Lord.

No matter how I needed the Church
to make it right.
I now know it was beyond its insight.

With prayers and words the healing
finally came, not from your ordained
but from the love of family, friends, and
Jesus Christ. Amen.

—*The Reverend Canon Margo E. Maris*

This is a poem written after listening, working, and reflecting on the stories and the voices of more than one thousand survivors of clergy sexual misconduct.

Healing for a Parish after Sexual Exploitation

God is with you at this time of trial.
The fabric has been torn but the weavers are among us.
We need only to allow them to begin to weave and make us
    whole again.
A patch is often stronger than the hole that it fills.

Let us also learn what is important,
What is our mission both corporately and individually,
How the cloth can be added to with softness and strength,
With color of diversity and pastel of unity.
Let us see the Holy Spirit present in the threads to make the
    fabric whole,
Knowing each thread by name, by color, by strength,
And let the fabric be offered to God in thanksgiving for the
    fabric of life of which we are all apart.

Amen.

—*Anonymous*

Phoenix

Silently
Life emerges from deep within.
'Neath raging walls of twisted Scripture.
She had languished there
Once.
Ties that bound, tempting her always
to back down, have severed.

Strengthened,
She arises yet again, giving voice
To those who dwell therein;
Darkness still.

Ashes to ashes, dust to dust;
"Be gone from me all who raise
Anger, fisted, in his Holy Name!"
No.
Arise again, Phoenix.

—*Ms. Melanie A. Seitz*

Prayer for Boundaries

O God, you set upon our borders sentinels who are never silent
and watchers who never sleep; guard and protect the boundaries of
my soul. You shelter us under the shadow of your wings; create
within me a safe place in which to heal. Speak tenderly to my
spirit, Holy Mother, and teach me to stand upright in the center
of my being. Comfort my fear, that I may walk freely within my
own sanctuary, and become a place of welcome to those who come
in peace. In the name of your dear child, Jesus. Amen.

—*Ms. Barbara Hughes*

Illness

The Singing Bird

> *If I keep a green bough in my heart, the singing bird will come.*
> —*Old Chinese Saying*

I tried to keep a green bough in my heart, Lord,
    tried to reach the cool shade of your arms,
    the cleansing sweetness of your tears,
    and yet, the pain so fierce, I could not see your tender eyes
    nor hear your soothing voice
    nor feel your cooling touch,
    but you were there with me.

You nourished and sheltered that bough—
    you, through my ministering angel . . . angels.

Can I but believe the singing bird will come?

—*Ms. Patricia B. Clark*

Suffering

Dear God,

I do not understand the reasons for so much suffering. I do not know what healing can be for her. I feel limited and inadequate. I only know that your love is present for all. Your love does not depend on answers or solutions. Use me, I pray, as your instrument. Let my presence be your love to this special child of yours. I pray in and with Jesus, whose suffering led to joy. Amen.

—*Ms. Trudy James*

Prayer for My Beloved

O Lord, bless my beloved who found torment in this life through HIV and AIDS. Thank you, O Lord, for giving my beloved the strength to carry his burden with dignity. Thank you, O Lord, for the love and the laughter, for the moments of joy, for unwavering faith, and for a death marked with great love. I rejoice, O Lord, in the gift of his life. Help me, O Lord, to set aside my painful memories and remember, O Lord, that my beloved and I are always in your sight.

—*Anonymous*

Goliath's Battle

Too many Goliaths out there.
They are laughing at me in my pain,
My murky clay,
My winter's rain.

Where are you, Lord,
Healer of my soul?

You had calmed my slumber once,
Freed my mind from the turbulence
Of its youth.

Too many Goliaths out there.
Their arrows sharpened,
Attacking my spine once again.

Once again, the pain
Torments this body, your temple,
This mind, your vehicle,
And
Questions your healing.

My battle starts with the morning sun,
When thanking you for your Light,
Which has changed my spirit from Darkness.

Goliath, the furious beast,
Lies in wait,
When I have not yet put on
My full armor,
And assaults me.

I'm confused in my solitude,
Trying to make some sense of war,
Where loved ones make no sense,
Where disturbing nightmares and
Worthlessness try to exercise
Their authority
And
Thoughts of assisted suicide
Run rampant through my mind.
No!
Goliaths be gone!
I am God's child.
God, am I your child?

—*Ms. Joanne Starks*

Prayer of Someone Facing an Operation

Tomorrow a knife will pierce my flesh
while I lie in slumber.
It is for my health;
nevertheless, I am afraid.
Honor my fear, O God,
and instill me with courage.
Bless those who tend my body
and grant them the power to heal me
as you make me whole;
in the name of the healer
Christ I pray. Amen.

—The Reverend Dr. Vienna Cobb Anderson

On Donating a Kidney

Generous Creator,
You took the sad barrenness of my body
And allowed me to give life
Not to flesh of my flesh and bone of my bone
But to my brother.

Now he can drink the cool water of freedom
Not tied to a machine
Free to wander landscapes only dreamed of.
You helped me give away a part of my body
And it made me whole.

—Ms. Judy Mood

The Lesson of the Blue Jays

It's "only" skin cancer I tell myself
While an unacknowledged cold fist of fear
Grips my gut.
I have seen what it can do;
I need only think of our dear neighbor.
And I try to push the panic back.

Breakfast. A cold, wet Saturday.
My mind is blank, waking up.
Then I hear it,
A soft bird call, faint and plaintive,
Almost a sob,
Sad and forlorn.

Lifting my eyes from my cereal,
I see it—the blue jay.
Wet and bedraggled,
Perched on a branch by the suet
Chirping his sad song.

I watch, gripped by some unknown drama.
Moments pass.
The sad song continues. Then!
We both hear it—the blue jay and I—
A responding call from up the gulch and
Into view swoops the mate.
Their separation is no more!

The two are together now.
And I learn in the deep way that
Only God can teach
How much I love my spouse
And how very sad I'd be without him—
As sad as a wet bird singing a sorrowful song.

—*Mrs. Gretchen Olheiser*

To the Cancer on My Father's Vocal Cord

I stand before you—you clandestine,
now no bigger than an acorn
with plans to stretch and swell in secret.
But I am David to your Goliath.

I bring an arsenal of words
with prehistory for a sack.
I come with sound and song and rhyme,
with dentals, gutterals, fricatives.
I come to declaim and recite

with psalm, petition, lecture, aim
to break your hold and make you go;
I come as tirade and command.

I come as voice that stakes a claim
to speak and tell and name this world.
I come to reclaim, stretch, and strum,
and to embody what I say.
I take this page and wad it tight,
make my own strong cords a sling,
breathe in a bellow's worth of sound
and hurl it at you and your kind.

—*The Reverend Penelope Duckworth*

A Prayer for Young Mothers with Breast Cancer

Lord, give me strength to bear this new sorrow
And hear always my thankful cry
That this unspeakable horror has happened to me—
And not to my child.

Lord, in this time of trial, grant me the wisdom to know
That this spiteful growing cancer will open doors for me,
That I'll understand more clearly what my life has been,
And what it ought to be.

Lord, give me the compassion to withstand
The voices of doom railing against cancer's evil march across our souls.

Give me the grace to smile, to offer my prayers,
That others may find the comfort I find
In the hollow of my shepherd's hand.

And, Lord, please grant me the blessing to stay with my child
For as long as he needs me.

—*Ms. Marie Fowler*

These were my prayers when I was diagnosed and was coping with treatment. My son was seven then and he's fifteen now. I have been granted the incredible blessing of watching that little boy grow up!

When a Woman Friend Faces Death

Sometimes we forget we were born.
We remember we were born only when it seems that life is no
longer on our terms.

We live life daily. We make our big decisions.
We love. We play. We fight. We lose. We weep.
We pretend for a while that we are in control.

How foolish we feel when a woman friend faces death.
How silly we are with our words and our thoughts.

We are scared. We feel pity. We feel relief, believing that perhaps
we are different, stronger, wiser. We still believe that we have
somehow escaped mortality, that life will never leave us. We will
have our moments forever.

Why can we not see the courage in their eyes,
their wisdom, their soaring souls?
Why do we not realize that they are the pioneers with
compassion for us?

For those who are remembering their birth have seen beyond life.
They have come face-to-face with their spirit. We must recognize
these living spirits among us. They hold in their heart what we
see and know not. They hold life. They hold courage. They hold
faith. They hold eternity.

They need us not.

For they are winged spirits, soaring a clear blue morn on a silver
note that sings to the world the silhouette of their soul.

—Ms. Karen Ott Mayer

Hospice

Today the therapist brought a Hoyer Lift,
that leviathan of rehabilitation equipment,
but a liberator for her.
It frees her from bed and the tiresome sheets,
faded like the dreams dissolved by cancer.

With gentle hands he maneuvers and teaches
until she is settled in the wheelchair,
a more benevolent captor.
It gives her freedom to move throughout
the home she created and kept.

Near the window, she asks:
"Did my husband remember to plant the flowers?"
He says, "They're out there."
He turns her slightly and she sees the blossoms,
some just opening and others already faded.
Hair lost, paralysis settling in, she hopes enough to ask,
"How long will it take to get over this?"
He defers to her doctor.
But a soft touch conveys his prayer
for a gentle death like the fading of her flowers.

—*Ms. Mary H. Eick*

Healing

Prayer for Forgotten Dreams

O My Beloved Creator,
My dreams have been packed away so long,
beneath my pain.
I thought I had to protect them
from those around me,
who would squash and bruise them
as carelessly as they would kill an insect.
In all those years the dreams have grown
quiet and dusty until I've forgotten they were there.
By forgetting, I'd hoped to ease
the pain of their silence and unuse.
Instead the pain had deepened until
it ripped through my body and left a scar on my soul.
Help me now to heal the wounds.
Help me dust off those dreams,
to bring them forth to live again.
So they may breathe and grow and dance in the sunlight.

Help me use them as a message of your love
and for the good of all your world.
Help me to find the courage to believe in them again
and to lead them into your glorious light.
Help me to heal.
Thank you, Beloved Presence.

—*Ms. Donna Marquardt*

The Woman Bent

And just then there appeared a woman with a spirit that had crippled her for eighteen years. She was bent over and was quite unable to stand up straight. When Jesus saw her, he called her over and said, "Woman, you are set free from your ailment." When he laid his hands on her, immediately she stood up straight and began praising God.
                                                                —Luke 13:11–14

My back has hurt for eighteen years.
Or is it eighteen thousand?
My back has all but given out.
I have looked down day after day,
looked at my feet,
looked at the dirt,
looked at these toenails lined with grime
and the calluses now hard as horn.
I have looked down
for I could not look up.

I have been bent for so long
I thought this was how I was made.
I'd forgotten what it was to stand straight.
I'd forgotten how this body felt
when the vertebrae stack one upon another,
nice and straight.
I'd forgotten what it was like to breathe in
and feel that good air rush through
heart, gut, lungs.
I'd forgotten what things look like if I stand up.

I had been so used to being bent
that being straight feels odd.
Feels like new shoes.
Feels like I'm a different person.
Feels like I can see, breathe, move, speak.
Feels like I can't be bent again.
Feels like I am a different woman,
and yet this body knows
being bent is hell.

Funny thing, when he laid hands on me,
he felt my spine.
Felt those bumps
that others flinch from.
Felt those protrusions.
Funny thing, when he laid hands on me,
I wanted to stand up.
Something in me remembered—
I have not always been this way.
I have not always been curved and twisted.

So now I can breathe,
I can take a breath and simply feel the rush of air.
I can see the sky.
I can speak because I can breathe.
And I have plenty to say.

The dirt taught me a lot, you see.
I spent so long looking at that dust between
my toes that I know some things.
I made friends with soil,
with grime,
with earth.
I made the acquaintance of the dust.
And she is my friend.
That dust will not let me go.
Now when I bend over to see her,
it is out of love and memory.
It is out of wanting to remember being bent,
so that I do not bend another.
It is out of wanting to receive whatever gifts
being bent gave me.

I had been bent so long,
that woman is a part of me.
She learned some things
in that distorted posture;
she knows.
So now, when I stand straight,
when those vertebrae stack gently one by one,
when the stretching of limb and ligament
frees this body of those age-old contortions,
I give thanks to the me who was bent—
for seeing it through,
for carrying on,
for birthing the one
who can stand up straight
and speak.

—*The Reverend Mary Earle*

A Meditation on the Twenty-third Psalm

Lord, you are:
A companion to my spirit—
Father and Shepherd of a life;
Perplexing at times for me.
Designing a purpose for me.

Fashioned in you,
I am in need of nothing
But the riches coming from
The depths of your love.

Lord, you are my Shepherd.
May your hands calm my rough waters
When I am tossed by swift currents
And
Fleeting wind.

May my soul be restored,
Healed,
Reconciled with body,
Delighting in its abode.

May the focus of my eyes stay fixed
Upon images of your face in all of
Creation.

Lord, you are my Shepherd.
Anoint my head with your oil;
Bathe me with the sweet perfume
Of your Word.
Penetrate my spirit with your truths,
That I may reflect such
To a hungry world.

Fill my cup overflowing
With your presence,
That my heart may sing in jubilation
Songs of your unceasing love.

Lord, you are my Shepherd,
The bosom of your temple
Will be my dwelling place forever.
Lord, my Shepherd,
Blest am I, your sheep!

—*Ms. Joanne Starks*

Healing and Blessing

Come now reviving Spirit of our God,
Breathe your healing strength upon those who suffer
And then, renew and bless all who
Proclaim and perform your liberating Word.

—*Fredrica Harris Thompsett, Ph.D.*

*I have learned that healing and blessing are kindred actions, twins in
the overall economy of God's grace. This prayer for healing grew out
of living with loved ones with AIDS and other illnesses.*

Prayer for Erin

Through this time of resting and healing of your inner being, may God's angels continue in their vigilance to watch and guide and to keep your spirit ever present and resting with Jesus. And when the time of reawakening comes, may God bring you back to us in wholeness, fully restored, to continue this life in testimony of his great Love. Amen.

—*The Reverend Sarah B. Crandell*

Erin was in an accident that caused multiple head injuries and many broken bones. She went into a deep coma and has been kept there until the swelling goes down. I asked God to heal her completely, working miracles in her to edify the body of Christ as a witness to him. In time, she moved a leg and blinked her eyes.

Prayer with Outstretched Arms: The Loss of a Limb and Its Healing

Lord:
My illness is gone, and gone is its threat to my life.
But for that cause is my leg also gone, and with it the life of my soul.
I have been hurled into the deep of depression,
into the heart of a black sea,
and the currents swirl over me.
All its waves and breakers sweep my head under and I cannot
    breathe.
Lord, you are gone from my sight and I have no hope.
I lie in my bed in the dark, alone and unable to rise.
My crutches mock me from their place against the bed,
taunting me with supposed means to walk,
condemning me with the sure knowledge that when I lean upon
    them I shall fall.
I cannot see you, cannot imagine you are there—
nevertheless, I lean upon you, O Lord, for I have no other.
The engulfing waters of fear
bring me down to the roots of despair.

But you, O Lord, saved your people with an outstretched arm.
Stretch out your arm to me, O Lord.
If only you uphold me, yet may I stand; yet may I hope.

Lord, you have brought my life up from the pit.
For in my anxious dreams there was a sudden, holy silence
and there I beheld your arm outstretched from heaven,
unlike the crutches, not mocking me,
no false promise this,
for you invited my hand into yours.
And in my dream, I stood!
Now it is morning, and it is I who taunt the crutches.
How dare they threaten my confidence? They will serve me,
     and you.
Leaning now upon your own arm, Lord, I lean also upon them,
and behold, I do stand, and I do not sway, nor am I brought to
     shame with a fall.
Now I rejoice with those who say to me, "Let us go to the house
     of the Lord."
For my feet will stand in your gates, O Jerusalem,
in the arms of Jesus once and forever upheld.
I shall praise you now and forevermore.

Lord, it is years since your arm first upheld me.
You have made me to stand with limbs not my own,
your arms filling my arms with strength,
your spirit uplifting my soul,
your will propelling me forth in freedom.
I now walk with a grace unlike that of other women.
It is grace nonetheless, a powerful grace,
a sure sign of your own presence,
and of the healing of that night.
You have given me freedom of spirit,
freedom of movement,
freedom to love, to enjoy, to climb the steps of the house
     of the Lord.
I rise up to celebrate you, O Lord.
I celebrate my independence
from all others save you,
and under my own power and yours,
I shall praise your name everywhere,
in the street, in the marketplace, in the appointed spaces
     of my work.

Wherever I walk—I walk, in some new way, in your way.
With every step, I shall praise you in my heart forever.

Amen.

—*The Reverend Kamila Blessing*

This prayer represents the experience of a real woman whose leg had been amputated because of cancer. Though physically well, she became literally disabled with fear, depression, and humiliation. Then one night she had a dream; after the dream, she was healed. Today she is as independent as anyone I have ever known. The genuineness of her healing is represented in the last section of the psalm, representing her looking back at it to tell the story, many years later. The prayer uses praise from Psalm 122 and images and expressions from Jonah engulfed in the sea.

Walking

Take a step,
Put one foot
In front of
The other foot.
Oh,
It is so hard to lift
One foot
Feel bone and balance shift.
To walk at all
Is just a series of arrested falls.
So,
Do not fall.
Put
One foot
In front of
The other foot,
And then
Again,
And go.

—*Mrs. Anna Tessaro*

One year ago, I smashed my right knee cap, and now I must learn to walk all over again. I am woefully lame. My prayer is for patience and for the knowledge to know that I need help, that I must reach out for support, physically, and otherwise, and to bless those who are learning more about disabilities so that those of us who cannot walk (or see or speak) can participate more fully in our world.

A Prayer for One Living with a Disability

Lord God, I thank you for the fact that you have given me the gifts I need to fulfill the ministries you have set forth in my life; that you have shown me how to put at ease those who are uncomfortable with what they see as incomplete; and that you have blessed me with the grace of those who see me as a whole and integrated person. I give you thanks for the quiet—and sometimes not so quiet—confidence you have instilled in me, and for the strength I derive from the oneness I feel with you, through Jesus Christ. Amen.

—*Ms. Antoinette (Toni) Daniels*

A Prayer for Renewal

You poor giraffe-like plants
Stretching out
your necks
Toward the light
How you thirst for sun!
I know what it is like
I too am
pulled
Away from darkness
Toward what's bright

Lord, do not let this yearning cease
Make me a resurrection plant
Soaking my roots
In your redeeming water
Turning my leaves
Toward your light
And sharing your rebirth

—*Ms. Anne Morgan*

Acceptance

May I remember, dear God, that I belong in your arms.
It is there that I am healed, and there that I am whole.
May all impurities be cast from my mind, my heart, my body.
May every fiber of my being be filled with your light.
May my cells vibrate with your divine energy.
May my body and soul radiate your love.
You are my divine physician.
In you I trust.
I accept your will for me.
I accept your healing.
I accept your love.
I accept myself.
Amen.

—*Ms. Glenna Mahoney*

A Psalm

Help me, O Lord, in this frightening hour of need,
When fear courses through me like dangerous,
bright white electricity.

I do not want to face this awful affliction.
But, apparently,
according to your divine plan,
I must.

I wish it were not so.

For the moment, I sorely want to rest
my battered body and
my bruised soul in the heart of your divine love.

I seek in you my own restoration
and resurrection,
Plain truth and the power to uplift the world
with my words.

Grant me strong courage then,
You who have the golden strength of a lion
and a roar to match.

You, who conquered all
and are All That Is,
aid me now
as enticement and submission
threaten my life.

Let my worrisome fears and
my evolving reality
be instruments
of enlightenment
and eventual
everlasting
peace.

In Jesus' name I pray.

Amen.

—*Mrs. Cynthia Horvath Garbutt*

Remember

I can't know the full extent of your pain, but I can offer to go with you just as far as I am able. I trust God to be with you all the way.

I believe that God understands that there will be times when you are really scared or angry or hurt, that God embraces you there, is patient and loving and will stay with you as long as it takes to move toward peace and trust.

I believe as you find strength and courage, days of fear will also come, but that as you find healing, the days of strength will lengthen and the days of fear will shorten.

I struggle with how to commit to you in the context of my human distractions, but once I have loved you in my prayers, you are part of the sacred context of my life. I claim that connection from me to you, and when you feel abandoned in your struggle, still I am there beside you on the day you feel you are most alone.

When you wonder if anyone really cares, remember that I am praying for you by name. When you feel too weary to even name your fears, still God will know all the pain that you may not even be able to articulate.

Your pain is a great challenge for you but also a great opportunity. It is in this crucible that you can discover the understanding and grace to minister to others in their pain; you can demand light from these shadows and shine brightly.

I have not known your exact loss or fear, but I love you from the part of myself where I carry my own deepest hurt. You and I touch in the dark and in the light.

I don't pretend to understand all the mysteries of disease and of healing apparent or elusive, but I ask to be open to unexpected forms of healing for us all. My prayer is that you will recognize and claim all the possibilities of healing in your life.

Sometimes the world crashes like a great tidal wave against the battered supports of our lives. Wave upon relentless wave pummels our trembling bodies, but always God is beside us, reinforcing us, surrounding us, substituting his own strength exactly where we are the weakest. He is a flying buttress for the cathedral we yearn to be.

I wanted you to have a tangible expression of my prayers for you, so you would have something to hold and touch when you feel alone. I claim God's words of peace and love, and they synchronize with the beat of our hearts. We are all part of one rhythm as God's shelter is sufficient no matter the storm.

Always remember that I am remembering you. Amen.

—*Ms. Anne L. Beach*

I originally wrote this "Remember" statement because my healing prayer group had talked about needing something to send people we were praying for so that our concern could be more tangible. When I send it, I ask the person to please hang it somewhere visible as a reminder that I am remembering them in this difficult time.

Eucharist

The Gifts of God

Into my imperfect body,
    Take I your perfect flesh;
Into my tainted heart,
    I drink the wine of
Your sacrificial love.
    And with this feast,
Once offered for salvation,
    I bind my human soul
    to thy Divine Purpose
    of Love and Purity.

—*Mrs. Carter Johnson*

Bread and Wine

Symbols of my Life, he says
    Wheat gnashed and baked
    Grapes plucked and pressed
Elements of daily living

Symbols of my Love, he says
    Shared sustenance and joy
    Sufficient sacrifice for all
Elements of God's grace and nurture

Symbols of my Truth, he says
    My body broken for you
    My blood spilled for you
    Bread of Heaven
    Cup of Salvation
Elements of communion and eternity

—*Ms. Kathleen Nyhuis*

Lord, I Am Not Worthy

Lord, I am not worthy—
Lord, I am *not* worthy!
But I have come under your roof, Lord,
So that you will come under mine!
I hold in my hand your body
So that you will ever hold mine—
As I believe you broken,
May I will to be broken too!
A reasonable, living, and holy gift,
A breaking for birth of the new—
Wholeness I sought and clamored for
In ignorance, panic, and pride.
But you required fracture—so

"Lord, I am *not* worthy

That you should come under my roof
But speak the word only
And my soul shall be healed and whole."

—*Mona C. Hull, Ph.D.*

Homeless Angel

Returning from the nursing home, I feel empty.
She who nurtured me no longer knows me.
Suddenly, I need to be taken care of.
The unkempt homeless man on the steps of the church invites
    me in.
"The food here is good," he says.
Trained early not to talk to strangers, I think only, "Do I look
    poor or hungry?
Why should he call to me?" It's his soup kitchen, and more his
    church than mine.
There is a noon Eucharist. How I've missed it. Communion,
    and the taste of my mother's kitchen. A meager celebration.
But the bread and wine feed my soul.
Outside, he calls to me again as I walk past. "Did you get to eat?
Did they feed you? Did you get what you needed?"

I glance back over my shoulder. He smiles.
"Yes," my heart silently shouts.
He nods.

—*Ms. Julie Krause*

Thanksgiving

How I Live and Why

Because I know
that Spirit matters
itSelf lavishly
into the Universe
I am committed
to packing
a lot of living
into a little life.
Some call this
ecstasy,
I call it love.
Love's favorite
word is Thanks.

—*The Reverend Dr. Alla Renée Bozarth*

A Prayer of Gratitude

God, fill my heart with gratitude.
Like a child, I cry for my wants, rather than my needs.
My sense of entitlement is immense.
Focus my mind on abundance rather than lack.
Keep me aware that I have all that I need—and then some.

Amen.

—*Ms. C. Lee Richards*

Morning Gratitude Walk
(briefly put)

O God, thank you for the sense of senses and the sense to sense them. Amen!

—*Mrs. Camille S. Senter*

Thanksgiving

Thank you   for constant rhythms,
                 for returning cycles,
                 for mysterious reappearances.

Thank you   for running fast and disappearing,
                 for disappointment too sharp to be held.

Thank you   for messages beyond expectation,
                 for learnings garnered without hope.

Thank you   for drifting sunsets and pregnant moon,
                 for loose shoelaces and soft scents.

Thank you   for possibilities tense with tears and laughter.

Thank you   for the scratching underneath, revealing the
                 shimmering dark.

—*Ms. Carol White*

Thankfulness

Thank You, God, for stars that glow
beyond the end of time, the sea,
the untamed flowers in the wood,
the gentle souls who walk with me,
and children who are born and grow
and learn to handle life's demands.

Thank You, God, for end of pain,
for final ceasing of the rain
that brought dire floods,
November's chill and drying leaf,
the gradual release from grief,
the understanding of a friend.

Thank You, God, for sun's great gift
that, being, caused life to exist,
seasons' cycles, morning mist,
and memories of times far past,
whose precious hours could not last,
but gave reason to be living,

and human gratitude expressed
each autumn in Thanksgiving.

—*Ms. Margaret Stavely Payne*

An Awesome Lord

How awesome to be in the presence
Of you, Lord, the One
Who brings Good News.

How lovely to sit at your feet,
To be nestled beneath your wings,
To suck from your bosom
Once milk, now solid food.

How skillful a Potter you are,
The Creator of this temple,
Who has fearfully and wonderfully molded me.
You have called me to Yourself.

How delightful the indwelling of
Your Holy Spirit,
Who has set on fire my battered heart,
Babbled my twisted tongue,
Strengthened my feeble knees
And
Purified my sin-sick soul.

How privileged am I to praise You,
To honor You,
To bless You,
And to
Love You.

Your name will be forever glorified
In the songs that I sing,
The tears that I shed,
And
In all of my afflictions.
Lift up my words.
Humble my pride.
Let my love for you be shown.
Not only with my lips,
But in the life that I live.

Let this meditation of my heart
Be acceptable in your sight, Lord,

For you are the Alpha
And the Omega,
The immortal, and the invisible One—
The Risen Lord!

—*Ms. Joanne Starks*

A Widow's Psalm

I will thank the Lord from the balconies;
From the rooftops I will shout God's praise.

Despair was the root of my existence;
Hopelessness was the core of my being.

I wailed in the emptiness of my dwelling;
I cried alone to the walls.

Then the God of those who live alone
heard my plea;
My mourning reached the ears of God's sanctuary.

God delivered me from my distress;
the Lord gave me companions;
my isolation was relieved.

With all my breath I will sing God's praises;
With all my time I will serve the Lord.

With all my mind I will consider God's mercy;
With all my heart I will love the Lord.

—*The Reverend Canon Barbara J. Price*

A Psalm of Joy

O Lord God, how wondrous are thy works in all the world!
The beauty of souls thou hast created,
The radiance of faces glowing with thy love,
The warmth and strength of arms reaching out to
    surround and support.

O Lord God, how wondrous are thy creations!
The homes thou hast blessed with thy love,
The homes thou hast filled with children,
The homes in which thou art Lord of all!

O Lord God, how glorious is thy love in all the world!
The love that touches the hearts of all people,
The love that causes souls to blend in harmony,
The love that fills hearts to overflowing.

O Lord God, with my whole heart I thank thee!
For beauty and strength,
For warmth and tenderness,
For sincerity and humility,
But most of all for love and for those we love.

O Lord God, protect and guide these loved ones I pray!
Amen.

—*Ms. Geraldine W. Dellenback*

Magnificat, or Thoughts on Singing in the Cathedral Choir

In the beginning
was the Word set to music
Venite and Te Deum, Kyrie and Gloria
Bach, Britten, Poulenc, Palestrina
Hyfrydol and Lobe den Herren
descants in the dark of Easter
chimes in the dim of Christmas Eve

My soul doth magnify the Lord

A galaxy of stained colors high on a wall
tidal marks of years in oaken sanctuary floor
needlepointed cushions, velvet kneelers, wooden lace
sermons heard backward, baptisms seen close
fanning and coughing and little upright naps
processional challenges in lining up
sideways telescoping into the Andrews Sisters
recessional glances of greeting
kaleidoscoping quartets
young relatives noisily doodling on service leaflets behind
    one's nervous back
Christmas parties, laughter-filled luncheons, Easter breakfasts
(oh, where are the grits of yesteryear?)
marriages, births, deaths, departures and returns

My soul doth magnify the Lord

For this blest communion, fellowship divine
this blessed company, this community
this chosen people, this tuned wind of God, this choir

My soul doth magnify the Lord

—*Ms. Mary Gilbert Sieber*

An Octad of Thanksgivings on My Eightieth Birthday

That I was born into a world that was simpler in its ways and in
   its visions.
*That I grew into a world of complications beyond the dreams of that
   earlier world.*

That I was born a woman, responding to feminine feelings with
   womanly strength.
That I live in a world in which women can reach for their own stars.

That I was born healthy and physically complete.
*That I lived with a mate, produced offspring, and nurtured them to
   adulthood.*

That I was educated in the classical manner to understand the
   masters of the past.
*That I have been given the opportunity to extend this heritage into
   the new order of thinking.*

That my life has been spent in a nation of freedom-loving
   people, without repression.
*That I have had the opportunity to serve my country in peace
   and in war.*

That I learned enough of body and mind to gain a certain wisdom.
*That I have been called to educate many and to heal the wounded
   and the broken.*

That I was given a longing to discover the source of my being.
*That this revelation has connected me with the world of others of
   like mind.*

That I know that the universe is good and of incomprehensible
   proportions.
That I am permitted to adore and worship that incomprehensibility.

Sunset here betokens the sunrise just beyond.

—The Venerable Shirley F. Woods

Thank You

Dear Lord, thank you for giving me the privilege of dropping a coin in a blue box each day to thank you for all my blessings. Lord, let me thank you for allowing me to do this part of your work. It makes me feel closer to you and to your people. Amen.

—*Ms. Muriel Holstead Dix*

The "blue box" is used by the United Thank Offering ministry in order to collect funds from individuals to support grants for mission and ministry.

Stages of Life

Self-Image

Mother Image

Mother, did you scar
When the world was born?
Mother, did your shoe size change?
Mother, did I mar your heavenly form?
Mother, do you show your age?
Tell me, Mother.

—*Ms. Melanie Lamb Robinson*

Body

This uniform could be much worse:
Three-layered skin, blood, sinew, bones.
When God came to work here,
God wore it, once.
When God comes to work here,
God wears it, still.

—*The Reverend Sharon K. Dunn*

The Beauty Contest

We stand together yet apart
The script written by strangers.
Time stands still at the judgment
While we await someone else's determination.

Fear of rejection squeezes through our pores
The forecast said, "Snow," and we're half-naked.
Refusing to fall, flakes hold tightly to swollen florid clouds
And the clock strikes the thirteenth hour.

Bright eyes, firm breasts and buttocks heat the room
Denying the cold outside this convoluted world.
Driven by appetites for approval, recognition, and dazzle,
When will we awaken and write our own destiny?

—*Mrs. Karen O. Poidevin*

Litany for Our Daughters

God, who created women,
> *Hear our prayer.*
God, who blesses us with daughters,
> *Hear our prayer.*

Help our daughters know that whether they have curly hair or straight, a body like a basketball player or like a teddy bear, they are beautiful and worthy of love just the way they are.
> *Creator God, hear our prayer.*

Give grace in abundance to mothers, fathers, sisters, brothers, teachers, clergy, neighbors, and all who touch the lives of our daughters. Help us all set standards determined not by television and magazine ads, not by manufacturers of cosmetics and diet plans, but by what is right and good for each individual girl.
> *Creator God, hear our prayer.*

Give us the words, the hugs, and the discernment to use them at the right time, when a daughter is in crisis—a real crisis, or one of her own making.
> *Creator God, hear our prayer.*

You who created us all in your image, remind us, when you see us frowning into our mirrors, that all each of us needs to be is the "me" that you created. Let us be good examples to our daughters.
> *O God, hear our prayer.*

> *We praise you and we thank you, Creator God. Amen.*

—*Ms. Lois Oller Nasdos*

All of Creation

Lord, may I learn to be just as pleased with me, your creation, as you are.

Help me to love my body and to cherish each part as the lovingly fashioned gift from you that it is. Let me not look with disdain or hate on that-part-that-would-be-so-much-better-if-only-it-were smaller, curvier, more toned, less sagging, larger, firmer, longer, shorter, straighter, or wavier. Let me not continually seek out faults in your work; instead, let me wonder in the perfection of your craftsmanship, declaring with you that yes, what you have created is indeed very good.

—*Ms. Vivian Lam*

Raindaughter

Raindaughter,
sorely weeping one, weep on,
but when your tears are done, rise up,
bind on your brow the fire of noon
    (your sister hawk will show you how),
and claim your kinship with the sky.

        Raindaughter, the fierce blood of humankind
        runs rough, and what are we
        but singers and slayers, makers of weapons,
        makers of intricate myths.

Raindaughter,
run with the hounds of royal heart;
the quarry is a truth that's hidden in the fire of time:
go softly where the dark will know your step;
search down forgotten rivers in the night
    (your sister serpent knows the way)
and claim your kinship with the earth.

        Raindaughter, think how darkness is our light,
        and light our darkness; think how God must love us,
        wild and wry and undefeated,
        weaving music out of our mortality.

Raindaughter,
sing against the dark; there are
no decorous battles and the fire within
sinks like the daystar at the end.
Then, rainchild, bare your teeth at death
    (your sister wolf will show you how),
walk proudly to the house of endless light,
and claim your kinship with eternity.

—*The Reverend Anne McConney*

Friendship

I Am Martha, I Am Mary

I am Martha
preparing the house
expectant
yet busy
cleaning
bustling
setting all in order.

I am Mary
preparing my heart
expectant
watching at the door
listening for footsteps
setting all aside.

Martha
welcomes with a smile
"make yourself comfortable
shed your shoes
relax into the cushions
of the couch."

Mary
welcomes with anticipation
"make yourself available
shed your burdens
relax into the presence
of the Spirit."

Together we embrace
the Spirit's presence
a trinity of seekers
beneath a cross of sycamore wood
before a candle flame.

Martha serves
a word
to start the conversation
Mary sits
at Jesus' feet
to draw the focus to him
Our guest begins
that conversation
her eyes on me, her heart on God
never noticing
as Martha slips silently
from the room.

After our guest's departure
Martha returns to plump the cushions
as Mary douses candle flame
No need for words
beneath the cross
in hallowed space
we count blessings together
instead of teacups
gathering mercies
from the crumbs of conversation
giving thanks
for the gift of hospitality.

A trinity remains.

—*Ms. Shirin McArthur*

We Shared an Umbrella in the Fall

It was cold and windy.
The rain was falling steadily.

How did it happen
That we shared the umbrella
Of our companion
To leave him
With the sole use of mine?
Just how did you manage that one?

You did.
He did.
We did.
I am still glad.

Adults, much too old
To be enjoying such fun in the rain.
Looking back,
It was in the sharing
And caring
That a happy memory was made.

Who could have guessed then
How much rain would fall on us,
In so many different ways,
To bring us to this seeming separation
Of our lives.

I wonder . . .
. . . do you sometimes think of me
When walking alone beneath your umbrella
In the fall?

I think of you.

—*Mrs. Ruth Brooks Silver*

Cheryl's Prayer

Thank you, God, for the people you provide for us when we need human contact and support. I am richly blessed and renewed each day with my sister in Christ, Cheryl. We both thank you for your outpouring of love to us. Thank you for our combined faith and for hearing our prayers in need and in gratitude. Please, Lord, continue to guide and direct us with knowledge, presence of your Spirit, and the wisdom of purity that we need to minister to those around us.

We thank you. We praise you.
We yield all to you, our loving Lord and God.
Amen.

—*The Reverend Sarah B. Crandell*

Intimacies
(three short poems)

the women held each other
against blare of train
and stare of rider

she slipped her arm
through mine
we skipped to the table
sharing food
and friendship

since we were not sisters
we became best friends
with twenty years between us
we have become sisters

—*Ms. Jeanette Adams*

A Prayer for a Friend Who Doesn't Fully Know You

Lord, I lift up my friend to you.

You know where she is, Lord, better than I do.
    I know only what I see on the outside,
    While you know what is in her heart.

I know you meet us where we are, as we are,
    And that you don't leave us there, thank goodness.

I know you are working in her life to draw her ever closer into
your love,
    Just as you are in mine,
    Even if she doesn't know it herself.

I know that you are doing better things for her than I can desire
or pray for, and
I know that you love her more than I can ever begin to,
    But she weighs heavily on my heart.

Enable me to be a godly friend,
    A living witness of your love,
    A channel of grace in her life.

I trust you, Lord,
    In Jesus' name.

—Ms. Patricia O. Horn

Love

Love at Seventeen

so full of their feelings
they cannot walk without touching
talk without kissing
they crawl under barriers
to scrawl their names in cement
they dance down river

in red silk and white gauze
moving from mambo to merengue
giving people cause to cheer

—*Ms. Jeanette Adams*

Prayer for Healthful Living

You, O Lord, who gave us
our breath and our bodies,
please help us to treat them
with tender love and good care.

Please let our physical bodies be
glowing vehicles of
your light and love,
refreshed by clean air,
bright sunshine,
and the joy found in simple pleasures.

Using vital energy
to create
more energy in which to serve you,
let us honor our bodies and spirits
through healthful eating,
appropriate exercise,
and mindful meditation.

May the care and keeping of our physical bodies
further our spiritual journey until one day,
having served their temporary purpose,
our bodies find rest and
with abundant joy
our spirits rise eternally.

May our healthful life choices
allow us always
to praise you, to serve you, and to love you. Amen.

—*Mrs. Cynthia Horvath Garbutt*

Love with Wings

There is that Love—
the one with wings,
that neither cages
nor clings,
but lets others in.
I know that Love.

—*Mrs. Betty Vilas Hedblom*

Sea Prayer

Lord, let me, in giving love, remember the seashore—
the ocean's openness. May I keep in touch with your divine passion
beyond my sight's limits on the water's surface—a passion
that ridges both the sea and the seashell.

Let me risk giving of myself—an exposure
like the crosscut section of the chambered nautilus.
Yet help me to understand how to use the power you have given me.
Remind me that I must know quiet moments,
cradling your gifts so that then I can pour them forth like the tide.

May I not be as the water lily that closes in on itself
at evening in its still pool. But may I become,
with time, strong and nourishing
like the brilliant breakers of the sea.

—*Ms. Mary Ann Coleman*

One

From this day we are one.

One, yet . . .

I linger; you hurry on.
I explain; your thoughts wander.
You react with excitement; I wonder.

Do we share?

Where is the level ground where we can see
Eye to eye to eye?

Can we dream a single thread and soar
With feet firmly planted?
You the kite, me the string.
We pull apart with force
Yet remain solidly joined.

Our dream becomes reality

As husband and wife.

—*Ms. Rietta Bennett*

Life Is Round

I believe that life is round.
                                        —*Vincent van Gogh*

Life is round,
a sounding river
always moving
beyond the silence of lake
and the sleeping pond.

It knows the depth of shallow
the measure of deep.
Not at rest, it holds to itself
both the quiet reflection of sky
and full coursings that whisper
a pulse unknown to time.

Love is a circle
of burning light.
When there is darkness,
when there is shadow,
though the light burns low,
it remains undiminished.

Who enters
the dwelling place of Love
will know
rain on the sounding river,
a circle of life
in the circle of burning fire.

—*Mrs. Annette Penniman*

Husband

My husband wraps his arm
Around my shoulders as we go to sleep.
Guardian.
He keeps away the howl.
I see the arms of God
Like this
Holy kiss.

—*Robin E. Turgesen, RN*

His Glance

His glance, my touch
We come together and I see my body defined
Stroked and held in a passionate embrace
The magnetism surpassing time
Two souls united, bodies entwine
Boundaries dissolve into the cosmic dance
Two different minds touching, seeing, smelling
Tasting hearing Oh love divine
Fully present, fully alive
Fully me and mine and yet his
Giving and receiving a transcendent mutuality
Two bodies and spirits playing together
Ignited by passion and sustained by love
The sense of self embodied, bathed, adored
Familiar in our marriage and yet new
Exploring the mysteries of the soul

Eros binding us to the universe
Floating, safe, feasted, holding and
Resting in the arms of God

—*Ms. Ann Smith*

Weddings

A Prayer on Going to a Wedding Reception Alone

Lord, I am going to another wedding reception alone.
Help me to share the bride's and groom's happiness without
    dwelling on my own loneliness.
Help me to reach out to others there, realizing they may need my
    fellowship as much as I need theirs.
Make me aware of the love I have from my family and friends.
Bless all of us at this celebration of commitment and hope;
    move us to support this couple, now and in the future.
And always, Lord, let me remember your love and faithfulness
    to me.

—*Ms. Dorothy E. Wynne*

The Bride

It is your wedding day,
Your wedding hour.
You are adorned with finest silk,
Jewels on neck, head, and feet,
With flowers entwined in your hair.
Beautiful bride,
Your future unfolding,
What lies ahead
That you cannot yet see?
Will there be blessings and joy?
How many curses?
Will sorrow cut short your laughter
And crease your face?
No one knows,
But in the face of the unknown,

You and your love make your vows:
To love and cherish
'Til death do you part,
In good times and bad,
In sickness and in health.
Your love is your strength
To guide you through
The days that are yet to come.
May your vows of love
Embrace you with courage,
Entwine you with hope,
Enhance your lives with grace,
And clothe you with fidelity.
May these be the jewels
Of your married days,
That in years to come
Your smile will still be full
And beautiful.

—*The Reverend Dr. Vienna Cobb Anderson*

A Prayer for the Mother of the Groom

In all shapes and sizes, icons of marital hope line the perimeter of the dining room. Wind chimes and wicker baskets. Candles and cookware and linens and hardware.

With each UPS delivery, the icons expand and mutate. They are a bittersweet reminder that soon her youngest son will marry.

God of the present moment, bring peace and courage to the mother of the groom. Keep her ever mindful that it's really okay to let go, that you are her son's rock and fortress.

One maid of honor. Eight bridesmaids. A photographer and videographer and limousine driver. One junior bridesmaid. One flower girl. One ring bearer. One wedding director. And, of course, a junior groomsman.

God of peace, shield the joyous during this time of feasting and merriment. Bless those who are about to witness the vows of brides and grooms everywhere that they may trust in your goodness all the days of their lives.

Fill the heart of the mother of the groom with tenderness and understanding, that she may grow in wisdom and compassion in her future role as mother-in-law.

At Mitchell's, the largest tuxedo rental business in the Southeast, the mother of the groom drifts into a catatonic state as the store manager explains to the bride and groom intricate differences between cutaways, tuxedos, and strollers. (And she thought strollers belonged only in baby stores.)

The bride wants the groom to wear gray cutaways with ascot and striped pants. The groom wants to wear his tuxedo. The bride says marriage means compromise.

The mother of the groom remembers her church's eleventh commandment, "Thou shalt not be tacky," and quietly hopes the bride and groom won't mix the prescribed attire with the wrong time of day.

Lord, have mercy on this wedding. Christ, have mercy on all weddings. Lord, have mercy on the mother of the groom when she bears the burden of being stuck in the middle and feels the pain of biting her tongue.

A summer stall in the marital jet stream launches a series of bridal showers. With each dramatic opening of gifts comes a mighty chorus of oohs and ahs, much like that during a Fourth of July fireworks celebration.

Loving Spirit, in all these wedding wrappings and trappings, help brides and grooms everywhere to look beyond their own families and concerns to see the world suffering and struggling. Keep their eyes and hearts always open to the needs of others less fortunate.

A family member suggests the newlyweds be transported from the church to the reception in the groom's 1979 stick-shift Subaru. The groom laughs. The bride doesn't, not yet understanding the quirky humor of the family she's about to join.

God of Love, mothers of the groom everywhere praise you for all the ways your humor quells these tempestuous nuptial seas. Keep everyone involved ever mindful of your playful presence. Bless brides and grooms with the strength to be loyal and faithful to each other and to be wise and loving in the nurture of their sons and daughters.

So that thirty years from now brides will know something of your love
and grace in being a mother of the groom.
World without end. Amen.

—*Ms. Mary Lee B. Simpson*

A Mother's Rehearsal Dinner Prayer for Her Son and His Bride

Loving God, Creator of all that is good and joyful and beautiful, Giver of every grace, accept our thanks for bringing together in safety these people dear to *N.* and *N.* to share and augment their joy. We pray that you will shield them in their happiness, Lord, nurture their devotion, and strengthen their commitment as tomorrow they give themselves to each other in Holy Matrimony. Forgiver of our faults, help them always to forgive each other. Source of all healing, preserve them sound and well in body. Fount of all knowledge, sustain their alertness of mind. Compassionate Savior, keep them tender in heart, devout in faithfulness. Holy Spirit, make them ever conscious of your presence with them, that each of them will be eager to rise to the best in the other.

In the midst of such abundance and joy as blesses us this night, let us not forget the physical and spiritual needs of others and our obligation to them. As husband and wife, inspire *N.* and *N.*, in the fulfillment of their mutual love, to reach out to others in your love. In Jesus' name we gratefully ask these things. Amen.

—*The Reverend Canon Jean Parker Vail*

One Road for Walking and Sun for the Sky

As the sun is held and reflected
In the east window of morning
And in the west window
Of late afternoon,
So hold while reflecting light
Each one of the other.

Take to yourselves
The random fluting of small birds,
The dance of stars on ancient rivers,
And the storming gold of butterflies.

Take to yourselves and carry
Branches of drifting flowers,
Branches of snow.

Let the hearth fire be burning,
The kettle on, the cups and saucers out
For when we stop by.

We want to be with you.

When the fringe of time wears thin
And clouds wrap the dream song of night
Turn to the dawn and walk the road
Under a sun-filled sky.

—*Mrs. Annette Penniman*

Pregnancy

Sarah Laughed

In the tent,
Sarah hovered,
    eavesdropping on
    Abraham's conversation
    with a stranger
    who said Sarah would
    bear a child.
    She laughed
    then denied it
    when the stranger
    asked why she laughed.
    Who was this stranger?
    Was it God?

Later,
Sarah pondered,
    why laughter
    followed by denial
    at this miraculous
    revelation.
    Was she afraid
    apprehensive
    anxious
    uncertain
    embarrassed
    that she might have
    pleasure
    in her old age?

Time passed,
Sarah remembered,
    years of waiting
    hoping
    aching
    for new life to spring up
    inside her
    empty arms longing to
    cradle a child.

Sarah wondered
    about Hagar
    how would she react
    to the news
    would she have the
    same feelings Sarah
    had when
    Abraham took Hagar to
    his bed and produced a son
    sadness
    anger
    unworthiness
    unloved
    unwanted
    frustration
    or
    would a new bond of
    sisterhood emerge

from the shared
experience of
giving birth?

Questions, more questions, still more questions.

Sarah prayed,
    on her knees
    fervent prayers for
    understanding
    patience
    strength
    wisdom.

Finally,
Sarah trusted,
    knowing that in the fullness of time
    all her questions would be answered
    her fears and doubts quieted
    her fondest hopes and desires
    met
    for with God
    all things are possible.

—*Ms. Marjorie A. Burke*

For Comfort When the Pregnancy Test Is Negative

Dear God,

We are heartbroken.
We have cried so many tears
    for our unborn children.

The pain we feel
    is so deep and raw that
    there are no words
    to express our sorrow.

Lift our hearts from this sadness.
Comfort us with your love.
We ask for your peace for we have
    tried so hard to succeed.

Help us to accept that there
    is so much we may never understand.

Grant us your guidance
    in making a decision
    for the next course of action.

Restore our courage
    so we can see tomorrow
    in a brighter light.
Amen.

—*Ms. Janice Cave*

Pregnancy Prayer

O God, thank you for the miracle of new beginning life. Bless the mothers, and let them know that you are ever with them throughout their pregnancies, labors, and deliveries. Bless those eagerly awaiting their opportunities to love and nurture. Especially bless baby *N.* Keep these, your tiniest souls, safe in their mothers' wombs and under your heart until they are old enough, big enough, strong enough, mature enough, and healthy enough to be born into this world to be shining examples of your love and grace. It is in the name of your own dear child, Jesus Christ our Lord, that we pray. Amen.

—*Mrs. Camille S. Senter*

Birth

Of Birthing

Human birth,
pain, messy, sticky, sweaty,
push—breathe, push—breathe,
no pain, no gain,
push—breathe, push—breathe,
finally, new life.

Spiritual birth,
what does this mean?
pain, struggle, water, sweat,
no pain, no gain.
Trust in God.

I push against my own will.
God breathes new life into me,
push—breathe, push—breathe.

Wind and water.
No, I don't want to go,
the wind blows,
God's breath surrounds me.
I resist
push—breathe, push—breathe.
The water of baptism engulfs me.
I am made new.

Human birth, spiritual birth.
I don't remember the first.
I don't remember the second, either.
It happened gradually—a long litany of
push—breathe, push—breathe,
not willing to fully give myself over to God.

—*Ms. Marjorie A. Burke*

A Child Was Born This Day

A child was born this day
in a moment of quiet
in a moment of strength
in a moment of sighs
in a moment of pain

A child was born this day
glowing
pink
warm
crying
his mother
reaching

loving
her new child
against birth-tired skin

A child was born this day
and
God
rejoiced
danced,
white robe and hair flying,
laughing
crying
singing
songs of praise

A child was born this day
and that
child
was you

Welcome
to the
world

Rejoice
sing
laugh
love
play

for
this
is your day
and
it is time
to
celebrate

Happy Birthday

—*Ms. Susan Fariss*

Written for my nephew.

Her Parent's Prayer at Lisa's Birth

Lovely Lisa,
Child of light,
Sent to make the years
    glow bright.

Little Lisa,
Gift so small,
Yet gift enough
    to bless us all.

We who loved you
    at conception,
Joyfully waited
    for this reception,
Now adore you
    while you lie there
    gazing from your
    baby eyes.

To God we pray
    that in your life
He in his way
    will give you back
    the happiness
    we cannot repay,

For Lisa,
    you were born today.

—Ms. Patti Dewing

Already

Her body pushes
    straining to give birth
    to God's gift
    her first child.

"Not yet!"
    the doctors cry,
    "It's too early;
    the child isn't ready
    to survive on its own."

O Lord,
    still her birth pangs
    let *your* timing prevail.
May your presence support her,
    uphold her,
    endow her with patience—
    body, mind, and soul.

Already
    she is a mother
But not yet.

Her soul strains
    aching to receive
    God's gift
    of ordination.

"Not yet!"
    her mind cries,
    "It's happening too fast;
    I'm not ready
    to shoulder this divine responsibility."

O Lord,
    calm her fears
    let *your* timing prevail.
May your presence support her,
    encourage her,
    enable her to serve you completely—
    body, mind, and soul.

Already
    she is ordained
But not yet.

—*Ms. Shirin McArthur*

Baby's Coming

Contractions have begun.
I'm terrified.
O Lord, please help me
Through the hours coming up.
Minimize the pain, because,
As you well know, I'm not
Quite ready for all this.
Lord, squeeze my hand—
Direct my thoughts
From agony to those
Grand days and years ahead
When giggles will abound
In playful hours
With my child.

> O Lord, I feel another pain—
> Squeeze my hand.
> Lord . . .
> Please . . .
> Right NOW!

—*Mrs. Ginger O'Neil*

A Prayer in Celebration of Childbirth

Dearest God in Heaven,

With awe and wonder,
I look down upon this tiny face tonight.

It is snowing.
It is two o'clock in the morning,
and this breathing miracle at my breast
suckles with raptured contentment.

Pure magic, pure joy, pure love,
A living testament of your divine existence.

In my heart,
in the deepest part of my soul,
I give thanks to you,
now and always,
for this most sacred gift.
My child.

Let me lovingly nurture my child,
whom you have graciously lent to me,
as you lovingly nurture me.

Grant me wisdom, especially when I am tired.
And grant me laughter, especially when I am tested.

Thank you, O Lord, for entrusting me
with your Creation and for making me
a mother. Amen.

—*Ms. Cynthia Horvath Garbutt*

Making Connections

Such a wonder it is for me,
　　to see my baby nurse her baby.
She is full to overflowing,
　　milk spilling from her swollen breasts.
He roots and gropes urgently,
　　his very eagerness making it difficult
　　to "latch on."

She aches, as I do, to be emptied of her
　　fullness; such superabundance can overwhelm
　　a little one.
What utter relief it is for all
　　when the connection is finally made,
　　a holy moment of joyful union.
I wonder if God so aches until
　　we finally "latch on."

—*Ms. Diane M. Abbott*

Adoption

Grace of Adoption

A teardrop as large as the world
    suspended midair between mother and child;
    joining with others and falling on the sleeping baby,
    sealing with crystal clarity the blessing of child by mother—
    signifying heart-wrenching choices.

Cradled in her mother's arms,
    with family and friends cradled in God's presence;
    giving and receiving.

God's ever-present and unquestioning grace revealed
    in the wonder and miracle of new life.

Courage to bring this beautiful child to her new parents,
    to be enfolded by them
    and to entrust her to their care and keeping.

Tears, laughter, caring, hope, sadness, trust, acceptance:
    Unconditional Love.

—*Ms. Charlene Tiffany Higbe*

Thanksgiving: On the Adoption of a Child

We whose hands have cupped open and empty for so long,
awaiting the gift of a child,
now clasp (*him/her*) close in joy and thanksgiving
for the mercy of your plan.
We have waited for this moment, Lord,
for this tiny hand nestled in ours,
our shadows melding at long last from three into one.

We are family now, O Lord,
and we thank you, forever, with our tears and our laughter,
for this child you have brought into our lives.
Amen.

—Ms. Julia Park Rodrigues

A Prayer for Baby Dylan

Welcome to our family, precious little gift from God.
Your mommy, daddy, and big sister are on their way to get you.
I am picking blueberries on Blueberry Hill.

It is very hot.
The sun is beating down on me.
I try to hide from it on the shady side of the bushes
as I pick those luscious big blues.
Will you love blueberries as much as your cousin Andrew does?

The branches of the bushes are bent low to the ground,
heavy with ripe berries.
In the center of the bushes there is much new growth,
Slender, tender, pale green stalks with shiny green leaves.
They are tenderly surrounded by last year's growth
and
with the more mature branches of many years.
Much like you will be,
the tender young baby surrounded by the many loving arms of
your family.

As God nurtures the blueberries with warm sun and gentle rain,
we, with God's help
will nurture and care for you,
with all our hearts, and souls, and minds.

Welcome, little Dylan. Amen.

—Ms. Marjorie A. Burke

Written on the adoption of my biracial grandson.

Prayer for a Birth Mother Letting Go

O Eternal Spirit, we implore you to bless this child always *(touch or bless the baby possibly being held by mother)* and bring comfort, strength, and peace to _____ [birth mother's name] *(touch or bless birth mother as appropriate)* as she lets go of this little *boy/girl* she so dearly loves. Give the baby's adoptive parents the gentleness, wisdom, and strength to provide all the opportunities and stability _____ [birth mother] dreams of for her baby but knows she [or they, if a couple] cannot provide at this time. _____ [birth mother] has said that this is one of the most difficult and painful decisions she's ever had to make. O Creator Spirit, you and we know how much she loves this baby. Help her to remember this in moments of doubt. She cannot raise this child, but *he/she* will always be part of her family. _____[birth mother] is giving her child what every mother wants, the best she possibly can. May _____ [birth mother] have many brighter days as her own life continues to unfold, and may she remember this moment with peace. Amen.

—The Reverend Rosemary H. Lillis

Mother

In this still place
wreathed in early
morning mist, I
grieve

for what I remember
and what I do not
remember still haunts
me

Mother, you elude me—
your face, your color,
your frame, your
touch

Your sorrow matches
my sorrow; your
longing matches my
longing

I have gratitude
that you gave me
life and placed me in
a basket.

I see now that your
letting me go freed me
to become—to live into
my destiny

The cord you cut that day
was visible and shed
real blood, yet we are
still bound by the invisible

Many of these cords
I have cut
by diligence and by
Grace

I go on doing my
work—discovering the
truth, embracing it,
accepting what was,
what is

I pray, and do my
priestly things, covering
the past with a
blanket of redemptive
love

Dawn breaks and a
new day begins.

—*The Reverend Canon Gwendolyn-Jane Romeril*

Mothering

In Mary's Arms

The boy is protected
from the cold
in the warmth
of Mary's arms,
safeguarded
from all fears
in the comfort
of her breast.
Gentle mother,
against the cold,
against the fear,
hold us tighter.
Shelter us,
enfold us,
hold us closer
to your Son.

—*The Reverend Marie Louise Webner*

Thank You, God

for the gift of this sleeping child.
    Head on my lap—her hair spills across my legs
    in sparkling rivulets of gold.
Her busy hands lie still . . . I hold one,
    kiss its softness,
    marvel at its smallness.
A fleeting smile makes me wonder
    what merry games
    she is playing in her dreams.
Soon she will awaken and chatter away,
    absorbed in her child's world.
In time, she will fly away,
    a young woman on her own—
    more yours than mine.

But for one brief, oh so tender moment,
    she is mine, all mine.
    A moment to cherish.
Thank you, God.

—*Ms. Carol Dunagan Husbands*

Blessing for a Child

May God protect you from every danger that you face.
May God give you the strength and courage to take failure,
    not as a measure of your worth, but as a chance for a new start.
May you care for the body that God has given you and thus be
    filled with health and wholeness.
May prosperity come your way, so that you are free from worry
    about food and drink, about home and shelter, but
May you never be so caught up in material things that you forget
    that the essence of life lies not in possessions or money,
    but in love, and in God.
May you find the joy that is ever-present in God's creation.
May you find fulfillment in whatever you choose to do.
May you use your talents to serve in the way that God intends
    you to, helping your fellow humans and walking in the light
    of God.
May you fully love and may you be fully loved.
May your happiness be unmarred by evil, spite, or maliciousness,
    either your own or someone else's.
May your path be one of goodness—leading to changes for the
    better in the lives of others.
May you be a source of light and inspiration to your family and
    friends, and may they be the same to you.
May God fill you with wisdom and grace, with virtue and
    knowledge, with patience and action, and with understanding
    and love.
May you be forever comforted by a strong and enduring faith in
    God, who created you and who sustains your life.

—*Ms. Elizabeth K. Camp*

A Mother's Prayer

O God of boundless love, make my love strong,
    that I may perform with joy the duties of motherhood.
Help me persevere through times of fatigue and frustration.
Help me see the work of mothering as a sacrament,
    bringing your love to life, making it tangible.
Help me become ever more aware of your countless blessings,
    so to fill my heart with continual thanksgiving.
Dear Lord, I receive such joy from you.
Grant that I may find the time I need
    to sit at the feet of Christ and listen,
    to feel his closeness, to learn of his love for me.
Teach me to make all my actions prayer,
    that busy or at rest I might always be near you.
Fill me with the quiet power of your Spirit,
    so that through me, those I care for
    may experience your most tender and merciful love.
Grant these my prayers for the sake of your Son Jesus Christ,
    who loves us without measure. Amen.

—*Dr. Karen A. Eshelman*

Twilight, 1/4/99

The sun is hidden by the grayest clouds of evening.
This bleak midwinter wearily weighs down
    the heaviness of the heavens upon your shoulders.
As my shoulders droop I wait for your crescent face
    to enlighten the sphere of my world.

Reflect the power of you in me tonight,
As the stars that are your children,
and the children who are my stars
await.

—*Ms. Melanie Lamb Robinson*

The Commissioning

She was there.
She had flown into town; found out about the
commissioning,
and she was there.
I faced the front of the church; they said some
words about being a Chalice Bearer;
they placed a cross around my neck.
We turned and faced the applause of the
congregation.
She smiled a pleased and happy smile.
My smile was crooked as it is when I hold my jaw
in that certain way so that tears of joy don't
streak down my face.
Later, casually, I tell my daughter I'm glad she
was there at the church of my youth today,
tell her that someday this cross will be hers
in memory of this day we shared together.

—*Ms. Dottie Jo Davis*

Milk
(*for Clare*)

Pulled by your cry, it surged out.
Welling from the nipple's pores, it was thin,
bluish, sprayed in tiny streams,
caused a slow, drawn, homesick pain.

We laughed in astonishment as it kept coming
until your shining mouth let go
and you drowsed in sunlit bliss.

You, at seven months, nurse and pedal
rhythmically, your hands explore the air.
I fill to meet your whitest need,
the hind milk now, grown thick and creamy,
will hold you sleeping with its weight.

Dame Julian, in her mystic state,
perceived Lord Jesus as her mother
offering to nurse us all,
milk flowing from his giving breasts.

It is a glory, this feeding from the body:
Take and eat this simple meal.
This is my body given for you.

Take and be full, my daughter,
from this white vein of sharing.
Take nourishment in all its forms
as it comes generously down the years,
from this first food to banquet fare,
in memory of me.

—*The Reverend Penelope Duckworth*

Lament

O GOD, will it all end?
    Playground battles
    Bloody tatters
    Sullen pouts
    Sibling shouts
    Interrupted sleeps
    Dirty clothes in heaps
    Jelly smears
    Nighttime fears
    Barbie clothes
    G. I. Joes
    Clutter, clamor
    Incessant chatter.
    When can I be alone?

O GOD, will I be alone
    When they bandage their own knees?
    When they find their own shoes?
    When someone else soothes the pain,
        and strangers people their universe?
    When I am no longer needed?

How bittersweet, Lord.
    I must give up their pain
        To receive my joy, alone.
    I must give up the joy of them
        To work through my alone-pain.
    Somehow, it just isn't fair.

—*The Reverend Diane Moore*

After Littleton

Eleven years old, he believes, one day
shootings will come to his school, too.
And that I cannot stop them.
I, his all-powerful mother
who kept his little fingers from the fire
and that sweet rear end from rashes.
And the sun in
and the cold out.
I, who warmed the casserole and
sorted the socks.
Pencils and binders bought, applications in,
immunizations done. Vitamins,
the prayers. The sandwiches.
He tells me I cannot stop them—
the guns, the culture, the bombs.

But he is wrong this time.
For I am his mother.
AND GOD WILL LISTEN TO ME.

—*Robin E. Turgesen, RN*

Meditations of a Karate Mom

Lord, I have nothing to do but sit here and watch that extremely
young man with the black belt at his waist teach my child to
stand, to move, to block, and to yield. Kee *Yah*.

First they learn to bow—to the room, the flag, the teacher,
each other. "Just like in church, Mommy!" Well, almost.
Kee *Yah*.

A little girl, very well padded on head, hands, and feet, jumps and blocks the teacher's hand. Kee *Yah*.

The teacher laughs. I wince. He picks her up. She giggles. Controlled chaos. The plaque on the wall quotes 1 Corinthians 13, and it doesn't seem out of place. Kee *Yah*.

I realize, Lord, that I too have taught my child to stand, to move, to block, and to yield.

Teach me, Lord, to do the things we must do for our children— to stand, to move, to block, and to yield. Kee *Yah*.

—*Ms. Julie Krause*

Young Hearts, Strong Hearts

Such young hearts
Strong hearts that beat like eagles' wings
looking for good to behold
trying to understand sorrow
They rise at midnight
sleep when all else awakes
Not afraid to say or do
just give, take what is given
laugh at mistakes
cry when heart is touched
feel pain of each other
feel happiness of one
Bright eyes seeing something
mind turning like fish wheel
slow and steady
with current of holy water
take in good fish, throw out bad fish
back to the holy water
they know all is sacred
And when I look into their eyes
I see something of long ago
Something I once was
that still lives on
Something so good that when rest is here
I dream of rainbows and peaceful things

When I am with them
they are my reason for being
and when they go
they are my reason for going on . . .

—*Ms. Ginny Doctor*

Dancing in the Rain

Staring out the window
watching you dance there in the rain,
seeing your smile,
imagining your laugh.
Watching you dodge raindrops,
and catch them in your hands,
watching the amazement,
on your tiny face.

I smile
as our eyes meet,
and laugh
when you give a cheerful wave.
You turn to play some more,
and I watch you,
praying that these days
will never come to an end.

I wouldn't give you back
for anything in the world.
They told me to wait,
that I was too young.
But to see you smile,
and hear you laugh,
and watch you play in the rain,
I fall deeper in love.
I couldn't have given you up,
not seeing you today,
for I never would have known you,
I'm glad I didn't wait.

—*Miss Colleen Lynn Prittie*

Teeth
(for Emma)

Bite, you say.
Your four teeth flash,
bright as new-minted
pennies, the unexpected
white of ponies
prancing through
poppy fields. *Bite*.
And you bite
your own hands, laughing,
then cry betrayal,
displaying small fingers
ringed with teeth marks.

The world spreads feasts
before you. Expecting
benevolence, you crunch
geranium leaves, marigold
blossoms, marble-hard
cherry tomatoes, ignoring
my call, from five feet
away: *No, No. Not ripe*.
Bitterness shocks
you like pain or anger;
your flower-face crumples
toward tears.

I thought myself hardened
to beauty's betrayals,
but watching I know
myself vulnerable
to the bright world
once again. Emma,
I want to give you
the world to eat.
I want to promise
that it will always
be sweet.

—Ms. Rebecca Baggett

For Anna

My daughter says
that the night is
God's black cloak
spread across the sky
and that unseen stars
are halos hidden deep
within its folds.

My daughter says
that the earth is
a small brown box
held with care
in God's great hands.

My daughter says
all that.

—*The Reverend Nancy Baillie Strong*

Praying with Play Dough

Flour for sustenance
Salt for life
Drops of food coloring
Become her rainbow
Perched on a kitchen chair
She stirs as the sticky mix takes shape
On a white speckled cutting board
We knead the warm turquoise dough
Blue green for the sea

In her hands, it will become
Cookies and cupcakes
Pizza and apple pie
We taste the salty goodness of it all

On this Wednesday afternoon
We celebrate the Eucharist
Giving thanks for all things
But especially for
Play dough.

—*Ms. Marcy Darin*

A Prayer for Bronte

Thank you, O God, for the wonder of this child:
for the stillness of her listening
    as the words of God are spoken
for the confusion in her voice
    as she tries to understand
    why they would want to kill Jesus
for the energy of her hug
    as we speak the words of peace
for the sureness at the altar rail
    as she tells me just how much
    God loves us
for the shining in her eyes
    as she reaches out her hands
    for bread and wine.
Embrace her, O God; protect her
from people who would tell her
what to believe
and how to live.
Keep her wondering and questioning,
and listening for the call of your voice.
Amen.

—*The Reverend Raewynne J. Whiteley*

Pistachio Children

It came to me slowly—year by year by year—
    the realization that my child is not Vanilla.
All those years consternation grew in my heart.

But no one heard my fear.
All they offered were bland assurances—
    He'll grow out of it.
    It's just a phase.
    Just be firmer.
Phrases met my mother's knowledge
        of the deeper reality of my Pistachio child.
    He perceives the world through lenses
        different than you or I
        or other people's children.
    His wiring bewilders Vanillas' mothers.
    His mold struck differently than other children's.
A Pistachio mold, it seems to me.

Other parents—those with Vanilla children—
    they cannot know the pains and heartaches
    living in me and other mothers like me,
Pistachio mothers grow slowly into acceptance,
    through things like
        understanding, naming, claiming
    the who that circumstances have christened him.
To have him named, acknowledged, claimed is comforting.
To know I share the pain with others somehow helps.
    They know my heartaches, griefs, and tears,
    Know the dreams and wishes others never see,
    Know the knot of anger at our future here.
Do they also share my inmost betrayal
    when late at night, I confess
        I ordered Vanilla?

O Lord, show me the essence of this Pistachio,
    help me nurture the gifts you have placed within him.
O Lord, help me enable him to become the child of your
    dreams and yearnings.
O Lord, help me to look beyond the frustrations and pain of today,
    towards all your tomorrows for him.

—*The Reverend Diane Moore*

Granny's Treasure

Holding my growing baby once again is sheer delight.
Kept him a few hours, for a tired granny. What a sight!

Weariness slips away, coaxing smiles from sweet child,
Making busy, hectic, roller-coaster week appear mild.

Being a granny is a special gift beyond human measure,
Lodged in one's heart as the earth's greatest treasure.

Warm, sweet-smelling, cuddly, soft. Nuzzling his chubby cheeks,
Looking at his mama, marveling as her baby's eyes she seeks.

Two special treasures, what a miracle my baby and her baby can be,
Crowning me with unspeakable joy and gladness. Both are dear
    to me.

Life as granny, filled with wonder approaching awe and astonishment,
Blessing my life with love, warmth, and devotion, for a little
    while is lent.

Soon he'll grow and wander away from his granny's tender embrace.
Playing games, being a boy's boy, baby will be gone without a
    trace.

That's how it should be, as this granny well knows from life with
    others.
Treasured little ones reach, extending past mother and grandmothers.

—*The Rt. Reverend Mary Adelia R. McLeod*

Thanksgiving

My God, Father and Mother

Thank you for my grandchildren
    Thank you for their coming and their going home
    Thank you for my aching back and their slimy kisses
    Thank you for my rattled nerves and their sleep of innocence

Thank you for my life that will endure forever, in Christ's name, your Son. Amen.

—Diane Jakel, M.S.W.

First Days

Mothers' Early Autumn Prayer

Poured out of our deep summer pools
    (elegant observation, refined reflection)
into autumn's waterfall:
    school buses, meetings, lessons, practice.
We are awash, tumbled in the rapids
    (kicking and screaming
    or enjoying the ride)
in the long rush to winter.

Wellspring of Life, Object of Our Longing,
Save us from drowning! Remind us to breathe.
Open our eyes, that neither beauty nor violence escapes our notice.
Give us the wisdom to know when to go with the flow
    and when to swim upstream
So that we may arrive at Thanksgiving
    with thanksgiving. Amen.

—The Reverend Lesley M. Adams

Off to School

Dear Father/Mother of us all,

Please keep in your loving care
This child of yours as s/he goes off to school.
It is without reservation that I know I cannot be with him/her.
However, I have taught him/her that s/he is *never* alone
You are always with him/her.
Bless his/her teacher, who I am sure is going through his/her
    own trauma.
Let the teacher be kind and loving.

Let my little person "fit in,"
know the answer to at least some of the questions,
make new friends.
Let him/her get home soon so that my heart will stop beating so
    fast.
This I ask in the name of your holy Son, Our Lord, Jesus Christ.
Amen.
> P.S. Please add to that: In the name of All the Saints and All
> that's Holy.
> P.P.S. Help me! Amen.

—*Ms. Sarah Ann Sked*

Untying

Run along, little one, hurry on.
That school bell will ring before long.
    And you mustn't be late
    On your very first date.
Hurry on, little one, scamper on.

Now go on, brush that tear from your eye.
You know now you are a "big guy."
    Don't tarry or stray
    Or look back this way;
I don't want you to see Mommy cry.

—*Mrs. Ruth Brooks Silver*

Heart Strings Pulled

"Welcome to camp!
Your son's in Owasco Cabin."
Memories of my camp, the good and the bad
God, be with him in the uncertainty of new friendships.

"You can drive right to it.
Pick out his bed."
Names carved in wood, summer friendships still remembered
God, be with him as he sleeps.

"Can I put my shoes and bug spray
Here in the eaves, Mom?"
Gnats buzzing, bugs biting
God, be with him in the midst of your creation—bugs and all.

"Hey! I'm Willie, your Cabin Leader.
How's it going?"
Big smile, friendly eyes, but who is he?
God, be with him as he guides our child.

"You know, we have vespers every night
And hymn sing on Sundays."
Do my ears deceive me? Could this be?
Alleluia, the Lord is risen indeed!

"Hey Mike, wanna play kickball?"
Heart strings pulled, one last hug
God stay with us in the month ahead.

God, stay with us all.

—*The Reverend Elizabeth Rankin Geitz*

Adolescents

Prayer for Adolescents

Almighty God, designer of all that is good and worthy, look upon
my children and fill them with direction and purpose. Help them,
O Lord, to look into their hearts and minds and know that there
is a place for them in this, your world. Teach them once again to
love and trust you as they did as little children. They are growing
up, O Lord, in a world far from your design, and they are lost in
its quickness. You are the Good Shepherd; gather these your lost
sheep and lead them to a life of meaning and hope through your
never-ending grace. All this I ask in the name of your Son, our
Lord, Jesus Christ. Amen.

—*Ms. Mary Jane Miller*

Protect Them and Lead Them

Precious Father, I especially pray for our teenagers and young adults; where they are lost, find them; where they are afraid, bring them comfort and love; and where they are confused, show them your will. Protect them, Father, and be with parents as they ride the roller coaster of these years with their children. May they have the courage, the strength, the wisdom through your Holy Spirit to help guide them and in many cases just to hold on, and to be there as their children take on adult responsibilities in a chaotic, sinful world. I now place them under your loving wings. Amen.

—Mrs. Stephanie Douglas

A Collect for Clifton and Devon

Most dear and delightful Mother of all, you have blessed the world with the wonder of my teenage, all too soon to be men, sons. They have in them the gift of love, the power of change, the capacity for new life. You have wonderfully made them in the images of family past, family present, and maybe, someday, family future. They are the reflection of the stars at night twinkling with mischief. They are the heat of the day, lacking worldly control. Too soon they grow and change my life again. You are the God who parents them always; you are the Mother of their eternity. Bless them always, as you have all your sons of all ages, I ask in your name. Amen.

—The Reverend Catherine A. Munz

Adult Children

Child of Mine

Your life is yours to live,
Though living with me
Makes it also mine.

Your action gives birth to reaction,
Your words demand response,
Our lives remain entwined.

I, too, was once young—
And invincible—
Error and Misjudgment my teachers.

My hard-earned wisdom witnesses the futility of your footsteps.
As all who have gone before you,
You deafen to the din of disaster.

And I—I am to be silent.
Provide, nurture, maintain—
Without voice.
O child of mine,
No more could I be silent than cease breathing.

My soul, the mothering blood,
Instinctively begotten of Eve,
Reaches out in warning to Cain.
No, you are not your brother's keeper.
Nor am I yours.

You, and that which is within and without,
Must keep itself.
Turn to that strength,
Listen to that voice,
And go.

Your wisdom, too, will be earned.
Minutiae are outside a mother's realm.
Shield my soul from your growth and envelop me in your mirth.
In unseeing lies belief,
Free me from knowing.

Child of mine,
Your life is yours to live.
Take it away from me.

—*Mrs. Janet Hitchcock*

Poem for Mothers with Grown Daughters

all grown
but not gone

roles trade
without tears

distance dims
minds mesh

friends fasten
each other's earrings
and exchange gifts

—*Ms. Jeanette Adams*

The Gift of My Children

O Heavenly Father, thank you for the gift of my children.
Thank you for being with me as we taught them.
Thank you for being with them while they explored their big
    New World.
Thank you for taking care of them when I was busy, angry,
    or depressed.
Thank you for loving us so much that you gave your own Son,
    Christ Jesus, for our salvation.
Thank you for giving to me the opportunity to be their mother.
Thank you for giving to me the opportunity to enjoy their
    childhood and now their adulthood.
And Heavenly Father, I leave them in your care now that they are
    on their own, and I trust that you will be with them through
    the hard and easy times.
I ask for them love, peace, and your grace and that you will let
    them know that you are with them. Amen.

—*Mrs. Patricia D. Alwardt*

Our Mothers

For My Mother: 10 November 1984

You carried me into life
    birthed me into pain
    and rage

Now you kneel before me—
    carrying me in your heart
    birthing memory and dream
    —your own,
    still-born and half-forgotten and unnamed—

and bid your daughter's blessing.

What can I give you?
    only mumbled not-quite prayers
    and the laying-on of my hands

And now I carry you
    and wait for the moment of forgiveness
    birth into love

—*The Reverend Nancy Baillie Strong*

My Lost Mother
(an apology to my daughters)

It makes no sense
that I, always so eager to be curious
always looking, searching, asking . . .
that I never asked. The questions stayed shut up like a
trunk on which I sat.
I let slip away those bits of information
with which I might have fashioned her.
Now my hands are empty. I face omissions that I dare not
examine.
I sit, searching the blank wall, trying to find images.
I sort old photographs like playing cards;
their backs are always blank.

I play with words like *aprons, bushel baskets, crabs,*
cookies, Ellis Island.
I see the wicker baskets and leather hampers piled up
and the brown floors and the brown walls
that must have frightened her. I never see her
hanging onto her mother's hand,
her long brown curls shining in the harbor mist.
I just can't bring her up.
She's a photograph waiting to be exposed.
My images are but maybes.
I could have been holding a lapful of her life's pieces,
I could have spread them on the table and made
a whole person.
I could have given you endless stories of who she was.
Now I can only guess and sorrow
for not knowing more than that she was afraid
of thunder and that she had never taken
off her wedding ring.

—Ms. Lucy Germany

Choice

Prayer of a Woman Facing a Choice

Hear my prayer,
O God of love.
I am afraid.
I have a choice to make
that affects not only my life,
but the lives of others.
Do I carry this child
to full term?
Am I capable of being a mother?
What is right?
What is wrong?
I am frightened and confused.
Help me to know what to do.

Grant me wisdom
to make the best choice
for my life
and the life of a child;
in Christ's name I pray.
Amen.

—*The Reverend Dr. Vienna Cobb Anderson*

Unable to Bear Children

Prayer of a Woman Unable to Bear Children, Looking Back

Merciful Father, you were my source of comfort after the early loss of three pregnancies. How angry I felt. I longed for a family. You answered my need, by leading me into situations where I could help others with their children. For this I will be forever thankful. Amen.

—*Mrs. Georgia B. Krauser*

Miscarriage

So Little Time

There was so little time—
No more than dust—days, tossed
To the wind and in an instant gone.
The months of preparation,
From single cell, splitting, selecting,
Building from Nothing
To a perfect babe. Those months
Lay long: dawn shadows, heavy
Upon the fragile dew drops of my hopes.
Slowly, slowly the black night folded
Back upon itself. My aching eyes
Longed for light, the lightening
That would lift my child from womb to breast.

I slept, a drugged death-sleep and awoke
To empty arms, and pain, and finally
My child, sleeping upon my pillow.
All the long years of waiting,
The months of fear, the days and hours
Have brought me here at last
He lives, my son,
My tiny perfect boy. Time stretches endless
Before me. His childhood days, his restless
Adolescence, his bride—as yet unborn—
All flicker through my drowsed contentment.
Firmly I grasp each day, segment it neatly:
So many feedings, so much sleep, a little while
Naked upon my lap for play. So shall my child
My little one, so shall he grow strong.
So little time.

The dark curtain swirls about me,
Smothering, quenching my light.
Mocking my dreams.
Come to me now, my vaunted strengths,
Shore up my ruined hopes, rein in the panic
That would herd me screaming, shrilling,
"This cannot be." Never, never to see
Him stand, or run? Never, perhaps
To hear his babbling speech? Where now
His teenage days, his "bride, as yet unborn"?
So will I grasp each nettle-stinging day
Day after painful day. For this is still
My child, my tiny precious boy,
Bone of my bone—
Imperfect flesh of my imperfect flesh.
But, ah! There was so little time for joy.

—*The Reverend Iris Ruth Slocombe*

Expectation: A Duet

Prelude
    O unborn babe,
    in your mother's womb
    divine mystery
    knits bone to bone,

forms flesh to shape,
pulses a tiny heart,
and you become.
My own heart leaps
with love and awe
to see you,
to hear the melody
of your cry,
to know you.

Continuum
O unborn child,
bone of my bone,
flesh of my flesh,
child of my child,
you show me a mystery,
that as I move
out of all that is past
and all that is present
toward a time when
I am a memory
(or no memory at all),
you will carry within your
self the smallest part of me.

Coda
In the long view,
you were but an eyewink
on the face of time,
sweet mystery,
interlude of possibility.
And now you are gone,
heartbeat stilled,
lifeless tissue.
In the long view,
you were a breath of time,
but oh sweet babe-to-be
-that-was, I weep for you,
short-lived and finely loved.

—*Ms. Shirley Bynum Smith*

Miscarriage

I wanted a girl, one
who would sass and stick out her tongue,
take tennis lessons, and climb trees,
one who would have lived
in the room that's painted pale yellow. The
door is shut. Someone will take away
the white wicker bassinet and the teddy bears
and the nursery curtains. They'll fix meals for
me, they'll do my laundry and bring me
cheerful gifts, but they won't let me talk.
God, nobody knows how real she is to me.
They don't listen to me talk about
a girl who should have lived to tap dance and
read all my childhood books, a girl
with freckled nose and love in her heart.
They won't let me say how I'll remember
every year and celebrate her birthday in my
heart. You listen, don't you, God?
Amen.

—*Ms. Kristen Johnson Ingram*

Prayer for a Pregnant Daughter Fearing a Miscarriage

Blessed Mother of all humankind,
hear my prayer for my beloved child.
She and I are both afraid;
shelter us in the love of your heart.
We cherish this child of hers;
nurture it in her womb to full term.
We tremble for the safety of her baby;
hear our cries and soothe our anxieties.
Whatever happens,
let us not become cynical,
or hard of heart, or calloused
to the sorrows or joys of others.

May your holy name be praised
through all we say and do.
Amen.

—The Reverend Dr. Vienna Cobb Anderson

Menstruation

Prayer of the Woman with the Flow of Blood

Lord, O Lord, hear me: even now my blood is being poured out like a sacrifice in the service of the life of the world. Monthly I suffer this, and I tell myself that in it I participate with you, Lord, in creation. But that is not the way I feel.

Lord, I come to you in my distress; I can barely whisper a prayer. Like a woman with child and about to give birth, I writhe and cry out in pain, but no birth pain, for I give birth to nothing. I do not bring forth people for the world. Instead, I die within; my skin will not hold me. I suffer unreasonable panic. I feel a stranger to you and to the world in these days. With my blood flows away also my self, my well-being. I cannot bear to live in this body for this time.

Will you not rescue my body from this cycle of trauma, O Lord? Dare I ask to be healed of what is not illness, freed of what is your design? No, not from your design; rather I ask for release from this prison of pain, and for healing within my spirit for the effect of many years' suffering.

I dare ask one other thing. I ask you to accompany me. There is another who suffered a flow of blood for the life of the world. It was not merely a wound; it was a part of your design. It was not desirable, yet ever to be looked upon with love by those whose new life it portended. It was you, Lord Jesus, on the cross, with the flow of blood and water. It recalled your earthly birth, and at the same moment gave sign that you were fully able to bring new birth to the world.

I will step aside for a moment from the pain of body and soul and look at myself in a new way. I place myself on the cross with you, willing to participate in your own mother-potency, in the making of a new creation. I give thanks for my body, a holy place, and ask you to touch me and fill me with your healing Spirit.

Henceforth my blood will be my sign that I am made in your image, in the image of the Lord whose blood flowed from the cross for the life of the world. Amen.

—The Reverend Kamila Blessing

Monthly

Monthly, you come
And pay me a visit that turns my life upside-down!
With you, comes PAIN,
AgGrAvAtIoN,
IrRiTaBiLiTy,
TENSION.
It seems as if you are never ending.
Before I realize it,
You are leaving.
No more Tension,
Irritability,
Aggravation,
Or pain.
My life calms.
You leave. Phew!
Things are back to normal . . .
Until next month.

—Ms. Lori L. Coulter

Menarche Bewilderment

Today my mother
Told me I'd be
Bleeding every
Month like this
For thirty years.
I can't believe it.
Yet I must because
I have no say

About the
Circumstance.
I'm a female
And, as such,
Have parts of me
I barely knew I had—
Parts I won't be able
To control.

I sort of knew
About such things,
But never thought
I'd be involved
So soon.

To my great surprise
I really have a body
God can use for
Motherhood.

Lord, teach me
How to cope.

—*Mrs. Ginger O'Neil*

Hysterectomy

Psalm 7: Before Hysterectomy

Lord, I am wonderfully and fearfully made;
O Lord, I am a piece of work of yours.

In your image, God,

From my green time I have held worlds;
My flesh contains a universe for you,
an infinity of stars between my knees.

In my wet and salty substance you can kindle fires,
and I cup the new flame.

In my mantling darkness
Life and spirit and flesh can quicken,
At your call, O God.

In my deepest places
I can hold your Dance;
My heart beats out its rhythm.

I can form the notes you sing forth
With the breath of your Spirit,
A chamber for your song.

Hold me, God, with your stars and your worlds.
Keep me ever in your spinning dance.
Contain me even as the cup breaks.
Let not my essence spill and seep away
Unused, unsung, untasted.
Make of me a new song.

Cleanse me still in the blood that is yours,
That is shed in the rhythm of your tides.
Wash me in the light of your moon.
Hold me on the breast of darkness.
Encircle and enfold me; let me root in you.

Let me be filled.
Let the salt of my tears be seasoning,
Let my life find savor in the wisdom of the blood
That drums and beats in my veins.
Make of me a new song.

Let my heart still leap.
Let my soul still sing.
Let my thoughts still kindle.
Let me be a vessel still
For you.

—*Ms. Terri Jones*

The Leap

Waiting for my train near Filene's
I pull my down jacket around my shoulders
As if to hide
The hole in my gut
Left when they took my uterus out.

I think that everyone can see it, wondering
if I still count as a woman.

My head was still full of babies in pastel gowns
Toes peeking through the drawstring bottoms.
Babies in see-through carts
Heads covered by woolen caps.
Their rosebud mouths rooting for my achy breast.

I have reveled in my three pregnancies
Jubilant that I could create by being.
Yet I had leapt to October
In the season of Advent.

Her arm around me
A nurse helps me struggle to my feet,
Untangling the wires attached to my IV pole.
It is a strange dance we do
She who never had children, she says,
And I who never will again.

Four years later
I have
No regrets
But understand I can create in new ways
In mid-life.

And yet,
When I watch my six-year-old asleep
Her moon-shaped face still graced with babyness,
I know it will not be long
Before it all fades.

—*Ms. Marcy Darin*

Menopause

After the Manner of Women: The Prayer of a Woman in Menopause

"Sarah's womb was also dead."
Is that my lot, Lord? In the eyes of the Lord and of people, am I dead because my womb will no longer bear children? Like Sarah, I no longer look for children. But unlike Sarah, I have no urgent need to bear. So: Whence, Lord, such despondency?
Deliver me!

I am grieving, I am grieving, I am grieving. It never ends. They tell me it is the hormone changes and will pass, but the grief is real.
Deliver me!

My Self is changed forever. I grieve, even though, all of these years, I have secretly awaited the time of freedom from pain and bleeding and wrenching moods.
Deliver me!

I know: Lord, I shall become Anna in the temple. Inside my deepest Self, I shall always have one new child, one place in myself that is pristine and eternally young and fruitful. That shall be the place wherein I keep the child Jesus, ever newly presented by his parents, the hope of his people Israel. A small light this is but a light nonetheless. I shall carefully keep it burning until the wave of despondency and grief has passed. This little flame will keep the newly changed place warm forever.

Deliver to me, Lord, the knowledge of your purpose for me, for the continuation of my life—some new task, something not possible until now, a resurrection of my Self. Deliver to me, Lord, my well-being renewed, freed, disentangled from internal chemical storms, my Self all new once again for you. For this I thank you, Lord, from what is truly my inmost Self. In the name of Christ. Amen.

—*The Reverend Kamila Blessing*

Aging

Upon Retirement

Dear God,

Help me have the grace to understand, when my retired engineer
husband becomes an expert in dishwasher loading.
Let me grin and sweetly reply each time he asks where I'm going
and when I'll be back.
Let me ignore his accusatory words when I'm late.
Let me swallow my words, when he makes our whole house the
depository for mail, newspapers, and torn-out articles.
I love the man, God, so please help me adjust to his being here,
day after day.
Let me forget that I was solely in charge and learn to share space
and time with him.
You have been good to me, and I thank you for keeping him well
and with me. Just help us to remember why it was so
important to become a couple those many years ago. Amen.

—*Ms. Marie T. Obermann*

Growing Older

How often do we stop and wonder
What was it I was going to do?
What was it I came to get?
Was there something I wanted to say?
I can't remember.
I can't recall.

Where was that shop I liked so much?
Have they moved away?
Or have I grown old
And just forgotten where they are?
I can't remember.
I can't recall.

What was the name
Of that woman who greeted me?
I know that face from somewhere
And she knows me.
But I don't know her name.
I can't remember.
I can't recall.

Losing one's memory
Is more than the absence of facts.
A life is lost
In the process of forgetting.
Memories become
Broken fragments, shards,
And what remains is a dark hole
Where names and places
Cannot be retrieved.
I can't remember.
I can't recall.
It will happen one day
To us all.

—*The Reverend Dr. Vienna Cobb Anderson*

Of Losing Things

My days are filled with
    losing things,
    forgetting things,
    dropping things,
    spilling things.

But, please, dear Lord,
    may I never lose you
    or forget you, and
    when I drop, will you pick me up
    and spill your gracious love over me
    always?

—*Mrs. Nancy Baldwin*

Lost Keys

Most merciful and loving Father,

You care for the sparrow's fall and know "my sitting down and my rising up"; surely nothing is too insignificant for your loving attention. I lost my keys on my shopping trip to the mall yesterday. Finding them would be nothing short of a miracle, since I cannot remember where I was when I saw them last, nor do I know at what point in my shopping I no longer had them. I am not asking for a miracle, but I need your help.

Am I becoming too absentminded and forgetful in my old age to function safely? Should I be thinking of some step to take after independent living is no longer advisable? And will I know when that time comes?

I never expected to live into my eighties, but here I am. So far I have been able to see the humor in all the changes age has brought, and you know I have always looked forward eagerly to the future, including that last stage of life—death and whatever adventure follows. But worrying about my keys has not seemed funny at all, and I have even been tempted to depression—an old problem I thought I had put behind me long ago.

My reaction to losing my keys makes me concerned and a little frightened about growing even older. I am trying to let go and turn it all over to you, but it is so difficult. Please help! I ask in the name of your Son, my Lord. Amen.

—*Mrs. Helen D. Hobbs*

Bunions

O God, how I would skip to meet you,
But life is long
And flesh is weak
And I have bunions
On my toes.

—*The Reverend Jean Dalby Clift*

To Bend the Knees

I will bend my knee to you, O God, as long as my knees will bend. Keep my knees supple, I pray, and when my knees will bend no more, may I always bend my heart to you, my loving Creator. Amen.

—*The Reverend Jean Dalby Clift*

As I Enter My Eightieth Year

How do I thank you, dear God, for the unexpected serenity that comes with growing old in the faith? From my youth, you taught me, and turbulent at times was the teaching! Then, slowly, reluctantly, I learned that saying and living out "Yes, Lord" was all that mattered.

I've said "Yes, Lord" to some pretty hard things. You know that. And it didn't always come easy. You know that, too! Mostly, I've tried, and still do, to run things my own way. But down deep inside, where you and I meet in the secret places of my heart, we've both known that the "Yes, Lord" will come—and with it, peace.

Growing old has taught me that this divine serenity doesn't necessarily mean lack of pain or that things will be as I want them, or think I do. I still tell you how I want things to be and kick against the evils I perceive. I even use what gifts I have to work against a few of them myself. The world continues to be full of violence and suffering. There is no promise in what the future may hold for me and mine.

But, this I know: my "Yes, Lord" will *always* be there, somewhere, and with it the many ways I may find to proclaim your might to the generations coming. Thank you, Lord, and one last *Yes!* Amen.

—*Mrs. Eleanor B. Spinney*

Psalm on Aging

There is a shock in growing old;
Friend after friend fails and dies,
Couples become singles,
Houses and beds become empty.

"What can you expect when you get to be our age?"
NO!
Others will never define who I am.
Only you, God, may do so.
In you I am more than body.
I am spirit, ever young and vibrant.
Praise to you, the God of new beginnings.
I delight in your possibilities,
Knowing there is much more left to be done.

—*Mrs. Nancy H. Miller*

Home Away from Home

O God, our great parent, when we come to the point in our lives when we can no longer ignore our need for assistance, help us! Take our hands! We are so accustomed to being independent and ordering our lives, but we now must face our limitations. Help us look and see those who are reaching out and willing to help us in so many ways. Help us see new doors opening for us in new living situations where life is not ended but is on a new dimension. We grieve for the independence we have lost but hold fast to the memories of the joy in that part of our lives. May we come to celebrate those same joys in the lives of our children and grandchildren, nieces, and nephews, friends and neighbors, and share with them our wisdom of the ages. In Jesus' name we pray. Amen.

—*The Reverend Jean M. Scribner*

The Sadness in Your Eyes

Walking closer to you while you
gaze intently out the window, I wonder what you see.
As you turn to me I see
the sadness in your eyes.
We talk for a while about what
saddens you.
It's your memories of Alabama
and times past.
The two husbands you've loved
and buried.

Your three children grown and
gone on to their own lives.
And a home that's now sold,
the home you lived in and
lovingly cared for while raising
those three children.
While you tell me of those years
your sadness briefly lifts to let
in a smile, a beautiful smile.
And those sad eyes now sparkle.
Those were your happy times.
Those long-ago days on a farm
in Alabama. Your young years.
While we're standing together
looking out that window,
I wonder how many more days
of sadness will pass,
days before the welcoming
embrace of our heavenly Father
brings back the smile and
the sparkle to never leave your
lovely eyes.

—*Mrs. Caroline Wing Fresoli*

Marjorie

Her face is blank now,
But in its lines I read
A lifetime of kindnesses
Given and received.

I say her name and smile,
And watch a distant pleasure
Light up her vacant face—
Echoes of long ago.

We walk together; as we pass
A radio, her restless hands
Beat out the rhythm of the song
Of their own accord.

An angry word can cause
Her pleasant face to frown,
Her mouth to swear in response
To the anger in the air.

Empty of her own thoughts,
Her hands and face and heart
Respond to the feelings they sense
In those around her.

—The Reverend Karen E. Gough

"Marjorie" is a fictitious name given here to an elderly woman of my acquaintance who suffers from Alzheimer's Disease.

A Prayer for Elderly Parents

Lord God, Father of us all,
I thank you for the life of my parents,
    For their love and care for each other and for us,
    For their example of godly living.
    For the model of their sixty-five-year marriage.

It has not always been easy for them;
    Perhaps it has never been easy.
    Certainly it is not easy now, as they are in their eighties.

They have lived longer than they ever thought they would.
    As each year passes, their world shrinks a bit more.
    As the circle of their world grows smaller, I thank you
        For television, newspapers, and magazines to keep them
        aware of what's going on in the outside world,
        For the telephone, which enables them to reach out to
        others and others to reach in to them,
        For friends who come to the door and send cards to
        keep in touch,
        For all the ways you bless them and brighten each day.

I lift them up to you, Lord.
    Encircle them with the light of your love.
    As their world continues to diminish,

let them feel the embrace of your everlasting arms
surrounding them, upholding them;
enable them to rest under the shadow of your wings;
give them such an awareness of your presence
that all fear and anxiety will be driven from them
so that they may abide in your perfect peace.

I entrust them to you, Lord; love them home.

—*Ms. Patricia O. Horn*

A Caretaking Wife's Prayer

Abba, Father, my body is tired, my mind is tired, my spirit is tired. My husband is tired and disagreeable. I resent him. I resent my position as caretaker and breadwinner. I mourn for the times that we anticipated earlier in our life together and that I know now can never be.

Very often I do not like myself. I do not like these feelings, and I feel guilty.

Lord, lift me in your arms and help me realize that you are truly with me. Give me the strength to endure and the will to be what you want me to be. Please let me be as Christ to him, loving, caring, tending. Let him be as Christ to me, suffering, thirsty, and allowing me to serve. Let me see him as you see him.

Thank you, Lord. Now I understand. You love me enough to allow me to serve. Here. Now. Him. Because you are with me, I have hope. I can endure and know joy. Amen and Amen.

—*Mrs. Nancy L. Burns*

Caring for a disabled husband and working full-time gave me the "poor little old me" syndrome. This was my way of reaching out for support and love to persevere. It works!

Tender Courage

I think of those I know
Who are walking shadowed paths
With a loved one.
Illness, disease, and time
Have taken their savage toll
In one so loved, who has loved in return.
A circle, a bond unbreakable
By cruel reality.
Shared joy, pain,
Tears, laughter,
Hope and despair.
Are they not the same
When bound together in love?

Those I know walking this path
Display astounding courage,
Dressed in tender strength and awe-inspiring
devotion.
Angels stand guard and watch in wonder
At such love.
A hushed world bows its head
In respectful silence.
May they know peace.

—*Mrs. Gretchen Olheiser*

Written for friends serving as caregivers to their loved ones.

Prayer for Midlife

As the winds of change
Caress her face,
Her soul goes searching
For a resting place.

For a circle of stillness
That is yet to be,
In hopes of finding
Her own epiphany.

As she smells the sun,
She remembers the rain,
And the taste of hope
In the midst of pain.

Her heart and spirit
Cry out for grace
As her soul goes searching
For a resting place.

—*Mrs. Yvonne Osborne*

Of Busted Buttons

Lord, I don't mean to complain, but this really is too much of a good thing. I always wondered how some women could let themselves become "pouter pigeons" with a bosom deep enough to put potted plants on! Now I know: they didn't. It was foisted upon them by a cruel fate! Why didn't anyone warn me? At the very least I could have been mentally prepared, and I wouldn't have bought all those pretty clothes that now cannot contain the bounty that's been forced upon me. I would have waited. You and my parents taught me to use my resources wisely, Lord; that isn't thrifty, to have all those blouses and dresses in my closet that I can't wear.

I don't understand why women don't tell those they care about, Lord, the ones who are younger, what to expect. We instruct our daughters about menarche, we see countless books and articles on weathering menopause, but nobody mentions the changes in our bodies as we begin to age. I know not everyone has the same problems I do; some women get so flat-chested, they lose whatever shape they might have had. You know, Lord, we're practical, and none of us expects to retain a girlish or even a matronly figure. But you might leave us some dignity as the years mount up! I don't like the way my shirt strains across my bust even when I buy a generous size, even when it's falling off my shoulders.

One can tell by looking at my wrists and ankles that you intended me to be slender, Lord. I intended to stay that way, too, and I wasn't prepared for the fact that glandular tissue that once fulfilled a high and holy purpose would one day turn to *fat*. I don't seem to be able to do anything about it, either; there's no way to exercise that portion of my anatomy that I know of. Is this your sense of humor at work, Lord, or is it an exercise in humility for me?

Of all the changes I thought life might bring as I aged, Lord, the one I never foresaw, and am not suffering graciously, is that I'd be busting my buttons. Please, dear God, is it too much to ask that I might go back to being just an ordinary 36C?

But if it *is* too much to ask, I understand. You have so richly blessed me that maybe this expansiveness is just symbolic of your generosity. If that is so, I'll try to praise and thank you. So be it.

—*Ms. Florence F. Krejci*

In a Mirror—But Darkly

O Lord,
if I did as much for my soul
as I do for my face
on a daily basis
I'd look better for eternity.

—*Ms. Lynne Atherton*

Golden Wedding Anniversary

Golden Wedding Day

Fifty years have raced
through my life
since that June evening
when, pale and trembling,
utterly ignorant of
the real nature of marriage,
I waited to enter the church.

Almost none
of my then-ideas
about a happy marriage
were realized.

Nor were his.
And yet—
we built a structure
that sustained us both;
we built a home
that gave us refuge;
we were friends;
we trusted each other,
and sometimes
we even understood.

—*Thayer W. Beach, Ph.D.*

Blessing for a Golden Wedding Anniversary

O God of days and of years,
    You have blessed your children in their togetherness
        with days of sun and years of gold.

    Now, at this golden time, let your blessing once more
        be upon them:

        the blessing of the Parent who created them and who,
        out of their love, created new souls to your glory;

        the blessing of the Child whose redeeming love shelters
        them in the arms of Holy Mother Church;

        the blessing of the Spirit whose strength sustains them
        through times of darkness and of light.

    The all-holy Trinity bless you, at this golden time of your
        togetherness, with golden treasures for all of your
        remaining years.

—*Ms. Patricia B. Clark*

In Times of Trouble

Prayer for Loss of a Relationship

Lord, I offer you my hurting heart and all the stories of the life and love that I have known with this very special companion. In your hands I place the loneliness, the emptiness, the pain, the despair of this brokenness. And especially, I give you the incredible sadness that has no ritual to mark it. By your power and grace, may I have the courage to meld this experience into my life story, that I may become an encourager and enabler of those who also will walk this solitary way. Fill me, please, with the abundance of your Presence, and grant me peace. Amen.

—*Dr. Kay Collier-Slone*

Dancing with Grief

When I think of her
Time and the universe
Lose their boundaries
And collapse
Into the here and now

What never was
What never can be
The cards we were dealt
The difference in our wiring
The cruel fact

We are two separated
By season
By role
By generation
By loves

And yet brought together
By one chance meeting
Now a journey
Long consecrated
by the years

All these converge upon
The structure of my heart
Where she inflicts
A great joy
and a great wound

—*The Reverend Joan E. Beilstein*

During Troubled Times

In the wilderness of my pain I look for the pillar of
cloud and fire to guide me,
But they are not there so I stumble ahead blindly over
Rocky trails, one foot after the other.
Somewhere I know God is there leading me
With his comfortable presence.
In spite of the beauty of God's fabulous creation,
My spirits are not lifted to rejoice in him.
My ears are tuned to hear a word of love,
Encouragement, or praise,
But they hear only words of criticism.
The more I try to please, the more I feel ignored,
Misunderstood, unimportant, and unvalued.
God is my refuge and strength, a help in all my
trouble.
It is easier not to reply than to be slapped down for
my response.
I hold my tongue and ponder these things in my heart.
I say nothing rather than condemn myself.
Is this sharing?
Others tell me their heartaches and receive comfort
and support,
But my heartaches are locked in my heart in the
darkness.

—*Ms. Geraldine W. Dellenback*

A Psalm

O God, how can this be happening to me?
I have been abandoned and rejected by the
    one to whom I gave my life.
Now I face the world alone.
I am afraid of what is ahead of me.
I am confused and unsure—of myself,
    of life, of you.
Come to my rescue, O God.
Then I heard you speak,
"Trust me. Trust me."
Did you really speak to me, O God?
Yes. I know I heard the words, your words,
"Trust me. Trust me."
How can I give my life again to another?
But my life is yours—and mine, too.
You gave me life, to live to the fullest.
We will live my life together, O God.
I do trust you.
Now I see many blessings.
They are from you because you have lived
    my life with me from the beginning.
I give thanks to you, O God, for my
    creation, for my life;
For the grace of your love, for your wisdom;
For your empowering Holy Spirit, which
    sustains me. Amen.

—*Ms. Judith P. Yeakel*

During an Argument

Lord, my husband and I are fighting. We need you here at the center of our conflict. We can't resolve it without you. We can't forgive each other unless you show us the way. Please be with us! In Jesus' name. Amen.

—*Ms. Frances M. S. Sturdavant*

Divorce

A Mother's Prayer for Children of Divorce

Dear Lord, bless my children, whose hearts were torn by this division in their lives, and who must live in this division. Help them to know the love of both their father and their mother, and above all, bring them to know the fullness of the love of you, their heavenly Mother and Father. Amen.

—*Dr. Kay Collier-Slone*

Beyond

Infinitely I wait for beyond
Beyond the screaming voices
The madness that drives to distraction
Beyond the steel-toned professionals,
acting only in my best interest
and the children's.

Beyond the mockery of the well-slitted eye
that self-righteously counts the years in numbers
Their marriages roosting on a borrowed perch
a black crow's ledge
Waiting for everyone else's to drop
mercilessly into the emptiness below
they make their money swooping and cawing

I wait too my voice speaking with an edge
it has never sounded out before now
Waiting for beyond
waiting for anything but now

And then the beyond happens
and it is over
the dreams tucked away
like the corners of an apron

When folded just right
they make a pretty white square
the right shape to be stowed
into some drawer marked "eternity"

And I too fold up on myself
applying the deadening needle of anesthesia
every time I utter "The Celebration and Blessing of a Marriage,"
I do not make as clean a shape in the hidden drawer

—*The Reverend Kerry Holder Sibold*

Now Is the Time

Now is the time to take off the mask and open your eyes,
to look into the face of darkness,
to step out of the muddy ruts and forge ahead.
Now is the time to shake the dust from your heart,
to open the back door and let the gypsies in,
to welcome home the cast of characters you left behind long ago.
Now is the time to hear the sweet sound of solitude,
to put on the coat you know you'll never outgrow,
to move on firm ground and arrive at the place that is yours.

—*Ms. Diane Janes-Tucker*

Beseechment Psalm

I need a miracle today, O God
My heart is troubled
and I'm scared
Having bade goodbye to the man I love
The work to which you called me
has become a nightmare—
like trying to cross
a highway
with the traffic bearing down
while I on hands and knees

can only inch my way
I need your Way
a miracle of faith and peace
Today

—*Ms. Lynne Atherton*

Home

Ancestral Home

Dancing grass
of the Plains
You call to me

Echoing the pain
of long marches
to the land of
milk and honey

Which was taken,
traded, cajoled
away from all
the old ones

And the young
radiant, regal
ones who
loved your Mother

Earth and her
gifts of nourishment
and beauty—full,
ripe, and sweet

Given tenderly
earned by teamwork
preceded by ritual

Always honoring
all as holy
living as one
with, in harmony
with, receiving
from . . . with
Gratitude

Dancing grass
of the Plains
You call to me

Echoing the footsteps
that converge the
ruts of generations
who walked with
travois to the
next place

The winter place
the summer place
the safe place
the place of Reverence and Respect

Where fires were
kept and stories
were told
where the elders
taught and the
young listened
and learned
the old ways

Dancing grass
of the Plains
You call to me

echoing the
sounds of wailing
women who
mourned their

beaten and
brutalized loved
ones

who walked
to their death
in a strange
land, who
gave up their
spirits to age,
starvation, illness,
heartbreak

who kept on going with
babies on their backs
against all
odds and whose ghosts
still march and
walk and wait

for new life
new hope

Dancing Grass
of the Plains
You call to me

—*The Reverend Canon Gwendolyn-Jane Romeril*

For Those About to Die

Provision
(for Candy)

I remember
when you were five

and went to visit
in Columbus.

You had a small
red pocketbook

of patent leather
all your own.

Mom gave five dollars
to put inside

and we sisters
watched with wonder

as you went away
alone.

Now you're going away
again

and we stand by
wanting to help

with only prayer
for provision

only love
in the red purse.

—*The Reverend Penelope Duckworth*

Written during my sister's last illness.

Friends Remembered

Why would I not
    dress you in daylilies
spin gold pillows of light
    on which to rest your head
wrap you in the royalest of purple silks?

If you think not having voice, word, air
    red lip
    soft laugh
    blushable cheek
    would keep me from this
    you are mistaken.

I would weave you hairpieces of blue diamonds
    glisten your skin with the sweat of fresh love
    careen your mind with all that is new
    Let you come alive again.

For now, I will read you poems
    paint your nails red
    and kiss you goodbye.

I will take the screaming of your eyes and love it as I love you,
    helpless in my ability, dumb.

If you think I wouldn't love you because you are dying
then how can you believe you love me?

—*Ms. Laura Scheerer*

Grief

She stands serenely
facing death
as I look on
in frozen fear
wondering if it really will be
better there than here.
There are no answers
for the pain
no well-put words
that might explain
this brevity of breath.
I wonder why
it comes to this,
why suffering seems
such senselessness
stealing life-blood
with its kiss
of pain,
slow tears,

and agony
leaving lives crushed
in the wake
of waves
of grief
too steep
to take

—*Mrs. Sandee Story*

Written as I watched a dear friend succumb to the ravages of breast cancer.

A Prayer of the Dying

Sweet Jesus, I know that I am more than the body, because you are. Like me, you suffered pain and faced death. Like you, I shall pass from darkness into light.

I hear your knock. I open the door. You invite me out of my life into yours. I come, Lord, I come.

—*The Reverend Dorothy A. Greene*

Death of Relatives

Michaelmas 1998: For My Son's Godfather

> *and flights of angels sing thee to thy rest*
> —*Hamlet, Act V, Scene ii*

When did you hear them?
Was it Gabriel's honeyed, golden voice,
the lily-sweet "fear not,"
or was it some choral *Ave-Ave-Ave*
beating in the echoing chambers
of your heart?

When did you see them?
Was it the reflection of Michael's sword
now shining in your eyes,
cruciform,
or was it the glimmering band
that bore you up
on salvation's shield?

When did you feel them?
Was it the brush of Raphael's wing
upon your brow, a healing kiss
gentling on your lips
to which you answered—
or was it the longed-for
strong embrace of their beloved Captain
and your soul's King?

I wish you could tell me:
when you listened,
what you heard—
when you looked,
what you saw—
when you reached out,
whose hand grasped yours
and led you home?

Across the fields,
the mountains,
and the great river,
some autumnal Angelus
now rings—
and I hear the echo of its call

and am thankful.

—*The Reverend Nancy Baillie Strong*

My Mother Died Today

Be my mother tonight, God, because my mother died this afternoon.
Our close moments came only when we fought;
I never confided in her or made her my friend; we didn't laugh at
    the same moment or exchange glances across a room,
    the way my daughters and I do.
I was angry at her a lot, and she at me.
She wasn't wise. But she was my mother, and I loved her
    and now I don't have her.
I think maybe you've been my mother all my life, God.
Stay close, please. I need you tonight.
Amen.

—*Ms. Kristen Johnson Ingram*

A Memory Poem

I stood beside my dying father's bed
and heard my mother say,
"We love you, Daddy,"
wondering at her need
to clothe herself in childhood.

As "Daddy" he was mine, not hers,
but she had long refused
to be his wife.

Was it duty,
or compassion for his needs
that brought those words?
Or was it recognition
of a withered love
that somehow still survived,
a small, cool flame
beneath wasteland
of the years?

—*Thayer W. Beach, Ph.D.*

Gone to Glory

Grandma Hannah's
gone to glory

give us a shout
give us a song

Grandma Hannah's
final story

read us a verse
lead us in praise

ninety-five years old
it is well with her soul

she has let go
frail bones folded
shallow breath broken

she needs no
help to hear
lens to see
teeth to talk

Grandma Hannah's
gone to glory

we grieve
we groan
we weep
we watch
we remember
we believe

God's done something
divine with her

lead us in praise
let us rejoice

Grandma Hannah's
gone to glory

—*Ms. Jeanette Adams*

My Dad

I met you, my father-in-law, just six months after my dad
    passed away.
It seemed we had met somewhere along the way.
I knew the instant I saw you that I would no more be alone.
For you brought joy and comfort into our home. I've enjoyed
    having you as "my dad" from the bottom to the top of my heart.
You are the apple of my eye, the joy of my heart.
The laughter we shared will never part.
The love I had for you was from the heart.
I will miss you.
You will never be forgotten. The memories will live on forever.
Have a safe and joyful journey and someday, somewhere, somehow
    we will meet again. For now you will be my special angel.

—*Ms. Ramona Burroughs*

Grief

Mud Song

"Careful of the mud, ma'm."
Not to worry, she thinks.
"Thank you. I'm wearing my cemetery shoes."
She watches her feet
as she patters through the rain . . .
Step, jump; sink.
She witnesses the red clay droplets
enclose the worn, black shoes.
Goooshy mud now:
it squooshes and bogs her down;

nowhere else to walk but through it.
How many babies have I buried in my cemetery shoes?
How many people even have cemetery shoes?
She remembers that once the shoes were new.
The sun is hiding today
longing for rebirth
as is the weary mother
anguished by loss so deep
that no tears can touch the pain.
Tears, rain. Rain, tears.
Which are falling on my shoes?
She sang today,
this woman of the cloth,
beseeching the Son to appear.
Mistress of ritual; officiant
Singing in a black rain hat.
Will the hat—
brim turned back to see the huddled faces—
become a Vestment,
as oddly reliable as her soggy graveyard shoes?

Go home now.
Dry out. Get warm.
Clean your shoes for another day.

—*The Reverend Mary Anne Akin*

In Remembrance

As I walk
through the mauve delight of sunrise
you're there:
together we see
the profoundness of nature—
in soaring herons
and songful birds.

It's as if you never left
at these moments.

But streaming tears
and the desolate return home
belie that time of love—
lost forever in a mystic dream.

Please, God, help me
through these aimless years.
Let there be another sunrise.

—Martha Pearman Sharp

*My husband died January 12, 1985. These walks give me solace and
a small degree of peace.*

The Lost Ones

The Christmas candles burn
and eager voices
float in through the door
trailing frosted air.

The wine begins to flow
as laughter
and happy murmurs rise.
The halls are decked,
the table bountiful,
and Christmas cheer incarnate
fills the room.

'Mid colors rich and scents
    delectable
the glass is raised in toast,
each missing guest evoked.

Gray shapes begin to gather
just beyond our vision
in the corners, on the stairs,
called forth by love and memory.

They draw near
as if to drink the wine
and find,
like Homer's dead Achilles drinking blood,
a moment more of life.

—*Thayer W. Beach, Ph.D.*

The Wilderness of Quiet

and let your widows trust in me.
                    —*Jeremiah 49:11*

She explains that she "is alone now,"
that she's used to shopping for a *family*.
But now all is quiet. All is in order—
the stairs swept, the ironing basket empty.
There is a wilderness that is all quiet, all order—
nothing but the desert of daily routine:
The mailman comes at noon.
Wednesday is trash day.

Satan sneaks in at 5:00 bringing despair.
Should she just bow out—quietly?

No. Angels guard her choices:
the paperboy, the sparrows on the walk.
Maybe they'll be hungry.
Maybe for the paperboy she should leave cookies.
For the sparrows she thinks
she'll scatter bread crumbs
made from this morning's toast.

The sparrows' "chip-chip" enters upon the silence;
then the paperboy rings his bike bell
as he calls out, "Thanks."

—*Ms. Rosamond Rosenmeier*

Curve

So we live here, forever taking leave
                    —after Rilke

Wherever I look these days
something is leaving.
The wispy ash grass, its green
lost to sun, sinks back to earth;
maples open handfuls of yellow and rust,
toss their farewell under bushes,
across sidewalks still shiny
from dew withdrawing its shawl.
On a limb a nest breaks apart,
disappears at the touch time makes
on the way from one loss to another.

Now words are clusters of dry weeds
without nourishment or sense,
their sounds mimic melodies once
known, forgotten like a baby's babble,
pleasure's inflection outgrown,
worn by the world's seasons.
At night starlight leaves little
of its dim past in a sky slowly
weathering black. Even in
my dreams since your death,
I meet myself running away.

—Annette Allen, Ph.D.

Leaves from a Woman's Life

She's lived
in an apartment for forty years
with her memory of leaves
falling at certain times.
Age ten, she stripped her feet bare
and walked in them, sank deep
letting her ankles wear them
like drooped stockings.
She's not seen them since

but remembers their soft descent
their feel under her feet,
the thick untidiness of rumpled rugs.
She functions well
in her walled garden,
called a "patio" in the ads.
Two pine trees prosper
but nothing wafts now
in slow downward spirals.
To her the leaves were wind
made visible.
She's asked for leaves
over her casket
instead of lilies . . .
to be dropped slowly.
That's to be her pall.

—*Ms. Lucy Germany*

Untimely Death

Meditation on Untimely Death

It hasn't taken long for our leaves to turn from green to gold and then to fall and form the winter blanket for this good earth. I know Nina has been making moose head soup and that Eli's son has been cutting fish. I know that Kathleen is preparing for potlatch and threatens to make me smell porcupine while it's cooking. I know Edna is sewing beautiful items and most of us are doing autumn things, waiting for winter's rest.

Two years ago here, you'll remember, life was not so orderly. Two years ago, the snow fell heavily on yet-green leaves, bending the trees, burdening the branches. Things were out of order and the sight of leaves blowing across the snow was a strange sight all that winter long.

Many of the bent trees managed to straighten, more or less, but are not quite the same. And some trees, of course, even in these two intervening years, haven't straightened at all and remain alive, but turned to the ground forever.

We are accustomed to a natural order of things, with seasons that follow each other in turn, with chores for each season, and beauty different to each season. We know what to do then; we know how to be summer people and how to be winter people.

But when the order is disrupted, we're uncomfortable, confused, not sure of what to do. Two years ago, with snow on every green leave, Judy said, "Oh, it will go away. It's too soon for winter." No, not that year. We just didn't have the time we expected to get things done. We went from summer to winter before the wood was all cut and stacked, before the freezer was full, before the boats were out of the water. We were caught unaware.

So, too, does death sometimes surprise us, coming too soon to be believed, coming to freeze blossoms, fell saplings, remove beauty before its season. We feel this, I think, at the death of any child, for we never desire to outlive the next generation. It is out of the order of things. It is out of season.

The death of anyone our own age or younger nudges our awareness of our own end. Death by accident too is sudden, unreal, unsynchronized with our notion of the world. And when death is by choice, the impact of its suddenness, the unimaginable reasons, the implied insult of being so suddenly and cruelly left behind, is like that early killing frost, leaving petals in the ice.

With the dying of our fruitful harvest season, with the last of the fish, meat, and berries put by, with a sigh for a departing summer and yearning for a long-deserved winter rest, let us remember those too soon gone: the young, the victims of accidents, and the victims of their own sad terrors. Let us remember the losses of this year and of past years, our losses and those of others. I ask you to pray for them, rushed from us outside of the proper time and season.

And we, those left behind, whose only choice is to say farewell, unready and unarmed; we, who like those fragile birch, struggle to stand again, alive yet not as before, let us pray for one another. May we stand through another year of seasons, frost-damaged but steady and growing still.

May winter bring rest as faith brings peace.

—*The Reverend Barbara Deane Price*

Alaska, with very high rates of substance abuse, child abuse, violence, suicide, and accidents, is ever in mourning. This was written on the sixth anniversary of my son's last day in this life. He died by his own hand on September 26, 1988.

Psalm (Lament)

O God, where were you on an ordinary night
In the great dark city? Where were you
When a young woman, one of your own,
Was robbed and stabbed in a random act of evil?
Where were you when she, worth more than
The sparrows I am told you notice,
Was left alone to bleed and die?
O God, where were you then?

Unknowing, I said my evening prayer,
And I slept. You were with me then,
When my world was in place.
Now all is chaos, and I look for you.
If you are love and compassion,
If you are justice and mercy,
I know where you were that night.
You were on the dark street with her.

You held her hand, and you wept,
As now you hold my hand and weep with me.

—Ms. *Shirley Bynum Smith*

Grief

Your absence fills the room, this house, my heart,
I hear your stilled voice clearly in my head.
I am afraid I will lose the sound of your laughter.

I bury my face in your old sweater, inhale its scent.
I want to sit with you and talk, to touch your arm,
To watch your hand lift a cup to your lips.

Instead, I hold the string of pearls you wore.
I turn the pages of a photo album to see you.
I pore over your artwork, trying to find you there.

My life is forever changed, as on the day
You were born. I was overwhelmed then, too.
Hope, joy, and fear mingled with innocence,

With awe for a small being cradled in my arms
I was no longer my old self, but I was willing then,
Eager to change. Now I want my old self, unchanged,

Not this slow-moving body, heavy, wooden, going nowhere.
Sometimes I am weightless, liquid, as if dissolving
Into nothing, swimming inside a terrible current.

If I find my way out of desolation, I am afraid
I will move too far away from you. I am trapped.
O God, I cry, I am unprepared. It is too much.

O God, I cry, I do not want to do this.
O God, I must give myself up to grief.
I am forced to wait for grief to do its work,

To help me bear what I cannot bear;
To trust that when the awful grief is done,
And a more gentle heartache settles in

Through grace, I will be made a new creation, the fruit of sorrow.

—*Mrs. Shirley Bynum Smith*

Death of Children

A Mother's Prayer

Hail, Mary, full of grace.
Pray for me, now, in the time of my grief.

You had a son. You lost a son—in the prime of his life.
I, too.

Were your tears bitter, reflecting the injustice?
Were your tears a torrent, reflecting the anguish?
Were your tears hot, reflecting your anger?
Mine are.

Did your soul become barren in the salty river?
Did your faith grow dark, extinguished in tears?
Did your love shrivel as your tears dried?
Mine has.

Did you withdraw to nurse a wounded heart?
Did you curse and shake your fist at God?
Did you retreat into the past grasping at memories?
(the feel of a baby, new in your arms
the smell of a boy, sweaty from play
the sound of a teen, raucous and gay
the look of a man, who is ever your baby)
I have.

Did your weeping stop?
Did you live again?
Did you love again?
Did you believe again?

O Mary, full of grace.
Pray for me, now, in the time of my grief.

—*Mrs. Joanne B. Galbraith*

Lisa

I thank God each day for the sweet tiny baby she was on the day of her birth; for the darling brown-eyed girl with golden curls whose smile and laughter warmed my heart; for the young woman she became who never saw a stranger and who touched the hearts of those who knew her—family, friends, and strangers; for the courageous, terminally ill woman who fought the great fight and when the end was near said, "the Lord has always been good to me and I'll be waiting for you all in heaven." As I held her hand and felt her body grow cold, I commended her spirit to you, O Lord. As my tears fell, I thanked you for allowing me even this short time with her here on Earth.

—*Mrs. Diana Born*

To Live Again

> *It is no longer I who live,*
> *but it is Christ who lives in me.*
> *And the life I now live in the flesh*
> *I live by faith in the Son of God,*
> *who loved me and gave himself for me.*
> —*Galatians 2:20*

When our twelve-and-a-half-year-old, Susan, died, I felt like one of Picasso's painted women, with a hole in my middle—empty and grotesque. There was no way I could go about every day, living in my own strength. Only God could fill that void and make up for what I lacked.

The words, "it's no longer I who live, but Christ who lives in me," were daily in my mind and on my lips until the emptiness began to fill and I stood again, alive and whole.

—*Mrs. Nancy H. Miller*

A Grandmother's Requiem

We decided early on, dear Nathan,
that you were a gift of God.

A gift that brought patience
as we waited for the time of your birth.

A gift that made us remember
we are all a work in progress.

A gift that reminded us to pray
as all things are possible with God.

A gift that instilled courage
so that we could be an example of faith.

A gift that taught us to mourn
and know that we are blessed and comforted.

A gift that brought us together
to form tight, unbreakable bonds.

As you rest now in your new, perfect body,
intercede for us. Pray that we remain faithful.

Our life journey is difficult,
but we have the promise of eternal life.

So remember us,
until we meet again.

—*Ms. Rietta Bennett*

Death of a Pet

Goodnight

You came home, skin and bones
Lived at the end on the left, away from wondering eyes
And every day I came, I saw you.

I cared for you, cuddled you,
Held you the only way I knew
Your head on my shoulder, your only response.

Breathing into my ear, trying so hard to tell me,
"What? What is it?" I cried.
Now I know what you were trying to say.

"I'm leaving you. I have no choice, but know I love you.
Move on, be happy, and I will always be with you.
Don't worry about me; take care of yourself;
Everything will work out. It's all for the best."

I kept you here as long as I could and then I could keep you no longer.

I said goodbye.

No tears were shed that last long hour,
Hoping you would come back home, knowing you never would.
And now, whenever I gaze at a sky of soft pinks, purples, reds, and oranges,
I say goodnight,

Knowing you're up there with God, watching over me
and I smile.

—*Ms. Charlotte Elizabeth Geitz*

Prayers for the Loss of a Pet

In the following prayer, the People may respond with the words in italics.

O God, creator and sustainer of the birds of the air, the beasts of the field, and the fish of the sea, sustain us in our sorrow. Help us to recognize the fragility of all life, and to therefore cherish the precious time we are given. In Christ's name we pray. *Amen.*

Psalm 148:7–13

A Litany

O God, our maker, we pray for all the pets of the world that they may have good homes.
Lord, hear our prayer.

Grant that all pet owners may provide loving care for your creatures.
Lord, hear our prayer.

We pray for all who serve our pets, that they recognize our pets as truly members of our family.
Lord, hear our prayer.

Grant us the wisdom to recognize the blessing of having had *N.* with us in our family.
Lord, hear our prayer.

May the owner(s) and friend(s) of *N.* receive comfort and peace from the knowledge of your eternal love and grace.
Lord, hear our prayer.

We praise you for the pets of your saints, who have gone before: for Dame Julian's cat, for the dolphins who led St. Brendan safely to land, for the wolf tamed by St. Brigid, for all the animals who loved St. Francis and for all animals everywhere.
Lord, hear our prayer.

Closing Prayer

Dear God,
We give thanks to you for the life of *N.* and the love and companionship we shared. We will miss *her,* but in the midst of our sorrow we recognize the blessings *she* brought to us. Just as you are aware of every sparrow that falls, be with *N.* at this time.
In the name of Jesus Christ, your Son, who died for us. *Amen.*

—*Ms. Madelyn A. Stella*

Spirituality

Naming God

Meditation on the Names of God

To you who laid the foundations of the earth, I dare to speak.

We have called you by many names,
in many languages,
through many centuries.

Living in this transition time,
none of those names seems sufficient,
expressive, easy to speak
when I try to bring myself before you.

"Jesus," I can say, yes, and "Jesus Christ"—
Son of the Most High, Redeemer of the world,
Incarnation of the divine in human form—
crucified and risen to show us the way home.

"Holy Spirit," I can say, no problem—
wind and fire anointing the Apostles,
your still voice at the center of the whirlwind,
caretaker of this strange thing we call the Church.

But what of you, O first person of the Trinity?

If I don't pay attention during church
I can roll through all those names without a hitch:
Father, Lord, King.

But when I hear myself, or focus on the words upon the page,
I falter, resisting the baggage of human fathers, lords, kings.

But human baggage cannot weigh you down.

You were enigmatic when directly asked your name:
just "I AM, tell them I AM sent you."
What kind of name is that? I AM what?

Is this an elaborate game
in which the goal is to discover what is hidden?
Or do we know instinctively
that to name something is to control it
as Adam named the animals?

Is that why your name is a mystery,
must remain a mystery,
lest we imagine even for a moment
we can control your beauty and your power?

God forbid.

Speak my name, lover of souls,
that I may be wholly yours.
Then none of the rest will matter
at all.

—*Dr. Pamela W. Darling*

How Do I Name You?

How do I name you, O God?
With the venerable, comfortable, awe-full language of tradition?
Almighty, Eternal, Everlasting,
Creator, Redeemer, Advocate,
Father, Son, and Holy Spirit?

With the language of flesh and blood as it mirrors your
Incarnation?
Mother, Sister, Father, Brother,
Maker, Lover, Keeper,
Friend?

By what name will you hear and answer me?

O God, I call upon you from the depths of my soul!
For you have touched me and I must seek you,
Naming you with the Voice, the Love, and the Need within me.

—*The Reverend Glyn Lorraine Ruppe-Melnyk*

Who Are You?

God is not rescuer.
God is not safety.
God is not benevolent or critical Father-knows-best.
God is not puppet or puppeteer.
God is not who I thought/was taught he is.

God is lover—reckless, spendthrift, indiscriminate, passionate.
God is pursuer—relentless, determined, tireless seeker of
    my soul.
God is challenger—demanding movement, journey, change,
    growth.
God is creator—delighted in me, her creation.
God is nurturer—feeding her hungry children at the breast.
God is teacher—eager to share her knowledge and wisdom.
God is dancer and music maker—creation responds joyfully to
    her choreography.
God is spirit, wind, and fire—uncontainable, she will not tolerate
    the tidy boxes we painstakingly construct for her.
God is light—exposing, revealing, searching out all that I would
    hide.
God is unknowable yet constantly revealing herself to me with a
    richness and intensity I cannot ignore.
God knows me, penetrates and forms me, recognizes and claims
    me as she has from my mother's womb.

—*The Reverend Virginia Going*

God Is Not a Single Parent

Father God, Creator of us all,
How long will we see you as a single parent?
Send your loving wisdom to fill our hearts
and minds with new words of inclusivity.

Open our eyes to see images that nurture and heal our brokenness.
Grant us courage and your freedom to try new words that
restore balance in all our relationships.
And like baby swans being guarded and cared for by both parents,
let the wholeness of you be illuminated in us.

Mother, Father, Creator of us all. Amen.

—*Ms. Ann Smith*

Father/Mother God

Dear God,
you are no more male
than I am God,
even though I have been well trained
and my instinct
has always been to address you
in the masculine.
You are as much—
no, more—mother than father to me,
and yet I still find Father
my instinctive address.
You nurture me at your breast
as I have nurtured my own children,
and yet I am more
and less than your child.

I am more willing to accept
traditional masculine understandings
of who you are
than to explore new,
more inclusive ways
of thinking of you
and, by extension,
of myself, as your creation.
I forget that it is all of humanity
who are your image,
and not man
or woman.

Teach me, O Lord,
Father,
Mother,
Lover,
Beloved,
teach me to be open
to all that you are.
Teach me to hear you
in the joyful voices of children,
in the wisdom of the grandmother,
in the bravado and confidence
of the beardless youth,
and in my own yearning for truth
and meaning.

Fill me, Beloved,
with the passionate
and powerful desire to share your life
and live only for you.

Know me
as only a lover can
and make me exquisitely aware
of your knowing and your love.

—*Ms. Marty Conner*

Metaphor

Godde*, I think you
are a metaphor
for all that we love:
your presence in
the beloved's heart,
the lake's mystical beauty,
the healing touch.

—*Mrs. Betty Vilas Hedblom*

*Godde *is a feminine spelling of* God.

The Tangled Road Toward God

I am searching for the divine Sophia.
I want to trust in her for a change.
I yearn to look up and see the face of a loving mother
to know if she has a plan for me.
Do I dare ask what next, gentle goddess?
I have often cried out to God,
"Show me what to do and help me do it."
I once asked to be cracked open.
I forgot to ask to be put back together.
I'm wondering what it would be like to
cry out to Sophia, to Ancient Wisdom.
Would I be cracked open again, but gently this time?

—*Ms. Jane D. Smith*

God of the Night

God of flowing skirts and tender eyes, you fill the dark places of
my life with power and compassion. In your presence I am a child,
naked and vulnerable. Yet you find me, and your strong hands lift
me into your presence. You are as large and indecipherable as the
night, yet as near and touchable as a mother's hand. When you lift
me, I am suspended in the midst of that night; but your eyes as
well as your hands hold me, and my fear is contained in your
tender compassion. As the stars twinkle with delight, your love
clothes my nakedness with joy. God, you are so enormous and so
full of power. Once I thought that your grasp might destroy me
and that your voice would be like thunder. Yet you stoop to earth
and open yourself to my presence. You speak in tones that I can
hear and hold me safely in your presence. God of the night, I
praise you.

—*The Reverend Elizabeth T. Wade*

Holy Woman

O holy woman
you are everywhere
but most of all you are here

surrounding me
in gentle, loving
women and men

A robust woman
with large breasts
and strong arms
whose very body
says: I Am hospitality

A tall, regal, black
woman whose
eyes see far and who
prophesies and
says: I Am on
The journey

A gay man
whose eyes shine
out from hidden
pools of pain and
who wears honesty
like a cloak saying:
I Am who I am

A lovely young woman
with flaxen hair
whose lap is filled
with children and who
says: I Am mother

A slender man
who moves like
a dancer embodying
the beauty of movement
saying: I Am full of grace

An older man
in worn-out
Corduroys and shirt whose
Fatherly ways and
sparkling eyes say:
I Am the storyteller
and my stories never wear out

A quiet, white-haired
woman whose wisdom
girds her fragile frame
like fireflies on a
summer's night, who
says: I Am here

—*The Reverend Canon Gwendolyn-Jane Romeril*

Mother God

Sovereign God, Mother of the Universe, you alone are my nourishment and salvation. Nurse me at your breast, fill me with your
Spirit, and, like a she-bear with her cub, protect me with your awesome power and might.

—*The Reverend Alma Terese Beck*

Spirit Stroke

Holy Spirit
    Unexplainable in words
    Yet WORD here experienced
God—*verbed*
    Humanity sensing
        Movement
        Breath
        Presence . . .
        Here—Now—Today

Flutter of comfort
    In my sorrow
Inner affirmation
    In my turmoil
Enfolding warmth
    In my being
Nudging me
    Into myself

Presence
    Inexplicable
    Ineffable
    Indescribable
Yet invisibly present
Cloud of murmurs wafting WORD

I know Spirit surging . . .
    Soft enfolding . . .
        Breath of wingtips
        Whisper love
        Flowing otherness
And I yield . . .
    Melting anxiety
Ultimate God Centered-ness

I am whole-wombed SHE
    Born in expiration,
    Born through inspiration,
    Born in exhalation
Becoming EXULTATION . . .
    Of the one "I AM"

—*The Reverend Diane Moore*

Being Known by God

Begin by thinking of the many names you know for God: Lord, Creator, Jesus, Light, Mother, Father, Savior, Love, Abba, Bread, Thou, and so forth. Decide on a particular name for this time, one that suggests the quality of God's presence you wish to call forth now. Repeat that name over and over softly to yourself for a minute or two, even moving your lips.

Continue saying God's name softly to yourself. To begin, think of what you know about the God who bears this name. Ponder all you know about God's essential being, and especially as One who chooses to be here for you now.

Continuing to say God's name, let your awareness of the name gradually sink down into the region near your heart. As you experience this passage, let go of your *thoughts about* God. Simply use the name as an arrow of longing cast forth from your heart toward God's heart. Don't think; just experience God's presence as the name repeats itself in your heart.

Allow yourself to be aware that this One in whose presence you are now enfolded knows you through and through. What feelings does this awareness bring? Let the feelings come as they will, noticing them but not grasping at them, so that they also go as they will, making room for whatever will come next.

Hear God say to you: "I delight in you. You are my beloved." Receive the truth and the empowerment of this reality as fully as you are able to right now. As you breathe in, take in God's word: "I love you." As you breathe out, give God your love. Continue this rhythmic breathing and loving for a time.

Rest peacefully in the quiet for some moments.

When you are ready, open your eyes and return fully to this now.

—*Norvene Vest, Obl. O.S.B.*

Prayer

Centering Prayer

Hidden God, ever present to me,
    may I now be present to you,
        attentive to your every word,
        attuned to your inspirations,
        alert to your touch.

Empty me that I may be filled with you alone.

—*Ms. Patricia B. Clark*

prayer of devotion

still my soul, that i might pray Thee
calm my mind, that i might hear Thee
light my vision, that i might see Thee
unveil my heart, that i might truly love Thee

bend my knee, that i might adore Thee
loose my tongue, that i might exalt Thee
come within, that i might know Thee
give me wings, that i might ever sing Thee

—*Dr. Karen A. Eshelman*

Mother Godde Prayers for the Rosary

Holding the medal in your hand, speak to Mother Godde offering
your praises, and noting your needs and concerns.*

*Then, on each of the following three beads, and on the single bead
between each group of ten, pray:*

Blessed are you, Mother Godde
For you calm our spirits, strengthen our hearts,
and fill our bodies with the power of love.

On each of the ten consecutive beads, pray:

Mother Godde, bearer of Creation,
Birth in us your love and peace.
Mother Godde, Lover of Creation,
Share through us your love and peace.
Mother Godde, Guardian of Creation,
That all may dwell in love and peace.

—*The Reverend Glyn Lorraine Ruppe-Melnyk*

*Godde *is a feminine spelling of* God.

How Do I Pray?

Very carefully . . . irrationally . . . and in thanksgiving; in pain and in sorrow . . . in the pure joy of living and laughing. Asking for magic . . . begging for a miracle. I am seeking, searching, forgiving, repentant; looking for answers for the sick, the lonely, the hungry; looking for direction, asking for mercy; seeking silence and trying to listen, listen, listen. On my knees, in the dark of night; while peeling onions; on my walk, with the Psalms and to the Father.

Those are my Alleluias and my Amens.

—*Mrs. Jean M. Hicks*

Silent Prayer

Eyes closed, we sit in silence,
Three women praying.
Seeking your voice, we go within.
Silent, we hear our breathing.
I see you on the cross,
Arms open for the world.
Your body suffering for us all.
I understand your humanity.
I believe your divinity.
As always, I pray for strength,
Strength to overcome timidity,
Strength to do what I must for family,
for friends, for you.
I am still; I listen.
I hear you say, "I am your strength."
I say to you, "You are my redeemer."
My Lord, my God.

—*Mrs. Sallie Cheavens Verette*

My Sequoia Prayer

When I feel tiny, weak, and trembling
Or pulled this way and that by swirls of change,
Too insignificant to be of service,
Too "uprooted" to hold my ground,
    I pray my Sequoia Prayer.

Sitting quietly, breathing normally, becoming centered in the
      present moment—
in this holy instant—
My mind's eye gradually forms an image of a giant Sequoia.
My Sequoia prayer takes form in my heart and soul
As the image forms and fleshes out to fill my being.

      Centuries-old roots so wide and deep they have become part
         of the earth,
      Supporting enormous, gnarled trunk that soars into the sky,
      Eternity wrinkles carved into its surface, holding character
         markings for the ages,
      Thick, porous bark skin covering the body, letting the trunk
         breathe,
      protecting it from the fires that must come to support its
         growth,
      Green leaves gushing out the top, reaching to the heavens,
      Nurturing birds and other beings, offering up limbs as if in
         prayer.

        Awareness of God fills my soul.
        Sequoia image fills my being.

Spreading
      Down into the earth,
      Deep into the soul,
      Strong into the body.

Breathing calmly, sitting quietly, praying trustingly, becoming
      Grounded in humanity,
      Rooted in God,
      Striving ever upward.
My Sequoia prayer fills my cells, my lungs, my heart, my brain,
      my soul, my being.

With love, grace, light.
With joy, hope.

With the strength of God I need to go on! Thank you, God!
Amen.

—*Dr. Monteen Lucas*

Creation

Bornings

Infinite depth
Unspaced in nothing
Explodes in patterned chaos.
A universe is born.
In the beginning
Word of light
Smashes through the darkness.
And the visible is born.

Out of the formless void of darkness,
Light reveals a world.

But always first the darkness,
Still for us, the darkness,
Womb-cell-shells of darkness,
Humming hives of darkness,
In hidden places, taking
The stuff of our creating,
Forming, shaping, making,
For the stab-bright light
Of birth.

And what births still are waiting,
What matrix webs are spinning
Casting shape to new beginning
Within our dark and secret souls?

—*The Reverend Daphne Grimes*

Mother Earth

Mother Earth, Queen of Heaven,
we celebrate with your many names.

Within the earth that is your body,
the waters of your living womb,
the air that is your sacred breath,
and the fire that is your radiant spirit
life is born, grows, dies and is reborn.

Instill in us an awareness of
the cycles and rhythms of nature.
As seeds sprout in the spring,
so should the inspiration of new ideas.
From summer's fiery heat we shall
harness positive energy and
celebrate the abundance around us.
When the days grow short in the fall
we will listen to the wise intuitive inner voice
and honor our feelings.
During winter's cold days and long nights
we will acknowledge our bodies' wisdom
and the healing power of dreams.
The moons celestial light and sacred dark
keep us in balance as our bodies cycle in harmony.

We will dance around the tree of life,
listening to your leaves whisper words of wisdom,
and celebrate your abundant beauty.

—*Ms. Judy Coates Perez*

Workshop of God

Like a lump of clay, soft, malleable, without definition
    the act of creation renders us
    other than indefinite.
At the center of this workshop, at first invisible within the liquid
that cradles us,
    both slowly and with speed
    we grow

from the beginning,
a being known and preordained
in secret
with our own special name,
and with a mission to achieve.
This being, form and spirit,
briefly consigned to earth,
goes through a transformation that consists
of living,
of becoming,
and of leaving something
on returning to the primordial dust
where our existence has its start.
The body is transformed according to ancient plan.
As the brain develops,
does the spirit also, having contact
with the temporal,
become more human
in its union with our form?
Does that also render us the more divine?

—*Ms. Lynda M. Maraby*

The Rocky Beach

When first birthed
From its mother rock
Each stone was sharp, jagged, unbending.

Now, eons of storms and pounding surf
Have rounded the edges,
Smoothed the surfaces.

Each stone different.
Some black, others white—
Speckled ones abound.

Many flat, more round—
Mica glitters from granite globes.
None shaped like its neighbor.

All together make the rocky beach—
A rough-hewn edge to the sea
Sparkled by the sun.

May one stone chosen from many
Be a reminder that we are *each* like this—
Born of the same Source.

Each is unique,
Each is being worn smooth
By the storms of life.

Together, with our various shapes,
Sizes, colors—and our varied gifts—
We return beauty to God's world.

—*Ms. Susan Mixter Blanchard*

Healing at the Well of the Wethers

Pilgrims banded by that yearning, that fear,
looking for intimations of presence
yet not knowing
if we can bear such inbreaking,
we gather thirsting,
encircling this age-old well
whose waters have washed many a parched heart.

We are hoping
for an elemental simplicity,
a meaning beneath all appearances,
steady as the craggy rocks that rim the well,
tenacious as the climbing roses
that fence this space of encounter,
piercing us through with beauty.

Peering down, we see our faces mirrored,
mossy green and rippling.
Waters that have flowed for centuries
promise to quicken,
intimate a rippling life in us

that we'd all but forgotten,
stumbling beneath wounds old and new
and stupid guilt bearing down without remorse.

In the Well of the Wethers the waters move,
unseen angels disturb the surface.
We press forward,
mouths already tasting the ancient water
of life,
the water from which we emerged,
new and dripping,
so long ago.

—*The Reverend Mary Earle*

Speak to Me

Even now,
In the muffled voice of winter
Buried deep under frozen leaves
Hushed by a blanket of clouds and snow,
Even in the unyielding silver-glazed ice,
You are there, I know.

Speak to me
Even now,
When the birds can only whisper
in distinctive muted peeps,
Having forgotten for a time
their lovely songs
As they puff out their feathers against
the searching cold,
You are there; I listen.

Speak to me
Even now,
When the deer make no mention
of their majesty's presence
As they gingerly tip-toe by,
Their dull-shagged coats lost in the stark
brown-sombered forest.
But I see.

Ah, there you are!
Even now,
You speak—simply
In the listening-for,
In the yearning-after,
In the looking-deeper,
In the Being-with,
You speak.

And I have heard you
Especially now,
In the poignant stillness,
In the pregnant hoping,
In the mysterious Surrounding,
You have spoken in your warm-sweet embrace
Even now!

—*The Reverend Dr. Elizabeth L. Lilly*

Prayer for the Homelands

Creator, giver, and sustainer of all life, we come before you in thanksgiving for all you bring to us for our visit within your creation.

Yesteryear was a time
when the rivers flowed without poison
wind blew untainted air
sun shown brightly through not-hazed sky
everything was safe to eat
simplicity was the rule
technology had no say
But now I hear your cry
all is not as you created
We have made a different time
Forgive us for not using our minds
to remember the Seventh Generation
not yet born
Creator, we come before you
with humble spirit
Open hearts to see what we have done
Give us wisdom to
undo what we have done

Give us hope that we may
one day live where
river flows pure
wind blows free
sun shines brightly
and our bodies are safely nourished
Give us courage to change
Give us courage to return
to our Homelands
and remember those yet to come

—*Ms. Ginny Doctor*

Testimony
(for my daughters)

I want to tell you
that the world is still beautiful.
I tell you that despite
children raped on city streets,
shot down in schoolrooms,
despite the slow poisons seeping
from old and hidden sins
into our air, soil, water,
despite the thinning film
that encloses our aching world.
Despite my own terror and despair.

I want you to look again and again,
to recognize the tender grasses,
curled like a baby's fine hairs
around your fingers, as a recurring
miracle, to see that the river rocks
shine like God, that the crisp
voices of the orange and gold
October leaves are laughing at death.
I want you to look beneath
the grass, to note
the fragile hieroglyphs
of ant, snail, beetle. I want
you to understand that you are
no more and no less necessary

than the brown recluse, the ruby-
throated hummingbird, the humpback
whale, the profligate mimosa.

I want to say, like Neruda,
that I am waiting for
"a great and common tenderness,"
that I still believe
we are capable of attention,
that anyone who notices the world
must want to save it.

—*Ms. Rebecca Baggett*

Mother, Teach Us to Pray

Mother here
now and here
name us.

Here make your wild and messy household
your chaotic piles of branches and bones
with the grass always springing up between
and always the unseen bird calling from high in a tree
and rain falling somewhere and snow falling
and rivers meandering and earth shaking
and small wet joyful creatures jumping
and everywhere darkness and dust and stars.

Fill us with the fire of your desiring.
Teach us to yearn for what you yearn for.
Make us ache and burn and shine and split.
Let us leave the air dazzling wherever we pass.

And give us another chance.
Teach us to walk barefooted and easy.
Teach us to go to ground singing.
Teach us to open our hands.

When we come to the rim of the volcano
or slide out onto a skim of ice
or step onto a thin branch,
push us over, crack us under, let us fall,
and catch us, laughing, in your wide welcoming arms.

Amen.

—*The Reverend Mary F. C. Pratt*

A Greening Prayer

Godde
keep me always
greening

keep me rooted
in the dark
keep me turning
into light

keep me well
and deeply watered
keep me bending
with the winds

keep me growing
beyond fences
keep me leafing
budding blooming

keep me fruiting
keep me yielding
ever blessing
everything

keep me healing
calm and able
keep me still as
stillness calls

keep me always
greening
Godde

—*Ms. Nancy Adams-Cogan*

God Our Provider

Providing God of the wheat in the desert,
you nourish our lives.
Sustaining God, you sent food for your people—
you supply all our needs.
With honey from the rocks you fed them—
your presence is joy.
God of the manna from heaven,
you are bread for our souls.

Refreshing God of the rain and the dewfall,
you revive the land.
God of the rock and the river,
your love overflows.
Our God, you are healing and cleansing—
renew us in you,
God of the crystal waters,
the water of life.

Lord Jesus, by your life you feed us,
for you are our bread.
Lord Jesus, by your body broken
our souls are fed.
River of life-giving water,
refresh and renew.
Creator, Savior, and Spirit,
we thirst for you.

—*Sister Cecilia, C.S.F.*

*This poem has been used as a canticle by the Sisters of the
Community of St. Francis for the last twenty years.*

The Voice

The voice in the waves as they curl 'round the rocks
in a whisper both gentle and clear,
the voice in the clouds as they float in the dome
is the voice I continue to hear.
The voice in the sun as it burns through the mist
till it glistens on mottled grey sea,
the voice in the ancient, still, barnacled rocks—
can the voice be the One calling me?
The voice in the waves, and the clouds, and the sun,
and the rocks, when I ask, "Is it Thee?"
replies in a whisper. My soul floats and burns.
In the stillness I hear, "Taste and see."

—*Ms. Sally Edwards*

Magnet Pulling

Today, I have the sense of the sprouted seed,
Long in darkness, somnolent, confined
Suddenly *pushed* through the wet resistant earth
Popped to the wide blue of the roaring sky!

Blazing and warm and mellowing, the sun
Draws me, magnet—pulling—
There is only the upward, outward thrust—
Surge, our pulse, our beat and loving—
Flamboyant, new, this
Camouflage of foliage—
Does it belong to me? And what
of this heavy, bursting seedling
Inside?

"O Lord, how manifold thy works!
In wisdom hast thou made them all!"

—*Mona C. Hull, Ph.D.*

Earth

God is digging in the garden of my soul,
    the rich, moist dirt sticking under her fingernails,
    turning and blending the soil of my life,
    now and then adding the compost
        of tossed-out experiences
    that I believed were useless.

She seems to understand
    that this bed can sustain life,
    that the deadened seeds and withered sprouts
        will not be all there is.

Like the herb jungle
    in my friend Elaine's backyard,
my soul, under God's care,
        will grow green and wild.

—*The Reverend Helen C. L. McPeak*

Early Spring Night

An early spring night,
cool, clear, bright.
The old oak tree,
majestic in its splendor,
flawlessly silhouetted against the
brightly shining,
perfectly rounded,
magnificent full moon.
Thousands of luminous stars
twinkle in the heavens.

The fullness of time for the moon is complete,
still to come for the oak tree,
its buds of new life not yet formed.
The mystery of life's cycles
captured for eternity
in one perfect moment of time.

—*Ms. Marjorie A. Burke*

Divine Musician

O God, you sang creation into being
And then embraced it in the sacred dance.
You breathed your harmonies into its spirit;
Enchanted restless forces with a glance.

Divine Musician, you played us an Eden;
You filled its silences with notes divine.
But we grew deaf from discord we engendered
And heard no more your musical design.

Your melodies still hover in our beings
Like tunes that echo through a hollow reed;
Your Spirit's voice sets ready heartstrings ringing,
That choruses long buried might be freed.

Make us your instruments, tuned for your service;
Call forth a symphony of grateful praise;
Arrange our lives in rhythm with your music;
Sing us a new creation for these days.

—*Ms. Patricia B. Clark*

Refreshment

Floating in a pond on a hot summer's day
Your sunlight radiating within and without me
Bathing me in the warmth of your goodness.
Bullfrogs croaking
Dragonflies mating
Birds singing
Fish jumping
A splash of cool water—
Ahhh . . .
"Come to me all ye that travail and are heavy-laden
    and I will refresh you."

—*The Reverend Elizabeth Rankin Geitz*

Seasons of Healing—A Litany

The Leader and People pray responsively

God of all that lives, your creative love gives us the hope of renewal as we witness the beauty of your ever-changing seasons.
God, grant me the courage to live each day as it comes, accepting the grace you so freely offer through all the seasons of my life.

O God, your creative love sustains life in hidden ways even through the cold stillness of winter's icy days.
God, grant me the faith to know you are present in my life even when I cannot hear your voice.

O God, your creative love renews our world in the gentle power of spring flowers, reminders of your promise that new life will come forth from the darkness of our lives.
God, grant me the courage to trust in the signs of new beginnings in my life.

O God, your creative love gives us warmth as the dawning summer sun dispels the coldness of our hearts.
God, grant me the wisdom to look with a kind heart toward those who reach out to me with love and friendship.

O God, your creative love gives us beauty in the color and brilliance of fall even as we say good-bye to another season's foliage.
God, grant me the courage to embrace even the difficult changes that make way for new growth in my life.

Let us pray.
Spirit of the living God, look with mercy on us. Give us the grace to seek you in all the seasons of our lives and to reach out to each other in times of adversity as well as joy, giving, and receiving your love. Help us be a sign of your presence for others that they may know you have not abandoned them. As children of a loving God, may we care for one another with patience, compassion, and cheerful hearts.
Amen.

May we go in the peace of God's blessing, trusting that God's love will sustain us, heal us, and strengthen us through all the seasons of our lives. *Amen.*

—*Ms. Mari West Zimmerman*

Ministry

Church Life

Heidi's Prayer

Holy God,
source of light and life,
we pray for Heidi.

We ask
that she may hear your love for her
and know your presence
throughout her earthly pilgrimage.

We pray
also for ourselves,
that we may recognize in Heidi's presence among us
your call to love her
as you have first loved us
and respond
by nurturing and guiding her faith
in your Son, our Good Shepherd and Savior,
Jesus Christ.
Amen.

—The Reverend Joanna R. Satorius

To Kalyon
(on the morning of her baptism)

Dear Jesus, celebrate this child who comes to you this day. Let her come running to you and grab you around your knees. Greet her with the exuberance she already brings to her experience of life. Surround her with a safety that can cradle her spontaneity and accompany her explorations. Convince her of your original Love to enable her to love and love and love again, so that she gives generously and profoundly. Let her love be like a smooth stone skipping on the water with an endless series of ever-widening circles. Let her creativity synchronize with yours so that all that she would become and imagine and invent will be a testament to you and in the context of your will. When her harvest is bountiful and her companions loving and her hearth warm, let her fullness lead her to search for others who are hungry or lonely or cold. Watch over her in the dark, and when she cries, come to her and envelop her in your arms and stroke her hair and wipe her tears until she is calm and rests wholly with you and knows that you and she can transform any monster, real or imagined, under her bed. Bless Kalyon and nurture her gifts to new definitions of Beauty and Love. Amen.

—*Ms. Anne L. Beach*

For Kris, at Confirmation

May you go fiercely down your days,
Earth's daughter, burning like a star.
Christ is a hunting tiger, he is lord
of all whose hearts are wild and sweet,
reckless in love as pure things are.

May you go weeping down your days;
the world's a wound unhealed by tears.
Christ is the dreamer from an unknown shore
singing of life and towering peace
beyond our unredeeming years.

May you go bravely down your days,
and never fall or fail or tire.
Christ is the watcher on the hill who guards
all those who find no final rest
but in the heart of holy fire.

—*The Reverend Anne McConney*

A Meditation for Lay Ministers

I am walking on a worn path. I need not imagine I am blazing a trail. I am barely scratching earth. I need not think my musings are the plans for a world-renowned structure. Though the tracks of birds are small, their wings have given them the gift of flight. Ants work with determination and fidelity. Their place on the earth is almost invisible, yet one follows another and others continue to come after and the hungry are fed and the young are nurtured.

I am bringing in my arms the treasures of others more powerful than I. I am a distributor, less significant than many creatures; yet my work is blessed.

A radiant structure, this my church. I wake to it every day; the faith it gives me is a melody that stays with me all the day long. Its people are the greenery in a dry valley. I am one of the waterers. It is not an exalted job but a noble one. My church asks for attention to small details; it extends my hand to other hands. It clasps sorrow and despair. It opens to reveal the goodness of the people of my community.

I sometimes feel I am lost in a crowd; my head barely reaches to the heads of others. Yet because I am serving God I am tall. My stature is not a result of pride or ambition. I am stretched by love. God has a wondrous power to move me beyond my physical being. I feel it when I am answering the call of others or when I have climbed through the fences and over the walls that separate me from my own spiritual riches. As a lay minister I no longer need search for the repository of these riches. They are placed in my hands as I serve.

—*Ms. Lucy Germany*

A Collect for Communicators

God who wrote your words
on tablets of stone
with fingers of fire

God who gave your Word
the chief cornerstone
with hands of flesh

Help us who write
with fingers of flesh
through sparks of fire
to break open
hearts of stone

—*The Reverend Jan Nunley*

At a meeting of the Episcopal Communicators Board, much on our minds was the ongoing struggle to open the eyes and hearts of the Episcopal Church to the importance of the ministry of communications to mission, evangelism, and stewardship—to the proclamation of the Gospel at all levels. As I heard story after story of communications budgets under-funded and positions cut, my heart cried out in this spontaneous collect.

Altar Rail
(I don't know)

Someone is on her knees
not in a pew
but at the altar rail
asking for strength and courage?
forgiveness? healing for herself or another?
giving thanks and praise?
I don't know.
I turn away.
Dusting pew rails, watering altar flowers can wait.
Someone is on her knees.

—Ms. Dottie Jo Davis

Esau

I am the oldest child
They come to me for blessing

the sixteen-year-old girl with a baby and a three-hundred-dollar
    electric bill
the mummified beggar asking on his knees for three dollars for
    mouthwash
the old man whose brain has left him only the memory of loss
the mother by the bed of her tube-filled beautiful brain-injured
    child

I give them what I can
I tell them
God loves you God is with you even
in the dark even in places where you can't
feel your cross is carried

Jesus has overcome
all shall be well
and all manner of things

I lug them around
and I lift them up
and up over and
over praying in the
dark that I'm right

Hast thou
but one
blessing
my father
bless me
even me
also
O my
father

—*The Reverend Mary F. C. Pratt*

I worked as a parish deacon in a city church, and this poem grew out of my own feelings of futility and my identification with all those who seemingly are left without blessings of their own.

Saint Barnabas's Day, 1983

The bishop stretches out his hands.

I see gray and ashen fingers
      like kindling sticks—
do embers still glow and smolder?
will I see the light?

I bow my head beneath the bowl
      of his hands,
         disbelieving for hope—and pray:

come, comforter, come fire
come son of consolation and deep desire.
come river of life, come Jordan
and let me see the Promised Land.

Odor of prayer, incense rising
    heat and light and crown of flame
tendrils of hair singed and singing,
    "Glory!—glory to God and to the Lamb."

Firestorm of light and power,
    swirling and leaping,
gathering strength,
    climbing to heaven—

He lifts his hands from the upturned
    basin of bone—
and peace
    like oil seeps through
    the matted confusion of curls
    igniting in a heart ablaze.

—*The Reverend Nancy Baillie Strong*

A Prayer for St. Brendan's
(Sunday 1:00 P.M.-ish)

It's quiet, dear God,
    Moving through your house I remember,
    Check the thermostats
    Check the lights,
    Education, music, women's and men's rooms.

I am blessed, dear God,
    Their voices still in my head,
    Prayers of hope, pain, love and sorrow . . . devotion to you.
    Their music still echoes in my ears,
    Voices lifted, chants of ages old.
    Clear and sacred chimes of musical relations.
    Strings and horns . . . offered to you.

Ages of your faithful,
    On their feet, on their knees, bowed in reverence,
    Eyes lifted in witness.

A loud but young and small "amen"
    Wrong time, but right place,
    Always right.

Ninety-six years young,
    A beautiful woman,
      A beautiful tribute to your aging process.

Crumbs on the floor,
    New life,
    Smiles of greeting,
    Sign-up sheets . . . don't forget to sign up.

1, 2, 3 generations
    —a parish new in years,
    —older in wisdom.

Your hand at work in the world about me . . .

I give you thanks.

—*The Reverend Catherine A. Munz*

Jesus Is Taken from the Cross

Once I took a body down,
not crucified,
but hanging,
a self-imposed penance for great sin.

Three of us—2 criminals and I—
untied the cord
and felt the body slip warm and flexed into our arms.
We laid it on the prison floor.
I held your hand and prayed.

Jesus, you died for sin—
No, you died *as* sin—
not to make its end (there will be none)
but to stop it from destroying hope.

Your faith-full death says
this is not the end.

Watching you,
I believe.

—*The Reverend Donna Olsen*

I volunteer at a men's correctional facility. This poem reflects on my experience of finding an inmate who hanged himself on the Wednesday after Easter. His name was Bobby, and he was the sexton in our prison chapel.

Envisioning the Future

Time and time again, a priest is called upon to listen
    to people—sharing
      Pain. Fear. Shame. Guilt. Rage.
Time and time again, a priest is called upon to listen
    to people—despairing.
Looking for answers:
    Looking for God, who is hiding Lord knows where!
People asking: "Why? Why, God?" and "Does God really care?"
Over the years, I've listened.
Over the years, I've heard
    women sharing pain, fear, shame, guilt, rage,
    long buried deep within,
    thinking its expression would be a sin!
Because—that's the way it is.
    The way it's always been.
    The way 'twill always be.
    Or so "*they*" say, or have said.
But today, we're here to proclaim
    Loud and clear
    for all to hear
    Not so! Not so! It will not *always* be.
Recently, I've listened.
Recently, I've heard
    men sharing pain, fear, shame, guilt, rage,
    long buried deep within,
    thinking its expression would be unmanly,
    for to be unmanly is a sin!

Because—That's the way it is.
   The way it's always been.
   The way 'twill always be.
   Or so "*they*" say, or have said.
But today, we're here to proclaim
   Loud and clear
   for all to hear
   Not so! Not so! It will not *always* be.

—*The Reverend L. Jeannette McKnight*

A Prayer for Lesbian Clergy

O God,
who created me in love,
help me to be true to myself
when the Church
and the world around me
want me to deny
who I am
in all my beauty and uniqueness.

Give me strength
to minister among the people of God
to those
who accept me
and to those
who reject me.

Teach me patience
As I listen to and educate,
by word and example,
those who by their ignorance
don't think I should be a priest.
Help me to continue
to serve them well
in the midst of my hurt and grief.

Grant me guidance
in ministering
to those who come to me
seeking courage,

those who are afraid of coming out
to their families and friends
and parish community.

Bestow upon me wisdom
As I discern how to speak and act
in the face of confrontation,
with those who wish to
defame me, mock me,
and question my calling.

Fill me with power
To seek your justice and truth
and proclaim with all of who I am
the good news,
That all are valuable in your eyes
And that no one is considered outcast.

Inspire me with hope
As I live my life with integrity
And strive to serve as a role model
of inclusion and compassion
for all people.

Empower me with endurance
As I live and work among those
who want to deny me
and my gay and lesbian brothers and sisters
A place at the table
and the dignity we deserve as human beings.

And finally most gracious God,
supply my heart
with overflowing love
Toward all your children
Gay, Lesbian, Bisexual
Heterosexual, and Transgendered.
That all may find a welcoming place
In my ministry.

Amen.

—*The Reverend Joan E. Beilstein*

Commitment
(from the vows of a hermit)

As I dwell in the Nothingness, I pray to belong to you, dear God. I pray for the silent, the empty, the hidden, that when all else is gone, you will be there and I will belong to you completely. I do not know where this prayer will lead me, but I want to go wherever you desire to take me. Help me to dwell within your Presence and your sacred heart forever. I love you, my Beloved One. Amen.

—The Reverend Judith Schenck

Priest's Song

When I have no title I make
one up—irreverend.

When I have no collar I roll
my neck round.

When I have no church I steeple
my fingers.

When I have no pulpit I preach
running.

When I have no altar I celebrate
my backyard.

When I have no wine I weep
blood tears.

When I have no bread I am
a sacrament.

When I have no God I pray
anyway.

—The Reverend Lyn G. Brakeman

Reconciliation

Unsolvable Things

If you feel your life
needs solving, try
three methods—
absolve all that is
unresolved in the past—
yourself and others—
dissolve all that is
absolved and its residue—
resolve anything that remains
conflicted or incomplete,
by what means occur to you
in dreams or while in
the shower or walking
in the rain.
If these do not work,
then live with the mystery
as originally planned.
There will surely be,
as surely as tomorrow,
a way through or around
everything.

Pray for protection, then,
from your own hesitation,
so that you do not miss
the moment of Grace
when it comes to you,
and pray also to be delivered
from your own aggression,
so that you do not kill
this fragile, vincible Grace
when it floats over to you
like a pearl on seafoam.

Then simply keep moving,
stay alive by moving along
the rhythms of rest and
discovery, and be brave
in any event.
Every choice you make
holds its own secret
for redemption.

—*The Reverend Dr. Alla Renée Bozarth*

Evil

O God of grace, give us your grace that we may not savor the evil
in others in order to disguise the evil in ourselves. Amen.

—*The Reverend Jean Dalby Clift*

Anger

I sharpened my two-edged sword
of justice and truth
and took it to the altar
to be blessed by God.
"Why thank you, Ellen,
another pruning hook."
I wept,
knowing that God was not the blind one,
and realizing once more,
that if God has enough mercy to forgive me,
God has enough mercy to forgive my enemies.

—*The Reverend E. Ellen Adams*

Betraying Jesus

The Last Supper—The First Eucharist,
Miserable and majestic moment.
Who believed it to be the last?
Who knew their lives would never again be
the same?

Jesus knew. So did Judas Iscariot,
Judas the Betrayer, Judas the greedy one.
Thirty pieces of silver.
Did they seem so much
After that kiss in Gethsemane,
The awful betrayal complete?

Bad Judas! Shameful Judas!
Tsk! Tsk! Judas! Die, Judas!

My hand is in the betrayal.
I know Judas, my co-conspirator.
Recoiling from such thought,
I cannot get away.
I play my tragic part daily
In the betrayal of Jesus.

Jesus incarnate in the world and in others
Is betrayed daily by me
When I choose to ignore
Or, blinded by selfish concerns,
I do not see him in others.
I pass by the One who saves me.
Sometimes while in the very pursuit of him
I pass him by.

Forgive me and heal my vision, Lord,
So that I can see You
As I ought—in the world,
In others, and in myself.

—*Mrs. Gretchen Olheiser*

Prayer for My Heart

Dearest One,
Increase the capacity of my heart.
Take its edges and stretch them out
To include all in me that I do not love,
All in my family that I judge,
All in my Church that I fear,
And all in the world that doesn't fit.

—*Mrs. Phoebe W. Griswold*

This prayer is one that I use as I am flying off to a new experience with new people in new places. I want to be open to what lies ahead and let God speak to me about what I should do. I pray that my heart can join with God in loving all creation into God's Kingdom.

Listening

To hear—really hear—amid the noise

to risk being open to another perspective
amid the impacted certainties

to be able to listen to impassioned pleas
while owning the cries that come from our own hearts.

To hear an argument that does not resonate
disagree, if that be our call,
without demeaning the bearer of the words.

Amid the colliding words
injured by the words
injuring with our words:

help us to hear
your
Words.

Amen.

—*Ms. Helen Barron*

Prayer for a Vestry

Loving God, you are in the midst of us.
    We are tired. Lead us to rest.
    We are filled with doubt. Give us faith.
    We need renewal. Fill us with the Holy Spirit's fire.
    Our patience wears thin. Help us stay in relationship.
    We need healing. Grant us peace and wholeness.
Help us look beyond ourselves and reach out to those in need
    whether they stand next to us or a world away.
In all that we are, all that we do, and all that we say,
    help us claim the promise of your presence
    and lift our common voice to you
    in praise and thanksgiving.

—*The Reverend Elizabeth T. Wade*

Prayer for Someone Troubled by Church Conflict

Gracious and eternal God, I bring to you my unsettled spirit, my disillusionment, and my yearning for peace in our church. Our conflict seems to have taken on a life of its own. Like a fire, it blazes and sweeps through our church. Now friends are not speaking to each other, others have withdrawn and stopped attending, others are gossiping and assigning blame. Division grows among us. Our priest is frightened and defensive and talks about resigning. It is impossible on Sunday mornings to concentrate on worshiping you. We have lost the trust and creativity that has helped us to have a strong ministry in our community. We are paralyzed by this conflict. Visitors feel the tension and don't return.

Dear God, I ache for our church. It has been the place where I have found you, been found by you, and welcomed your redeeming love into my life. This church lifted me out of a deep pit at a hard time in my life. Now, the church has pushed me into a new pit. How can a church that has been such a vehicle of grace now be a source of such anguish? I sink into disappointment and cynicism.

I cry to you: Come and help us, God! Show us the way to break through our paralysis. Lead us into responsible paths for resolution. Give us grace to speak with truth and charity. Help me and each of us to examine ourselves honestly, to discern what responsibility we may have for the state of our congregation's life. Give us courage to enter into peacemaking. Help us let go of our pride and to accept help from others. Free us from making people into scapegoats. Help us to fall on our knees before we get on the phone to spread rumors. Teach us, O God, what we need to learn from our situation. Bring us to the repentance that opens us to receive your forgiveness. Move our hearts to rediscover the strong bonds that you have built among us. Pour upon us the fire of Pentecost, that your spirit may move among us. Heal us as a body, that we may once again live as the Body of Christ, your Incarnate Word, who is our Savior and our Hope; and in whose name I pray. Amen.

—*The Rt. Reverend Chilton R. Knudsen*

A Prayer for Repentance and Revival

I come before you, Father,
and beg your forgiveness for my sins. I
have turned inward and away from you,
your mercy and loving kindness. I
repent of my sins, known and unknown.
Lead me from the sin of judging others
into your peace. Empower me with your
Holy Spirit to love and serve all people.

Help me to pattern my behavior so that all
may see your image through my life. May I
shine forth as the light of Christ in the world.
Revive your church, Lord Jesus, beginning
with me! I ask this in your name and for
your sake. Amen.

—*Ms. Sue Z. Schlanbusch*

Our Shared Values

We value God's Word as it is revealed in
    the gift of Creation,
        the person of Jesus Christ, and
        the gifts of the Holy Spirit,

and as it is revealed through
    Scripture, tradition, and reason.
We value liturgy as a transforming reality
within our corporate and individual lives
        leading us toward lives that are more fully eucharistic,
        lives of thanksgiving in communion with all the saints,
        lives marked by reverence for God,
        one another, and all of creation,
        lives marked by prayer, reflection, and discernment,
        lives marked by openness
        to be surprised by God's grace
        and to be disciplined by God's love,
        lives marked by integrity,
        repentance, amendment of life,
        forgiveness, and reconciliation,
        lives marked by a hunger
        for justice and peace,
        mercy and truth,
        lives marked by hospitality even to the stranger,
        the needy, and the disenfranchised,
        lives enlivened by hope for the coming of God's reign on earth,
        lives marked by fidelity and trust,
        committed to being faithful stewards
        of all the gifts and talents
        that we have received from God,
        lives that proclaim in word and deed
        the Good News of God's love in Jesus Christ.

—*The Reverend Judith P. Ain*

Peace and Justice

Remember Christ's Call for the Least of These

Dear Lord, our Heavenly Father,
Help us to be your servants to those
    hungry for peace, not division; people whose souls
    clamor for the sustenance of justice, an end to crimes
    of violence and greed; to those longing for a night's sleep
    without gnawing hunger, the fear of starvation.
Empower us to feed your sheep, your lambs.

Help us to be your servants to those
   thirsty for water, unpolluted water, parched for
   understanding, for living water.
Enable us to quench their thirst, to offer them the Blood
   of Christ.

Help us to be your servants to those
   strangers who live next door, the handicapped, the
   addicted, the outcasts.
Remind us they are your friends, made in your image.

Help us to be your servants to those
   naked in their loss by fire, water, or tornado; exposed
   by the media; unable to hide their emotions.
Give us grace to clothe their needs.

Help us to be your servants to those
   sick grown-ups and children, waiting for diagnoses,
   transplants, or cures; people sick from the world's ills
   and disappointments.
Beloved Physician, heal them, we pray.

Help us to be your servants to those
   imprisoned, awaiting sentence or parole; imprisoned
   by debt or an abusive relationship, locked in prisons
   that have no bars.
Help us to free them, to speak of your love.

Forgive us our failures. May we see you in others each day
   of our lives.
This we pray, for Christ's sake. Amen.

—*The Reverend Marie Elizabeth Dyer*

The Outcast

He walks with an uneven gait,
Barely noticeable, really.
He cannot type; one hand
Doesn't work too well.
His balance is poor; he hates
Edges, ledges, and heights.
He likes to do things slowly
And carefully, preferably
While sitting down.

Raised on the sound of laughter
Directed at people like himself,
He has learned to hold back until
He finds a time and space
In which to dwell.
He doesn't need a lot of time
Or a large space, but in this
Hurried age of crowded places,
He knows he is unwelcome.

—*The Reverend Karen E. Gough*

Hannah Rose

I

I asked the man at the gas station
did he know who she was or where she came from
and he said no he only moved here from Illinois
not long ago and it seemed nobody knew much
about her but then he said
maybe nobody asked

So I found her and parked my car
down the hill and then prayed my way up
and said ma'am, and she said yes? And
I said, could I join you for a minute
and she said I'm ok, I just like
to sit here during the day
and I said do you have a place to stay

and she said (this time I could
really see into her eyes) she said
I just like to sit here during the day,
now you have a nice afternoon
she did not dismiss me abruptly
she claimed her space with dignity
and I could do nothing but move along
and so I said with my eyes and my voice
and you have a nice afternoon too

I will take her a flower another time

II

In my heart I call her Hannah Rose

Each day she has been there
when I drive by and one day I saw her
crossing the street to get
another cup of coffee
being a cool day I think so
I gathered sweaters from my closet
thinking I would take them
but something held me back
Over and over we presume to know
the needs of others
We think they need us

So I waited and each day I would think of her
and she would touch my spirit yes
I would pray for Hannah Rose
until what I knew was that
I needed her
I knew that Hannah Rose was the one
who'd touched my spirit and
seeing her again would only be
out of my need not because she was
asking anyone for anything
especially not me

III

So it was out of my need that I went to
see Hannah Rose again but first
I bought a long-stemmed red rose and
asked that the thorns be cut off (I figured
Hannah Rose had felt enough thorns)
and I wanted it to be beautiful and
without anything to catch her
weathered flesh
I know what thorns are like

And this time I knew just where to park
my car but when I got there only her
blankets and plastic bags were
resting on the grass under the
leafless trees so I went to buy a donut
and tell myself again it was ok to go
to see her because I needed to

She was there when I got back so
I took the red rose with me and said
can you talk with me a minute? And she
said ok and I said I brought this for you
to thank you and she said what is it
and I said it's a flower and her face
lit my whole day with her clear, clear
and piercing blue eyes crinkled if only a
minute with the smile on her face that
showed me her white teeth
but just for a minute

IV

She thanked me and then asked if I was
an Episcopal priestess and I said no and
wondered to myself oh God why did I wear
my collar, and told her I was an
Episcopal deacon and she said
she's a minister too of a different kind and
I asked her if she needed anything and
she said no

And she said some people come by
thinking she needs a baby-sitter and I
took that to mean that some people were
fairly condescending and treated her like
something other than the gift she is
So I said please know I just came to say
thank you because I'm glad you are here
and you have touched my spirit
and she said thank you for your concern
reverend
Over and over we presume to know
the needs of others
We think they need us

But there was no question that I need
Hannah Rose though I still don't know
her name and I asked her if it was ok
for me to stop now and then and she said
if you happen to be coming by but don't
go out of your way and I said ok and
thank you again and then I left.

V

As I got in the car I looked over and
she was tearing open the package and
holding that beautiful red rose in her hands
She made it even more beautiful
because it was stark and rich against
all her black clothes and her dark blankets
and I prayed my way home giving thanks
for her spirit and her mystery

And I thought about Hannah of the Bible and
how when she prayed and prayed Eli saw
her lips moving but didn't hear her voice and
so he thought she was drunk and scolded her
and told her to put away her wine because even
Biblemen presumed sometimes that they knew
the needs of others and Hannah said no
she was not drunk she was deeply troubled
but was pouring out her soul to God
and I rested in that

Pouring out her soul to God

I wonder if Hannah Rose is pouring out her soul to God
reappropriating the message and living under leafless trees
"there is no holy one like the lord, no one besides you
there is no rock like our God. Talk no more very proudly
let not arrogance come from your mouth for the Lord is
a God of knowledge and by him actions are weighed . . ."
Hannah Rose perhaps speaking the upside down
that is God's justice and if she is
today she prays with a stark red rose in her weathered hands

—*The Reverend Susanne K. Watson*

Lazara and Divés
(for women and children everywhere who suffer)

Disciples shoo the kids away.
Don't let them come so close, they say.
You called us then;
You call us still.
You suffered us with open arms.
But suffering is our lot instead
When stones are given us for bread.

O Lord, we grasp, we toil, we spin.
We trample others in the dust
To clutch the treasures that we trust.
Give us the open heart we need
To open hands, to open mind,
Releasing every worldly good
To succor others with our food.

—*Shirley Blancke, Ph.D.*

Confession of Possession

Blessed
are the poor, meek, hungry, weeping.
poverty.

Face to face with my own riches,
shamed,
humbled.
Why?
Why me?
Did you do this for me, God?
Did you bless me with this wealth?
Did you gift me?
Was I chosen?
Chosen because of my righteousness?
Chosen because of my heritage?
Did my ancestors rack up credit for me?
Can I rack up credit for my children?
Are they chosen?
Blessed?

I meet mothers with mouths to feed; clothes to rinse in the sink,
  hang in the window; holes to stuff with newspapers against
  the icy night; buses to catch; losses to mourn; uniforms to
  mend; floors to mop; who love when they should kick, who
  comfort when they might burst, whose faith dances lightly
  around them, blessing everyone they touch.
Chosen?
Blessed?
Do I know "Blessed"?
If I take more Blessing than my share
  will somebody get less?
Blessed with life and food;
  savor, consecrate, a miracle!
Blessed with life, food, health, family, friends, clothes, cars,
  designer labels, pets, gardens, gold hoop earrings, appliances,
  good looks, nice furniture, hair spray, video games, garage
  door openers, automatic toothbrushes, cleaning ladies,
  word processors, sterling silver toothpicks, personal
  secretary . . .
  the Blessing fades.
Possessed!
Oppressed!
Chosen!
Blessed!
the poor, meek, hungry, weeping.
poverty.
Chosen to act.

Chosen to shed all of my possession.
Chosen to leave den and nest behind.
Chosen to let dead bury dead.
Chosen to plow forward; don't look back.
Chosen to visit the shelter; searching, faltering
    into the sorrowful fear.
Chosen to hand out food at the center; letting the
    grateful hate hang between.
Chosen to watch and listen and find; pieces of
    them touching pieces of me.
Chosen!
I turn back.
Unfit!
Oppressed!
Possessed!
The Saving God will bring us out of our oppression.
The Redeemer will deliver us from our possession.
poverty
the poor, meek, hungry, weeping.
Blessed.

—*The Reverend Gretchen M. B. Pickeral*

A Prayer for Lesbians

O Holy God, the Living God, Mother and Father of us all, we ask
your blessing on all women who love women: lesbians, bisexual
women, and transgender women. Guide and nourish them as parents, children, sisters, aunts, friends, and colleagues; support them
in their daily work, both in the world and at home; nurture them
as members of a faith community; encourage them to do your will
as citizens of the universe.

We pray especially for their physical and emotional safety in a
world where they too often face violence, hatred, and misunder-
standing. Strengthen them in their resolve to live their lives in
truth, honesty, courage, and love. Let the world see your face
through them.

We pray that they will serve you, dear God, to your glory in the
name of our blessed Redeemer and Deliverer, Christ Jesus. Amen.

—*Ms. Constance Cohrt*

Prisms

Isms
Fit best in prisms
Perceptions from different angles
Reflecting the light of truth
and brilliance of color
All different
and of Supreme value

Changes,
bringing different hues
from scattered penetration

The light from within and without
So pure
So true
So lovely
So DIFFERENT

To block the light
casts a shadow
To choose one lens
limits our vision
While not destroying truth,
will keep us from experiencing
the wholeness of what we and
others are

While not destroying differences
will create an illusion of sameness

While not destroying our spirits
will imprison them

Divorced from diversity
Robbed of richness
Exempt from life's fullest experience
Shallow souls in search

The power to see yourself and
the "selves" of others
awaits you
deep inside

You have the power to
Shape the view
Create the angle
Reflect the light
Transform isms to prisms

—*Ms. Katherine Tyler Scott*

Invisible in Church

Mother God, here I am again. I feel pain right now. I came to this meeting to learn, and now I am feeling left out and invisible. I was hoping at my age and in this time a change would come. I found a seat that I liked and went over to sit down. The woman looked at me and said the seat was taken. I tried a few other open seats, but I was told they were also taken or being saved for friends. I finally found a lot of space in the front row. You know how we Episcopalians don't like to sit in the front.

This is not hospitality, but I must remember my friend Jesus was ignored and misunderstood. I am sure Jesus felt the pain of not being seen and not being wanted. O God, am I overly sensitive? Am I reading more into this and making snap judgments again? Can I just once go into a meeting such as this and feel acknowledged and welcomed? Prejudice and lack of hospitality hurt us all. God, you have made us in your image; can we just get beyond this? Help me on this journey, especially today with my sisters, to explain how attitudes can cause pain and feelings can get hurt. You have called me each step of this journey. Keep me believing in the power of the Holy Spirit that through my strength and joy I can help my sisters overcome prejudice and move into action. NOW! Amen.

—*The Reverend Argola E. Haynes*

Meditation in Black

O Lord, God of my salvation,
It's morning and the sun is shining brightly.
It makes the world seem good and beautiful.
But Lord, the coffee doesn't even taste good.
My paper's full of hate and meanness.
I think I need some time to think and pray and
Lift this burden off my soul.

Folks were expressing their concerns about welfare,
And minority contractors and affirmative action,
When up steps Mr. Letter to the Editor asking:
"What do you people want? We've given you voting
Rights and opportunities for education so you can
Better yourselves. I'm sick of you people trying to
Make me feel guilty about your failures."

I wanted to shout, "Who died and left you king?
Who are you to dole out rights and opportunities?"
My mother told me they only act that way because
They only feel good about themselves when they're
Looking down on somebody.
My Big Mama said, "You respect people because of
Who you are, not because of who they are."

I find there are those who are so sure I'm inferior
Goods they don't read my resume or listen to my ideas.
They say no before they even hear my questions.
Seems anyone can come from anywhere in the world
And get welcomed, but my people, working all these
Years, paying taxes, building this country
Are denied opportunities, told they're not ready.

Lord knows, I've tried to live out my creed
I've tried to be a lover, a learner, your servant.
I've tried to be worthy of trust. I've tried
To make the world a better place in which to live and grow
I know the gifts I've brought are small in the face
Of so much need, but I've offered them with sincerity
And hope . . . hope for today, tomorrow, and the future.

I'm so thankful to you for all the wonderful
Gifts I've received; for all the people who have
Loved me and supported me through the years.
I'm a bit ashamed that I was pleased when they
Said I was different; that I had a great future.
Now I ask, "What future do I have when so many
Are being left behind, have lost hope? They are me."

My Lord God, I don't want to seem ungrateful, but
I don't want to ask for more than respect for me
And for people like me, people still trying to
Shake off the shackles of slavery. I only ask to be
Seen as one of your children. I want to be seen
As worthy of hope. Life without hope is not much life.
Forgive me if I ask for too much, but I am your child.

It's a hard thing to face, Lord, but ever since I was a
Child, the world has given me the feeling that
Everything would be fine if I and mine would just go away.
I watched folks let their little dogs lick them
In the mouth, but they avoided looking me in the eye.
With all the washing and ironing I was still unclean.
I couldn't be right. I was born black.

Forgive me, Lord, but I've always hated being a victim.
I've tried hard to learn the rules of the game . . .
You've got to be prepared: I pursued education.
You've got to be patient: I waited and tried not to
Be too pushy. I tried to maintain my dignity.
You've got to be competent, a hard worker: I've tried.
Just when you think it's working . . .

The lady behind the checkout counter glanced at me:
"Food stamps?" How could she know how hard I'd worked
To learn to pay my own way, to escape the social
Workers and the rules and regulations that fed you,
But worked hard to take away any shred of dignity.
All that checkout lady could see was black, and
Her understandings told her to discount them.

My children are all professional people, and they've
Had it better in some ways; but the stigma of black
Dies hard. These days, it's impolite, to say out loud,

"We'd prefer not to have your kind here. You're just not
Good enough." But waits and curtness tell their story.
It's not hard to know when you're not taken seriously.
There are so many ways to say, "Not good enough."

It's taking me over, Lord. My heart is filling up
And on such a beautiful day. "When will it end?"
I want to pray, but I don't know what to pray for.
Shall I pray for patience? I'm running low on
Patience. Shall I pray for courage? for hope?
For some nostrum that will dull the pain? I know
I have no power but yours. Lead me, Lord.

I have no place of comfort but at your feet. Take me
To your bosom and warm my heart that is growing cold.
Renew my life, fill me with your love. Only you can
Help me find peace. Only you can help me love those
Who would spitefully use me, hate me, isolate me, take
Away my personhood. Remind me you created them, too,
Sisters and brothers. Hold me, fix me, Lord.
I pray you, don't let us fall apart. Bless us, Lord,
Those who live on the fringes. Strengthen us.
Show us the way. Bind our wounds. Heal our hurts.
Forgive us when we forget "to love one another."
Only in the power of your love and redemptive acts
Can we find the right thoughts to think, the right
Words to say, the right actions to take.

Lord, hear our prayer. We offer our petitions to you,
O God of Love and Mercy, of Healing and Renewal.
Thank you for another beautiful day. Amen.

—*Dr. Kathryn E. Nelson*

Surviving Discrimination and Persecution
(a prayer of thanksgiving)

Dear Lord,

I trod the wilderness—more in darkness than in light,
And yet I did survive.
Darkness of discrimination-isolation-brokenness,

Unaffirmed as your creation
By those who set a goal to rid us from this earth:
A "Final Solution" that would save the world.
Dear Lord, why did I survive?

I searched for years for my identity and self-esteem.
You saw me stand apart, afraid to love or to be loved,
Paralyzed and frightened as the evil of the past
Seemed locked within, never to be revealed.
Dear Lord, why did I survive?

How slowly, Lord, I saw your outstretched arms
Reflected by the love so freely offered
By those acknowledging my dignity and worthiness
As I emerged from hiding in a prison of my own,
Which robbed me of all self-respect and worth.
Finally, dear Lord, I looked into your eyes
And, like the sun that rises in the east,
Hesitantly at first I opened wide my heart
Surrendering to you my all, my fears, my doubts
And gaining courage, self-assurance,
Enlightened to the truth
That life can be a gift of hope, of laughter, and of joy.
I finally and fully trusted in your unconditional Love,
Which you so freely offer to us all.
I fell into your arms—a new creation
Thankful for the gifts you daily shower on humanity,
Praying to be worthy to reflect
Your Glory to the world around.
Amen.

—*The Reverend E. Anne Kramer*

This is probably the most difficult prayer I have ever written. I am of Jewish birth and fled Germany in 1939 to England. My grandmother died in Auschwitz. I became a Christian in England and didn't talk about my experiences in Germany for forty years, until one day: renewal! Freedom came into my life by the way of loving, patient friends.

Open Our Eyes

It was dark in the garden—
grief dark, bereft dark.
She had seen him laid to rest
and now he was gone.
emptiness—emptiness—
Mary stood weeping.

We, too, stand weeping:
we grieve for our world—
for suffering innocents, for pain inflicted,
for shattered bodies, lonely lives—
it is still dark in the garden.

With Mary, we know tears that blind;
we fail to recognize the risen Lord.
Holy Spirit, radiance of God,
open our eyes to Love's presence;
open our ears as Love calls us by name.
Show us the glory of resurrection
piercing the dark of our gardens.

—*Sister Cecilia, C.S.F.*

Remembering D-Day

I walked along the cliff tops,
gazing at the concrete boxes
from which the Germans fired
their volleys that June morning.

I walked along the cliff tops,
suffering the thought that
we had climbed those cliffs
riddled with German fire.

I walked among the gravestones,
wrung by the thought of youth,
of innocence, of doomed hope
now ashes beneath my feet.

I wept with bitter despair
for all that brightness gone,
for the loss of faith and hope
that has marked this fifty years.

—Thayer W. Beach, Ph.D.

A Prayer after the Oklahoma City Bombing

I am the building that was blown apart by a bomb in the "heart-land" of America. My heart is blown open. The front of me falls away: I am the gaping floors, the broken glass, the dangling wires, the film of concrete dust that rises into the air.
 This is my body.
I am the children who were killed: the little ones, the innocent, tender little people full of play and laughter. The babies.
 This is my body.
I am the women and men who were killed, the mother, father, husband, wife, grandparent, neighbor, relative, friend, startled by death on an ordinary day.
 This is my body.
I am those who mourn: the suddenly bereaved, the shocked, the bereft. I am the mother clutching a picture of her two children, the husband grieving his newlywed wife.
 This is my body.
I am the rescue workers, the medical personnel, those who hope against hope, and those who are faithful even when there *is* no hope, those who press on into the rubble, searching for the living, the wounded, the dead, searching for what is human, for what is loved.
 This is my body.
I am the ones who planned and planted the bomb: the hard-hearted, the fearful, the numb and angry ones who no longer care. (When Timothy McVeigh is shown pictures of the dead, particularly dead children, he has no reaction at all. Says one source, "[There was] nothing. Zero reaction from that son of a bitch. This guy is a stone.")

This is my body.

I am the ones who fill the airwaves with venom and hate. "Take them out in the desert and blow them up." "Shoot 'em." "I hope they fry."

This is my body.

I am the Holy Spirit, brooding over our bent world with bright wings. I am the wings of Jesus, tenderly outstretched above the city, sheltering everything and everyone beneath.

This is my body.

I cannot hold it all. I hand it to you, Jesus. Hold it with me. And suddenly I see that I am handing you the cross: here, *you* carry it.

I cannot.

And he has taken it up. He is carrying all of this, all of this. The dead, the wounded, and those who mourn; the killers and those who were killed; the frightened, the angry, the sorrowful—he is carrying *all* of this, all of *us*, every part of us, into the loving heart of God.

—The Reverend Margaret Bullitt-Jonas

Blessing
*(dedicated to the Rt. Reverend Nathaniel Garang,
Bishop of Bor, Episcopal Church of Sudan)*

The bishop blessed my Fiona, with hands, dark and strong,
hands that embrace the Cross where shrapnel shards—
MIGs and RPGs burning villages and forcing flocks to flee—
are by fusion and faith transformed.

The bishop blessed my Fiona, on his knees, eye level.
Eyes dark and strong, over-full with pain, and memory of a man
with cross and Bible
murdered and dismembered
his scattered pieces
multiplied into 32,000 martyrs-to-be.

The bishop blessed my Fiona and me, her mother.
How could he help but think of other mothers
and of children,

burlap sacks struggling, then quietly sinking in the Nile;
dying in desert dust and dung, or branded and sold:
the currency of the Cross.

—*Ms. Faith J. H. McDonnell*

My daughter and I met Bishop Garang at the New Wineskins Conference. I stopped and introduced myself as someone who cares deeply about and is fighting on behalf of the persecuted church in Sudan. He was very gracious and appreciative of my words. He laid his hand on Fiona's head and prayed and blessed her. I was humbled, and blessed, too.

Woman Against War

"Almost like Christmas lights"
the bomber pilot said
of last night's strike against I guess
Baghdad
I turned the television off, the sound
and did last night's dishes dumbly
reflecting on my Christmas lights
downstairs in semi-sacred storage
reflecting on how real had been the urge
last night to go and get the globe
to hold it in my arms against my heart
and rock and pat and comfort it

—*Ms. Lynne Atherton*

A Breath Prayer for Peace

Strengthen the hands of those who work for peace.

—*Mrs. Pamela Grenfell Smith*

This breath prayer is my best weapon against denial and withdrawal. I use it when I read the paper or listen to the news; sometimes, when the news is bad, I use it all day.

A Poem for Activist Insomniacs

What the world could be
is my good dream
and my agony.

—Wendell Berry

When I can't sleep, I imagine
hands tearing down the Pentagon,
broad-palmed, callused hands,
slender hands with earth-crescents
under nails, ink-stained hands,
the quick, eager hands of children.
I imagine us turning the Pentagon
over to the sun. I imagine
the pale generals crawling out
one by one.

The earth heaves a great sigh,
stretches and twists herself;
stones crumble. Squash and cucumbers
burst through cracks in the sidewalk,
twining tendrils through rubble heaps.
Five-year-olds leapfrog over glowing
pumpkins, mouths stuffed speechless
with new peas. Among the vines,
our naked babies creep, babies dark
as blackberries, brown as almonds
or cinnamon, pink and golden as
peaches. Strawberry plants spring
up beneath their knees. Babies sit
on the rumps and feast, juice
pouring down their chins.

Aimlessly the generals roam
until one by one they strip themselves
of uniforms, pallid bellies flopping
free. Beneath their feet sprout
clover, partridgeberry, maiden pink.
They lie back, remembering how
to breathe, and wriggle toes,
while toddlers twine violets
into their graying hair. Our babies crawl
to them and, sticky fingers gripping

knees, balance spraddle-legged,
dappling the old men's skins
with scarlet hands.

—*Ms. Rebecca Baggett*

Originally published in Painted Bride Quarterly *and reprinted in*
Still Life with Children *by Ms. Rebecca Baggett (Pudding House*
Publications, 1996).

Prayer in Time of War

Our Father, who art in heaven, slow to anger, and of great mercy,
lover of all the peoples of the earth,
Hallowed be thy Name.

Remind us that "all the nations are as nothing before thee," their
governments but a shadow of passing age;
Thy kingdom come on earth.

Grant to thy children throughout all the world, and especially to
the leaders of the nations, the gift of prayerful thought and
thoughtful prayer; that following the example of our Lord, we
may discern what is right, and do it;
Thy will be done on earth, as it is in heaven.

Help us to protect and to provide for all who are hungry and
homeless, especially those who are deprived of food and shelter,
family and friends, by the tragedy of war;
Give us this day our daily bread.

Forgive us for neglecting to "seek peace and pursue it," and
finding ourselves in each new crisis, more ready to make war
than to make peace. "We have not loved thee with our whole
heart; we have not loved neighbors as ourselves";
Forgive us our trespasses, as we forgive those who trespass against us.

Let us not seek revenge, but reconciliation;
Let us not delight in victory, but in justice;
Let us not give ourselves up to pride, but to prayer;
Lead us not into temptation.

Be present to all thy children ravaged by war:
Be present to those who are killing and to those who are being killed;
Be present to the loved ones of those who are killing and to the
loved ones of those who are being killed;
Deliver us from evil.

Subdue our selfish desires to possess and to dominate, and forbid
us arrogance in victory;
*For thine is the kingdom, and the power, and the glory, forever and
    ever.*

Amen.

—Ms. Wendy Lyons

Seasonal Prayers

Advent

Meditation on Advent

Waiting is something we do a lot. Women particularly have spent their lives waiting: waiting for the phone to ring, waiting for the baby to be born, waiting for someone to come home. My mother told me a good reason to learn to embroider or knit was because, as a woman, I would spend my life waiting and I might as well have something to do!

Waiting . . .

. . . those chairs near dressing rooms that are occupied this time of year by weary men sitting glassy eyed amid bags and boxes, waiting. Children checking their calendars, "How many days 'til Christmas?"—they're waiting. An eagle sitting comfortably on top of a bare tree, the light shining on his feathers, turning to show his profile to watchers with a touch of vanity—he is sovereign of this site, but he too is waiting.

And yes, the people of God wait, too. But we, O most fortunate ones, wait for joy; wait for the wolf to accompany the lamb; wait, hearts filled with laughter; wait to bear witness to the light. And we do not wait in vain. By the very power of our expectation, by our very faith, our willing welcome, we assist in the annual birth of love, of hope, of innocence.

This Advent, let us wait well, in faith, in hope, and in sympathy with one another—for together, we wait for joy!

—*The Reverend Barbara Deane Price*

The Annunciation: Conversations with Mary

- Mary, we've landed on your feast! Help us, we beseech thee, find common voice with you and with one another.
- Mary, *theotokos*, God-bearer, help us travel with our humor and our pain as we seek to be God-bearers in our own day!
- Mary, Sweet Mother, have we traveled this far only to be put in places where we are "acceptable," places where we "fit" as long as we "are seen but not heard"?
- Ah Mary, surely you know that reality all too well, the one about learning "in silence with full submission" (1 Timothy 2:11)!

- Blessed Mary, if we can hear your voice anew, perhaps we can learn to challenge those in our own day who fear and distrust women.
- Mary, Mother of Mercy, help us shed our placid timidity!
- Mary, Co-Redeemer, you give birth to a new humanity and a new community born of suffering and of undefeated hope. Help us embrace new life.
- Mary, Mother of Compassion, have we forgotten you said "*Yes!*" to the liberation of oppressed peoples?
- Mary, Mother Bird with a mature womb and hope-filled wings, push us out of the warm nest, help us fly onward and outward!
- Mary, Sister and Mother, teach us to proclaim hope amid the reality of aching pain.
- Holy Mary, are not we ourselves the God-bearers of this age: women stepping forward together and saying "*Yes!*" Let it be with us according to your word (Luke 1:38).

—Fredrica Harris Thompsett, Ph.D.

The Nativity of Our Lord: Christmas

Travail

Out of the depth and quiet
of this chill, stark night,
a gnawing ache, a yearning
deepens, rising
like a threatening wave.

The young woman trembles.
Every inmost part of her is
shaken, all comfort broken.
Her hand gropes for something firm to grasp,
but all that was certain has become
obscure, all encompassing,
racked with pain.
Scarcely able to catch her breath,
she feels each wave larger, more
frightening than the last.
And as the great wave breaks over her,

she is broken,
momentarily forgetting what she accepted,
what love she bears,
yet choosing to believe when all seems lost.

Suddenly and completely
she, still bathed in sweat,
enfolds love in her arms,
knows joy as one victorious,
sees clearly as one who has been
stretched and changed,
that peace is always
born of travail.

—*Mrs. June M. Schulte*

Maria Sacerdota— Mary, Protopriest of the New Covenant

Before Jesus
was his mother.

Before supper
in the upper room,
breakfast in the barn.

Before the Passover Feast,
a feeding trough.
And here, the altar
of earth, fair linens
of hay and seed.

Before his cry,
her cry.
Before his sweat
of blood,
her bleeding
and tears.
Before his offering,
hers.

Before the breaking
of bread and death,
the breaking of her
body in birth.
Before the offering
of the cup,
the offering of her
breast.
Before his blood,
her blood.
And by her body and blood
alone, his body and blood
and whole human being.

The wise ones knelt
to hear the woman's word
in wonder.
Holding up her sacred child,
her God in the form of a babe,
she said: "Receive and let
your hearts be healed
and your lives be filled
with Love, for
this is my body,
this is my blood."

—*The Reverend Dr. Alla Renée Bozarth*

Merry Christmas from Me to You

Her name is Shon,
She's due any day.
She works at McDonald's
For minimum pay.
She has other children—
One, two, and three.
She's tired, she's broke,
She has no time that's free.

Her kids won't have Christmas,
There's no money to spare,
She's too proud to ask
With no family to care.
She's struggled to learn
How to clean and to cook.
She raised her siblings,
And did what it took

To finish her schooling,
Get her GED.
It's been a hard life;
She's barely twenty!

So, I'm caught in a dilemma,
You are my friend.
It's Christmas, I'm shopping,
With little to spend.
We've had a great year,
Good times—you and me,
And there's much for us both
Under our tree.
I can't spend the money
To buy you more stuff,
When Shon and her kids
Have it so tough.
I bought you this candle,
And gave her the rest.
I fretted and stewed,
But thought it was best
To do it this way.
I know you won't mind
Because you are loving,

And thoughtful and kind!

Please light this candle
Each day as you pray,
And think of this girl
Who's not far away.
She needs more than money.
She needs someone to care,
To know that she matters,
Though life is unfair.
So I've given her you,
Through your gift from me.
And all through this year,
'Neath her Christmas tree,
She'll know with her heart
That someone is there,
Holding her up
In Spirit-filled prayer.
Merry Christmas, my friend,
I hope this will do.
Thanks from Shon and her kids.
Love from me—just for you!

—*Mrs. Janet Hitchcock*

Epiphany

Three Wise Women

If there had been three wise women, would the Epiphany story have been different? You bet it would! They would have asked for directions, arrived early, delivered the baby, cleaned the stable, cooked the dinner, and brought practical gifts. God bless wise women!

—*Adapted from the Internet by the editors*

Lent

Ash Wednesday

Stepping from the brightness of Epiphany
I enter an unfamiliar place called "Lent."
My eyes are slow to adjust to the change.
I blink back tears and stand still wondering
if my eyes are open or closed,
for nothing visible lies before me.

My senses tell me there are objects ahead—
prized places, sacred spaces.
There is no sense of urgency;
time has fallen away leaving
forty days and forty nights
to explore this unknown, yet somehow familiar place;
touching, feeling, knowing holy moments.

—*Mrs. Gretchen Olheiser*

Ash Wednesday Prayers for Women Who Have Been Abused

Provide a bowl of ashes, a garland of flowers, a safe place of healing.
One woman makes a cross with ashes on the forehead of another woman,
saying:

Remember, beloved daughter, that you are of the Earth, formed
of the primal stardust, and to Mother Earth you will return.
Amen.

Remember, beloved daughter, that whether you live or die, you
belong to God; you can never be lost, only more and more
found. Amen.

For it is written, "I am convinced that . . . [nothing] in all creation, will be able to separate us from the love of God in Christ
Jesus" (Romans 8:38–39); and again, "I will not forget you. See, I
have inscribed you on the palms of my hands" (Isaiah 49:15–16).

The first woman puts the garland over the head of the other woman, saying:

Beloved daughter, receive this garland as a sign of the joy into which God calls you;

as it is written "I have said these things to you so that my joy may be in you, and that your joy may be complete" (John 15:11); and again "[The Lord] has sent me . . . to give them a garland instead of ashes" (Isaiah 61:1–3).

All respond: Thanks be to God.

The ritual is repeated for each woman who wishes it, then all pray together:

O God, we ask that you bless us as we enter this holy time of Lent, that it may be a time of healing and nurture for us. Protect us from self-hatred, self-violence, and addiction; help us to be faithful to gentle, healing disciplines of self-care; and comfort us with your unconditional love. Amen.

Dear Christ, help us to know in the liturgies of your Passion, the sanctification of our own childhood terror and pain. Be with us as we remember our suffering and help us to find in your wounds, a place of healing for ours. Protect us from the power of evil, and bathe us in the hope of your Resurrection. In your holy name we pray. Amen.

Let us go forth in God's love.

All respond: Thanks be to God.

—Ms. Barbara Hughes

I created this liturgy while I was doing my own work of recovery from childhood sexual violence. Remembering my abuse involved facing the terror of my soul being lost. My childhood fear of physical death and of the nothingness of spiritual death was overwhelming at times. The wording of the traditional Ash Wednesday service triggered that fear. Yet being part of the liturgy was very important to me, as keeping Lent had always been important to me. What I needed was the acknowledgment of death in the context of God's steadfast love. I needed to hear that we will never be abandoned by God and that we cannot be lost by God. And because childhood abuse left me believing that I was less than nothing, I needed to have the idea of being "dust" redeemed and set in the context of the "stuff of life." Recent scientific understandings that we are all made up of the primal matter of the universe, the original "stardust," helped me re-ground the image.

Lent: The Mind's Extremity

Into this late winter time
Lent erupts its Wednesday ash;
black dust darkens our sky.
Return. Return.
We follow the lightless fire
down to a place
beyond the mind's extremity.

Lent leads us down to buried time,
down the mountain
onto a fenceless plain,
a dry savanna where all demons wait.
Lent's unwilled free-fall
plummets us through remorse
and clotted dreams,
into the scarred haunts of hurt,
blame, damage, loss.
We are released into ourselves, alone.

Lent returns us into depths
deeper than the dead are deep
where we come into openness: two crows
on the bare branch of a single tree—
black carrion birds,
guardians of a slate gray sky.

A cold lightning arcs down
into silence and dim light.
Moment by fearful moment
its sharp pulse flashes
in terror and prayer to the breath's end—
in dust we are returned
to the place where no secrets are hid.

Here the Spirit's slow alchemy
melts every easy expectation,
and a final expanse opens
its felt presence
to the edge of visibility.
We are returned to the rim
to look outward toward the cusp
of a new place.

—*Ms. Rosamond Rosenmeier*

Holy Week

Passion Sunday

We worship here in freedom and in peace.
No alien idols mar the holy place,
no Roman legionnaires patrol the streets,
and on our coin, no stamp of Caesar's face.
Fortunate people in a pleasant land,
we claim deliverance by God's mighty hand.

Yet when the hungry turn to us for food
and when the lonely watch with longing eyes,
our easy hands may struggle to do good
but sin stands strong against our sacrifice,
as though some hidden Caesar, still in place,
condemns the ransomed, holy world to waste.

And so we listen for the joyful shout
that calls us to the palms and the parade.
Hosanna, Son of David! Lead us out
of all the prisons we and Caesar made
while we were happy to be fed and blessed
but turned aside before you reached the cross.

—*Mrs. Pamela Grenfell Smith*

Listening at the Altar of Repose

When the Blessed Sacrament is placed on the Altar of Repose on Maundy Thursday, keep watch there. Watch and listen. Listen for God's voice in that holy place, for God speaks to those who listen.

Last year in my parish church, the Altar of Repose was like a pathway to heaven. The path cut through clusters of lovely, living flowers—daffodils, geraniums, lilies, petunias, wild carnations, and peace lilies—ending at the altar. Flanking the tabernacle were a basket of white, pink, and yellow blossoms and a solitary *aloe vera* plant springing from a cluster of ragweed. A burning votive candle honored the Real Presence of Christ within the tabernacle, but the healing *aloe* stretching heavenward from the weed-strewn earth evoked the vision of Jesus the Christ in the agony of prayer in the Garden of Gethsemane.

At the Altar of Repose we can be led through the beauty of God's created world, to the agony of the human condition, to the mystery of the Word made flesh, into the embrace of our Creator God. Listen. Whatever the circumstances of your present life, God will speak to your need. From the flowers of joy, from the agonized Christ, from the mystery of the Incarnate Word, or from the glory of heaven, God will speak to who you are and where you are. Sometimes God speaks in thunder, but more often God's voice is still and small.

On Maundy Thursday evening or Good Friday morning, keep watch with Jesus at the Altar of Repose. Listen for God's voice there. If you hear no voice, don't stop listening. God will be with you. By resting silently in God's arms, you can hear the heartbeat of God's unfailing love for you.

—*The Reverend Marie Louise Webner*

Rapture

Dark shadows circle through Good Friday:
Secrets whispered in dimly lit rooms;
Betrayals and deceit hover overhead,
(Death's keening birds of prey).

They watch me, ever closer
To pluck and tear at eyes that see the Truth,
Ears that hear the Word, at last.
Plunging deep into my solitude,
They grab at my heart to find my core.

The vigil is long: three hours pass,
While death approaches with stealth,
And with great cunning, grunts,
Its foul breath and heat rising, until I can only break free or die.
(Ever patient, these vultures await my still-beating heart.)

Now, there is only silence; it is almost finished.
Eyes closed, I strain to hear a still small voice crying,
Telling me to awake and shake off my raptors, predators of faith,
To behold, once again, the Spirit present.

With aching arms, I push away the stone—
Back toward the darkness from where it came.
I am at once blinded by the light
As I behold the risen Christ.

—*Ms. Penelope Ann Thoms*

The Seven Last Words of Christ

I. Father, forgive them, for they know not what they do.

This wheel: if it could slow and stop, and then
reverse,
if we could jet backwards, visit once again our crossroads,
catch ourselves in mid-divorce, in
mid-slap, before we
betrayed, and armed,
with what we know now, arrest the act,
we could undo it!
We could un-die. We could
un-kill. We'd un-enlist, un-strike.
But the wheel turns.
There is no brake.
We pick up speed toward ruin
that we ourselves precisely planned, yet don't expect.
It is our way.
Ashamed, we pick through what remains,
and salvage what we can,
from wreckage we have made.

II. Today, you shall be with me in Paradise.

Most people wanted some assurance of their status.
Will the number of the saved be small?
    that is, *Am I one of them?*
What must I do to be saved?
    that is, *Have I left something out?*
Life was hard enough: if Hell were in the future, they wanted to know.
It has long been clear to him that
most would not reach out and take the gift.
Most would stand outside and knock
on a door already open.
But for this one on the right, status is not on the table.
At the end of life, this one is free to ask,
because there is no harm in asking,
and you never know.
At the end of a life that knows it needs saving,
when there is no longer any chance for amends
the one on the right just asks for the gift
and, as always, the answer is yes.

III. Mother, this is your son.

This is *not* my son.
You are my son.
This is my son's friend. He is about your age.
He is strong and vital, as you were
just this morning,
before they began to do
what they are doing to you now,
Before they drove nails into your hands
as if they were blocks of wood,
before this happened to my baby.
Now, we stand and watch,
your best friend and I. I cannot bear to see,
but neither can I bear to leave.
And neither can he. And so, I *do* love him.
I love him for staying.
So I will not argue with you now about this.
I won't allow our last talk
to be an argument.
I want so much to help you get through this
it tastes like blood in my mouth.

And there isn't anything *else* I can do to help you since
they won't let me come *near* you,
let alone *touch* you.
They won't even let me give you a drink.
I can't even brush your hair out of your eyes.
You are going quickly now.
This cannot last much longer.
So all right. When this is over,
it will be John and I.
I will love him, because he will remember you.
And you will be all I'll want to talk about,
for a long time after this is over,
long after most people think it's time I got over it.
But there was a time you lived in me:
I held you safe right here,
under my heart,
in the place where you have an open wound.
You were part of my body then.
I would be part of yours now.
I would leap
to take your place up there.
I would laugh
if they drove nails into my hands
instead of into yours.
I would look down at you
looking up and I would see your chest
heave with your crying and mine would
heave with my failing breathing and I would
shout, "He lives!" and send my last breath to the sky,
Thanksgiving.

IV. My God, my God, why have you forsaken me?

No one will let me despair.
They assume that they've misheard.
"He meant to call Elijah."
"He's quoting from the psalms."
When they are old, they will tell each other stories of today.
They tell stories of me already. They've told them for years:
embellishing my childhood manners, my
boundless patience, superhuman wit.
Already they sell me, paint me
so far beyond themselves they need not seek to follow.

But I am truly man,
and truly, terror holds me in its razor teeth.
I am not an actor.
And this is not a play.

V. I thirst.

He tries holding very still.
He tries not to move his tongue.
His tongue is thick and dry, a log.
He tries to hold his mind still, too, tries not to think of water.
But it fills with pools.
In thought, he kneels and laps up puddles like a dog.
He hears water pouring into a cup,
sees the cup coming toward his lips,
opens his lips, but it is not water.
When he was little, he and his mother went to the well every morning,
with other children and their mothers.
He had a tiny yoke of wood his father made him.
From it, he could carry two leather bags of water all the way home.
Mary had a yoke, too,
a larger one, and larger leather water bags,
for she was young and strong in those days.
He would follow her up the dusty steps of the dusty streets;
her brown legs climbed easily under her heavy load, his little feet
traced her footsteps. Usually, he made a game:
he must step exactly where she stepped,
and not miss even one.
He supposes that little yoke is in the house somewhere, still.
It has been years since he saw it.
They used to make the trip twice, two bags apiece.
That was the water for the day.
Here there are no children with their mothers.
This is no place for a child.
And there is no water here.

VI. It is finished.

Latin words are much more dignified than ours.
They satisfy the speaker more, they feel
important on the tongue.

I'll speak "*humilitatem*" not "affliction,"
and of "*furore*," not of "wrath."
I'll say "*insipiens*" when I mean "fool,"
and I will feel less foolish.
And I'll have Jesus say "*Consummatum est*"
in Latin, just like that,
a stately word, so calm and unperturbed.
This is complete, it says.
All now is accomplished and all is well.
Like a consummate artist,
a consummate professional,
like a consummated marriage,
we'll have a consummate crucifixion,
with all the blood cleaned up,
and Christ, serene, will hang so lightly
on his sweet cross for our assurance.
We might be more concerned,
if we thought it concerned him.
So let us polychrome this whole event
and make it lovely
and hang those lovely Latin words
on dying lips.

VII. Father, into your hands I commend my spirit.

He can just lay it down.
He can just stop.
He has only just now realized,
in the lengthening spaces between ragged breaths,
that he can just not draw the next one.
He is almost there already;
the wall between the worlds is very thin.
Now he sees it's simple to go on from here: just stop the breath,
and let his spirit slip on home.
In every way, this death is ours:
the same fear becoming the same intentness,
the same directional change.
He has always said this, but we did not believe it.
We thought exception would be made for him
because we hope exception will be made for us.
But there are no exceptions.

We can lay it down or have it
wrested from us.
We are almost there already.

—*The Reverend Barbara Cawthorne Crafton*

These poems were first read in public as part of a performance, with the Alexander String Quartet, of Haydn's "The Seven Last Words of Christ" in New York City in 1999. That eighteenth-century composition was intended to provide opportunity for contemplation of each of the seven phrases recorded as having been spoken by Jesus from the cross. It is typical of its era: formal, emotionally restrained—not passionate.

The poems are different. They are intended to spark emotions in the hearer, to show her pictures, to demand a response. But interspersing them with music is still a worthy cause: music will give the hearer a chance to make each "word" his or her own, much more readily than could ever be the case if they were simply read, back to back.

What music? Many hymns about the cross come to mind, of course, so that a moving and quiet service of word and contemplation could be made of the seven, a hymn and a healthy period of silent prayer following each poem. Or perhaps another set of hymns could be chosen— a hymn about water, for instance, to go with "I Thirst," or one about contrition to go with "Father, Forgive Them." There is no shortage of material in The Hymnal 1982 *that could be well joined to these poems.*

Or maybe a series of simple chants would work well in your setting—those of the Taizé community come to mind: simple, repetitive, melodic sung prayers around a few relevant themes. Or a series of psalms in simple plainsong. Or, if you have such a talent in your congregation, a solo cello or thoughtful solo guitar, or a quiet organ improvisation.

Americans are scared of poetry. But all of our dreams, much of our Scripture, and a great deal of our prayer is poetic. We are more at home with it than we think we are.

Prayer for Not-So-Good Friday

Not again God
Not again
The stones cry out
a thousand meters down
in the depths
of the earth
They grind and groan
they scream
as chasms
roll open
gulping rivers and trees
humans with their animals
down
down
sucked into the black hole
the self-centeredness
of the dying earth
And God, you risked all
to close the chasm
to bridge the gap
to walk the walk
to lay your life
on the line
for us again

Make me worth the effort

—*Mrs. Marcyn Del Clements*

Good Friday

This is the day the Lord has made
in her wisdom, in his fruition.

Do we stare over the precipice
looking down on death?
Do we hold the poison cup to his lips
saying, "Take, drink, you will be my body"?

Do we weep into his hands
knowing, as all of us
left behind
that we are the ones unlucky?

This is the day the Lord has made
in her deeper wisdom, in his infinite fruition.

Do we take the nails and wood?
The brick? The mortar?
Do we make this wall with our own bodies?
Or are we, like all those
at the cross, stilled to snickering
our own death let loose
for a moment upon this thin
broken body, this man?
Are we finally, then, glad to know
that's not our problem
not this day, anyway?

This is the day the Lord has made
in her infinite wisdom, in his deepest fruition.

I will look upon that face
Judgment Day or no
and see my own tears reflected there.
And will he know my deepest wisdom?
My infinite fruition is in his touch and wonder
his letting loose of death
upon us all.

Gentle Friend, know that I love you
on this Lorded Day.
Know that I am with you here.
Your depth, your infiniteness refracts through us,
we who wait to touch your broken hands.

Amen.

—*Ms. Victoria Pearson*

Easter

Easter Vigil: **Yami** *(darkness)*

I'm often amazed by structure of Chinese characters. The character for darkness, *yami*, is made up of two characters, a character for "gate" and a character for "sound." There is a sound inside or under a gate. This is how ancient people tried to express darkness. The impression that I receive from this Chinese character is totally different from the English word "darkness." A sound in a gate. It is dark, but I can somehow feel resonance that I cannot see because there is no light. I can hear something, though. Something is there, something that makes a sound.

Yami, darkness, doesn't mean a void. Something is there, but it is invisible. What sound do you hear now in the darkness? How does it resonate? Is it an unpleasant one, or does it have a nice resonance?

When the Paschal Candle is lit in the total darkness of the church at the Easter Vigil, I feel a great sensation. It must come from the power of the risen Lord, and that power embraces me. When the fire stone makes the sound, the darkness in the church is shaken with joy. Sound comes first, then comes the light. In the beginning of Creation, God's words "Let there be light" echoed in the darkness.

—*Mrs. Kyoko Mary Kageyama*

Eastering

It was early in my Eastering that day I looked within.
    Shroud cloths lay discarded round me,
    Mute evidence—marking end of real time
    And new beginnings.

Now I stood
    Naked
    before the tomb of who I'd tried to be,
    of who I thought I was.
And tasted the bitter fact I was no longer *me*.

That diligent, industrious, ever-busy *me*
    saw her fibrous web of self-deceit torn away
    piece by painful piece.
Each piece held up for mocking,
    flogging, self-derision
By a self who knows her own truth—
Each tattered shroud
    mocked for the flimsy mask
    each had always been.

It has been insidious.
Shroud upon shroud,
    layer after layer,
    year after year.
Muffling me,
Entangling me,
Until that Holy Saturday I gasped for breath
    God's Breath
    Holy Breath
Praying her inspiration to fill my soul.

I then entombed myself with proper care and purpose
    until the sound of rolling stone
    brought me to reality.
Then I fell against my yesterdays,
    mourning and beating my breast
    at the falling of each winding cloth,
For each proclaimed mask of the person who would never again
    be *me*.

When I awoke I was empty-tombed.
God had drawn me into Resurrection
    reluctantly, fearfully.

All I could hear was God's soft voice, asking me to yield.
    In giving my obedience to her will I find myself
    Rising free from tattered shrouds
    Rising free from fear
    Rising free from falseness,
    As I yield.

Arisen I now awake revealed.
  Naked, vulnerable,
  No protective masks separating me from thee.

My tomb lies empty in my Eastering
  As I move to share Jesus' Resurrection reality.

—*The Reverend Diane Moore*

The Women

The women rise before dawn.
It was a restless, sleepless night,
their hearts heavy with sadness,
their bodies wearied from the
tensions and stresses of yesterday.
Sounds of the angry crowd at the trial
still ring in their ears,
their eyes red-rimmed and puffy.

Slowly, they make their way toward the tomb,
there is no spring in their steps.
The first glimmer of morning light dances
across the horizon,
the grass is still wet with dew,
the early mist begins to lift,
they arrive at the tomb,
they rub their eyes to be sure they are seeing clearly.

The stone has been rolled away.
The tomb is empty.
Their tears flow again,
as they wonder what happened to the body.
Angels appear and ask,
"Why are you weeping?"
Then Jesus appears and speaks to them.
Filled with wonder and joy,
the women run to tell the others,
"We have seen the Lord."
He lives!
Alleluia!

—*Ms. Marjorie A. Burke*

Risen

Burned by Fire,
Yet not consumed.
Cut by Fear,
Yet gives Forgiveness.
Ears that hear the truth.
Eyes that see the smallest beauty.
A mouth poised to deliver the Word.
These things fade not,
No matter how much time passes.
We will, as did he, pass on
To that place where children dance without pain.
There, an almost invisible being
With infinite love is waiting
With outstretched arms.
Run to him.
He is gone, but he is not dead.

He is risen!

—*Ms. Mary Gados*

Pentecost

Pentecost

Godde's Ruach
touched my spirit
set it ablaze;
banked embers
still sustain me.

—*Mrs. Betty Vilas Hedblom*

Godde *is a feminine spelling of* God.

Hymn to the Holy Spirit

Spirit, moving over chaos,
Bringing light where there was none,
Be to us a light, revealing
Where the work is to be done.
Praise to God, among us dwelling:
Praise the Spirit giving light.

Breath, instilling animation,
Giving life, informing soul,
Breathe into this congregation
Life that makes the Body whole.
Praise to God, among us dwelling:
Praise the Spirit giving life.

Wind, inflaming fear-filled bodies,
Sending them to tell the News,
Fire anew your church's spirit,
Show the path we ought to choose.
Praise to God, among us dwelling:
Praise the Spirit giving fire.

Power, Life-force, Inspiration,
Blowing, breathing, brooding here,
Call, enliven, and empower
For your work, both far and near.
Praise to God, among us dwelling:
Praise the Spirit giving strength.

—*Ms. Patricia B. Clark*

This hymn can be sung to the tune Regent Square, *Hymn 93 in*
The Hymnal 1982.

Corporate Prayers

Collects

Collects for the Church Year

The following Collects for the Church Year, except for Feast Days, were written by the Reverend Elizabeth Rankin Geitz, and were inspired by either Holy Scripture or the Christian tradition.

Advent

Advent I
Creator God, from whose womb the sea burst forth: Be with us now as we seek with your grace to give birth to a new creation filled with justice and peace, harmony and concord, unity and love for all; in the name of your Child whom we await, Jesus Christ, our Redeemer. *Amen.*

(source: Job 38:8)

Advent II
Life-giving God, in whom we live and move and have our being: Kindle your love within us as we await the coming of your Son our Savior Jesus Christ, that we might humbly serve others in his name, both now and for ever. *Amen.*

(source: Acts 17:28)

Advent III
O Hidden, Eternal, and Self-giving God, who became human for our salvation: Open our minds, liberate our hearts, and strengthen our souls, that we may live into the fullness of your desires for us; in the name of the Source, the Word, and the Spirit. *Amen.*

Advent IV
Blessed Jesus, born of our sister Mary, the first and most perfect disciple who fully accepted the will of God and acted upon it: Give us the faith to accept your will for us and the strength to carry it out, to the honor and glory of your name. *Amen.*

(source: Pope Paul VI, 20th c.)

Christmas

Christmas Day
Most gracious God, for our salvation you were born and manifested in a human body: Help us see your likeness in women and men of all nations,

races, and cultures, that we may rejoice in our diversity and live together as one; in the name of your Child, our Savior Jesus Christ, given to us this holy day [night]. *Amen.*

(source: St. Athanasius, 4th c.)

Christmas I

O Loving Creator, for our sake you became human and were born in a lowly stable: Help us always to remember the forgotten, uplift the lowly, and give strength to the powerless, all for your love's sake; in the name of the Source, the Word, and the Spirit. *Amen.*

Christmas II

Loving Word of God, you have shown us the fullness of your glory in taking human flesh, becoming like us, your sisters and brothers, in every respect: Grant that we may share in your divine life and reveal it to others in all we do, to the honor and glory of your name, now and for ever. *Amen.*

(source: Hebrews 2:17)

Epiphany

The Epiphany, January 6

Almighty Mother, you have the power to empower and the light to enlighten: Lead us, we pray, by the light of your star into your radiant presence, that we may worship you in honor and glory, both now and to the age of ages. *Amen.*

(source: St. Hildegard of Bingen, 12th c.)

Epiphany I

Beloved Son of God, baptized in the river Jordon: Guide us as we seek to strive for justice and peace among all people and to respect the dignity of every human being; in the name of the Father, and of the Son, and of the Holy Spirit, one God, Mother of us all. *Amen.*

(sources: Matthew 3:13–17; Ruth C. Duck, 20th c.)

Epiphany II

Beloved Christ, both God and flesh, the image of father and mother: Fill us with the splendor of your great brilliance that we may reflect the radiance of your light to all whom we meet; in the name of the Lover, the Beloved, and the Love that exists between them. *Amen.*

(sources: Byzantine Mosaic, 12th c.; St. Augustine, 4th c.)

Epiphany III

Never-changing God, honored under many names: Protect us from all harm as a mother bear protects her cubs that we may walk in the light of your glory and share that light with others; through your Beloved, our Savior Jesus Christ. *Amen.*

(source: Hosea 13:8)

Epiphany IV
O Eternal Light, you sent your Child Jesus Christ that there might no longer be slave or free, Jew or Gentile, male or female: Help us to respect the dignity of all human beings and to live in harmony with one another; all for your love's sake, both now and for ever. *Amen.*

(source: Galatians 3:28)

Epiphany V
Gracious God, giver of love and peace, you call us to live together as one family: Give us grace to learn your ways, that all people may have the necessities of life and no one must struggle to survive; in the name of the Source, the Word, and the Spirit. *Amen.*

(source: Delores S. Williams, 20th c.)

Epiphany VI
Everlasting Father, we your gathered people are your Church, for without us the Church has no reality: Guide us as we seek to discover the gifts you have given to each of us that we might minister to others in your name; through Jesus Christ, our Savior, the light of the world. *Amen.*

(sources: Isaiah 9:6; Hans Kung, 20th c.)

Epiphany VII
O God, who became vulnerable for our sake, you challenge the powers that rule this world through all who work for justice, freedom, and peace: Fill us with your passion that we may have the courage to persevere against evil in all its disguises; in the name of your Beloved, our Savior Jesus Christ. *Amen.*

(source: 2 Corinthians 11:14)

Epiphany VIII
O Lord of Light: Rain your abundant grace upon us, that when the dark night of the soul threatens to overcome us, we may hear the comfort of your loving voice; in the name of the Father, and of the Son, and of the Holy Spirit, one God, Mother of us all. *Amen.*

(source: Ruth C. Duck, 20th c.)

Last Sunday after the Epiphany (to be used on the Sunday before Ash Wednesday)
Eternal Wisdom, who makes all things new: Bless us as we struggle to transform our world through the light of your gospel, that women and men of all

races, cultures, and orientations may live in unity in the midst of diversity; in the name of the Source, the Word, and the Spirit. *Amen.*

(source: Wisdom 7:27)

Lent

Ash Wednesday
O Christ, our kind Mother, our gracious Mother, our beloved Mother: Have mercy upon us; deliver us from the powers of sin and death that surround us; show us that all is well and all manner of things shall be well, both now and for ever more. *Amen.*

(source: St. Julian of Norwich, 14th c.)

Lent I
O God, who knit us together in our mothers' wombs: Create in us a clean heart and renew a right spirit within us, that we may embrace the unchangeable truth of your Word, Jesus Christ our Lord; who with you and the Holy Spirit lives and reigns one God, for ever and ever. *Amen.*

(sources: Psalm 139:12, Psalm 51:11)

Lent II
Steadfast God, you search for us when we are lost like a woman who searches for one lost coin: Help us evermore seek your face, that we may reveal your glory in all the world; in the name of our Mother, our Wisdom, and our Comforter. *Amen.*

(source: Luke 15:8)

Lent III
God of Compassion and God of Grace, who comforts us as a mother comforts her child: Be with all who ache for the reach of your loving embrace in the midst of a broken world; in the name of your Child, our Savior Jesus Christ. *Amen.*

(source: Isaiah 66:13)

Lent IV
Draw us, O God, to your heart at the heart of the world, at once joyful, aching, expectant, and loving, that we may care for others as you care for us, each and every moment of our lives; in the name of your Beloved, our Savior Jesus Christ. *Amen.*

Lent V
Blessed Jesus, who counted among your disciples, Mary Magdalene, Joanna, and Susanna: Help us take up our cross and follow you as they did, that we

may proclaim your good news to all whom we meet; in the name of the Lover, the Beloved, and the Love that exists between them. *Amen.*

(sources: Luke 8:1–3; St. Augustine, 4th c.)

Palm Sunday
O Suffering Servant, whose crucifixion we demanded: Open our eyes to the ways we still crucify you today in the lives of the least of these, our sisters and brothers; for the sake of the One whom we have caused to suffer, Jesus Christ our Lord. *Amen.*

(sources: Isaiah 53; Matthew 27:23; Matthew 25:40)

Maundy Thursday
Beloved Jesus, Servant of all, on the night before you gave yourself up for the life of the world, you washed the feet of your disciples, even Judas whom you knew would betray you. Fill us with your love that knows no bounds, that we too may serve and forgive others in your name, both now and for ever. *Amen.*

(source: John 13:1–11)

Most Blessed Jesus, on the night after you were anointed by Mary of Bethany, you broke bread with your friends: Let us never forget the sacrifice you made for each one of us that we all might be saved; in the name of the Lover, the Beloved, and the Love that exists between them. *Amen.*

(sources: Mark 14:3–9; St. Augustine, 4th c.)

Good Friday
Almighty Father, whose beloved Son Jesus suffered the agony of crucifixion: Give us the strength to stand at the foot of the cross as did the women on Calvary so long ago; in the name of your Beloved, our Savior Jesus Christ, who gave his life for us and for our salvation. *Amen.*

(source: Mark 15:40)

Easter

Easter Day
O Risen Christ, your agony on the cross was the birth pangs of a new creation: Give us the courage of the women who first discovered your empty tomb, that we may marvel with them at the wonder and glory of your resurrection and proclaim that glory to others; in the name of the Source, the Word, and the Spirit. *Amen.*

(source: Luke 24:2)

Easter I

Risen Savior, you first appeared to Mary Magdalene, the apostle to the apostles: Help us hear you when you call our names, that we, too, may proclaim the good news of your resurrection throughout the world, to the honor and glory of your name. *Amen.*

(sources: John 20:11–18; St. Bernard of Clairvaux, 12th c.)

Easter II

O Risen One, you have broken the bonds of an earthly body: Be with us now as brother, sister, father, and mother, that we may see your image reflected in our own and in all whom we meet; in the name of our Mother, our Wisdom, and our Comforter. *Amen.*

(sources: 1 Corinthians 15:42–44; St. Clement of Alexandria, 2nd c.)

Easter III

O Wounded One, Risen One, Life-giving Lover of Souls: Guide us as we seek to build up your Church on earth, drawing others into the warmth of your saving embrace; to the honor and glory of your most blessed name, from this time forth and for ever more. *Amen.*

Easter IV

Jesus, our true Mother, who is all love and bears us into joy and endless living: Be with us in the breaking of bread, that you may dwell in us and we in you, both now and for ever. *Amen.*

(source: St. Julian of Norwich, 14th c.)

Easter V

Most Blessed Jesus, the only begotten Son of God's paternal womb: Give us courage to live your gospel without compromise, that your reign may be established on all the earth, both now and to the ages of ages. *Amen.*

(source: St. Ambrose, 4th c.)

Easter VI

O Gracious God in Heaven, you sent your apostles to be gentle among us, like a nurse tenderly caring for her children: Be with us now as we seek to care for the sick, the oppressed, and the broken hearted, that they might be healed by the touch of your saving embrace; through Jesus Christ our Lord. *Amen.*

(source: 1 Thessalonians 2:7)

Easter VII

God of power and might, love and hope, we lift our voices in praise to you: Help us to remember the abundant blessings you have given us that we may be empowered to share those blessings with others; in the name of the risen Christ. *Amen.*

Day of Pentecost
Eternal God, Consuming Fire, who on this day gave us the gift of your Holy Spirit: Fill us with the longing to speak your uncontainable word to a broken and wounded world, that we may lead others to the warmth of your light, both now and for ever. *Amen.*

(sources: Hebrews 12:29; Janet Morley, 20th c.)

Trinity Sunday
Most Blessed Trinity, the Lover, the Beloved, and the Love that exists between them: May we so share in your divine dance, that our lives may be for ever entwined with yours, both now and for ever. *Amen.*

(source: St. Augustine, 4th c.)

The Season after Pentecost

Proper I
Everlasting God, you sent to us your Holy Spirit, root of all being, absolver of all faults, balm of all wounds: Infuse our hearts with your unquenchable fire, that we may be filled with passion for your gospel; in the name of the Source, the Word, and the Spirit. *Amen.*

(source: St. Hildegard of Bingen, 12th c.)

Proper 2
O Holy Spirit, giver of all life through the water of creation and the womb of the cross: Guide us as we seek to give birth to you in our lives and in the world around us; in the name of God, our Mother, our Wisdom, and our Comforter. *Amen.*

(source: Isaiah 46:3–4)

Proper 3
God of Abraham, Sarah, and Hagar: Hold us accountable that we may never exploit the less fortunate, but will respect the dignity of all people made in your glorious image, to the honor and glory of your name, both now and for ever. *Amen.*

(source: Genesis 16:1–6, 15–20)

Proper 4
O God of Justice: Unite us as one people in our diversity, since working for righteousness in isolation from one another is a luxury we cannot afford; through your Beloved, our Savior Jesus Christ. *Amen.*

(source: Renita Weems, 20th c.)

Proper 5
Everlasting God of infinite power and goodness: Give us the wisdom never to limit your glory to one image alone; in the name of God, our comforting mother, father, rock, midwife, mother bear, and eagle. *Amen.*

(sources: Isaiah 66:13; Mark 14:36; 2 Samuel 22:2–3; Psalm 22:10; Hosea 13:8; Exodus 19:4)

Proper 6
Eternal God, who has spoken through the prophets Miriam, Deborah, and Huldah, Isaiah, Hosea, and Amos: Give us the courage to hear your prophets of today, that through their witness we may be inspired and strengthened to work in your name; through Jesus Christ our Lord. *Amen.*

(sources: Exodus 15:20; Judges 4:4; 2 Kings 22:14; Isaiah, Hosea, Amos)

Proper 7
Transforming God: Lay your sacred hands on all the common things and small interests of our lives; bless, change, and transfigure them and in them give us your very self; in the name of your Beloved, our Savior Jesus Christ. *Amen.*

(source: Evelyn Underhill, 20th c.)

Proper 8
Most Loving Abba, you gather the perplexed and seek the lost: Shelter those caught in evil; free those in bondage; strengthen those who struggle to survive; in the name of God, our Mother, our Wisdom, and our Comforter. *Amen.*

(sources: Mark 14:36; St. Hildegard of Bingen, 12th c.)

Proper 9
Most Blessed Creator: Help us never to forget that there is nothing we can do to make you love us less and there is nothing we can do to make you love us more; in the name of your Son, our Savior Jesus Christ. *Amen.*

(source: Archbishop Desmond Tutu, 20th c.)

Proper 10
Blessed Jesus: Send upon us the sweet rain of your humanity, the hot sun of the living God, and the gentle dew of the Holy Spirit, that our aching hearts may find eternal rest in you and you alone, both now and for ever. *Amen.*

(source: St. Mechthild of Magdeburg, 13th c.)

Proper 11
Compassionate One: Remove from us all hardness of heart that we may accept all people as your precious children, remembering that when we reject them, we reject you; in the name of the Source, the Word, and the Spirit. *Amen.*

Proper 12
Blessed Jesus, Comforter of the Afflicted, you yearned to draw us to yourself as a mother hen gathers her brood under her wings, yet we were not willing: Open our hearts to the truth of your never-ending love for us that we might share that love with others, to the honor and glory of your name, both now and for ever. *Amen.*

(source: Luke 13:34)

Proper 13
O Eternal Radiant God: Place our minds before the mirror of your eternity; place our souls in the brilliance of your glory; place our hearts in your divine life that we may live always in the presence of your being; in the name of the Risen Christ. *Amen.*

(source: St. Clare of Assisi, 13th c.)

Proper 14
Eternal Mother: Cover us with your protective robe that we may find warmth and rest in you; fill us with your eternal love that we may not be overwhelmed by the trials of this life; in the name of your Beloved, our Savior Jesus Christ. *Amen.*

(source: St. Gertrude of Helfta, 13th c.)

Proper 15
O Holy Spirit, love within: Kindle within us the flame of your burning passion, that we may work without ceasing for justice and peace on earth, and at length may attain to your love that never ends; in the name of the Source, the Word, and the Spirit. *Amen.*

Proper 16
Gracious God, whose Church is always and everywhere a living people: Guide us when we are in conflict with one another; help us to be energized by what unites us, rather than by what divides us, that we may be the Body of Christ in your world today; in the name of our Risen Savior. *Amen.*

Proper 17
Most gracious Lord, whose appearing is as sure as the dawn: Come to us like the spring rains that water the earth, showering your blessings upon us and all whom you have made, that we may be strengthened by your love and may share that love with others; in the name of the Source, the Word, and the Spirit. *Amen.*

(source: Hosea 6:3)

Proper 18
Eternal God, from you we come, in you we are enfolded, to you we return: Guide us on our earthly journey that we may reveal your glory in all the world; in the name of your Child, our Savior Jesus Christ. *Amen.*

(source: South Africa, 20th c.)

Proper 19
God of Love and Light: Bring to life within us the living, burning sparks of your brilliance, that your divine flame may burn within us, warming our souls and empowering our lives with zeal for your gospel, both now and for ever. *Amen.*

(source: St. Hildegard of Bingen, 12th c.)

Proper 20
O Gentle Guide, who leads us with cords of human kindness and bands of love: Help us evermore to walk in your ways, that we may lead others to the joy of your saving grace; in the name of your Beloved, our Redeemer, Jesus Christ. *Amen.*

(source: Hosea 11:3–4)

Proper 21
Baker woman God: Knead us, shape us, form and reform us, until we are wholly yours, that we may live into the fullness of your will for us, to the honor and glory of your most blessed name. *Amen.*

(source: Luke 13:20)

Proper 22
O Holy One of Israel, you have called us by name and we are yours: Remain with us as we endure the trials of this life, that we may not be overwhelmed but may see your light in the midst of darkness; in the name of God, our father and mother. *Amen.*

(sources: Isaiah 43:2–3; Job 38:28–29)

Proper 23
Most Gracious God, Mother to the motherless, Father to the fatherless: Surround us with your eternal goodness; protect us from all harm; strengthen us through the power of your Holy Spirit, that we may never forget that we are your beloved children, both now and for ever. *Amen.*

(source: African-American Spiritual, 19th c.)

Proper 24
Most Holy and Loving God, let the same mind be in us that was in Christ Jesus, who emptied himself taking the form of a slave, that we may humbly and devoutly serve others, to the honor and glory of your name. *Amen.*
(source: Philippians 2:5–7)

Proper 25
O Immeasurable Generosity, Eternal Infinite Good: Pour out your abundant grace upon us that we may share your blessed love with others; in the name of your Beloved, our Savior Jesus Christ. *Amen.*
(source: St. Catherine of Siena, 14th c.)

Proper 26
Ever loving God, we thank you for nurturing us with profoundly paternal love and thoroughly maternal caresses: Guide us as we share the riches of your grace with all whom we meet in your name; through Jesus Christ, our Redeemer. *Amen.*
(source: Martin Luther, 16th c.)

Proper 27
O God of our weary years, God of our silent tears, who has brought us thus far on the way: Lead us into the light; uphold us with your might, this day and for ever more. *Amen.*
(source: African-American Anthem, "Lift Every Voice and Sing")

Proper 28
O God, our midwife, you took us from the womb and kept us safe on our mother's breast: Guide us as you continue to bring new life to birth within us that we may grow into the fullness of your desires for us; through the power of the risen Christ. *Amen.*
(source: Psalm 22:9)

Last Sunday in Pentecost
Eternal Light, shine in our hearts; Eternal Power, be our strength; Eternal Wisdom, guide us as we seek to serve you in all whom we meet, to the honor and glory of your most blessed name, now and for ever. *Amen.*
(source: Ancient Greek Orthodox Liturgy)

Feast Days

Saint Mary Magdalene
God of light and hope, we honor this day your apostle Mary Magdalene, faithful friend and companion of Jesus, first to desire the power of the Christ, first to announce the resurrection to the world. Bring us face-to-face with the risen Christ that our hearts may break open and our hands break free. *Amen.*

—Ms. Nora Gallagher and the Reverend Anne Howard

Commemorative Collects

The following Collects were written by the Reverend Canon Lorna H. Williams and commemorate women who have witnessed to the love and justice of God in the midst of racism, sexism, and other forms of oppression. They may be used in conjunction with the lessons appointed for the Common of Saints in The Book of Common Prayer *or with other lessons of your choice.*

Pauli Murray
Lawyer, Professor, and Priest; Ordained January 8, 1977
We remember today, O God, the life and work of Pauli Murray, whom you called to pursue justice and equality for the good of your people: Grant that we, after her example, may have the vision and courage to challenge all forms of discrimination and to promote reconciliation; through your Child, our Savior, Jesus Christ. *Amen.*
Through her hard work as a civil rights lawyer, Pauli Murray challenged the system of racism and segregation. She was also a strong advocate of women's equality, becoming a co-founder of the National Organization of Women. In 1977 she became the first African-American woman ordained to the priesthood in the Episcopal Church.

Florence Li Tim Oi
Priest; Ordained January 24, 1944, Hong Kong
O God, you called Florence Li Tim Oi, who suffered heavy trials for your sake, to serve as priest in your Church: Pour out your Spirit upon us that we may not fail to answer your call to ministry through our various vocations; through Jesus Christ our Savior. *Amen.*
During Japan's war with China in the 1930s, Florence Li Tim Oi worked tirelessly bringing relief to war casualties and refugees. As the visits of a priest to the area of Macao became less and less frequent and the need for pastoral care and Holy Communion increased, Li Tim Oi was ordained to the priesthood in 1944, becoming the first female priest in the Anglican Communion.

Carmen Bruni Guerrero
Priest; Ordained January 25, 1985
Faithful God, your Son Jesus Christ came among us to proclaim release to those who are held captive: You called Carmen Bruni Guerrero to challenge your people to examine their hearts and address injustice and oppression; help us to heed the call to a renewed life of freedom and reconciliation, through Jesus Christ, our Lord. *Amen.*
Carmen Bruni Guerrero is currently the Jubilee Ministries Officer at the Episcopal Church Center. Before coming to New York, she served as Archdeacon for Multicultural and Congregational Development in the Diocese of Los Angeles.

Barbara Clementine Harris
Consecrated Bishop, February 11, 1989
O God, who raises up those who have been cast down to serve as leaders in your Church: You sent Barbara Clementine Harris to be bishop to your faithful people. Help us, we pray, to address the issues of justice and power in our world, that we may stand before you as a people dedicated to your way of love and peace; through Jesus Christ, the author of our salvation, who lives and reigns with you and the Holy Spirit, one God, for ever and ever. *Amen.*
After a long and successful career in public and community relations in Philadelphia, Barbara Clementine Harris studied for and was ordained to the priesthood. In 1989, she was consecrated Suffragan Bishop of Massachusetts, becoming the first woman in the Anglican Communion to enter the episcopate.

Anna Julia Cooper
Educator and Churchwoman; died February 27, 1964
Almighty God, your Son Jesus came among us to teach us to walk in your way of love: We thank you for Anna Julia Cooper whose life challenges us to not be blind to racism within your Church; and we pray that your Church may be a community where all are welcome, through Jesus Christ, our Savior. *Amen.*
Anna Julia Cooper was an African-American educator and churchwoman who did not hesitate to speak out about racism and sexism she saw within the structures of church and society. She died at the age of 105 in 1964.

Konwatsijayeni (Mollie Brandt)
Mohawk Peacemaker; died April 16, 1796, Canada
Everliving God, who endowed the gifts of wisdom and mediation upon your servant Konwatsijayeni: Help us to follow her example of peacemaking so that your Church may encourage and spread unity and understanding to all people, through Jesus Christ, our Redeemer. *Amen.*
A daughter of a Mohawk chieftain, Konwatsijayeni was well known for her efforts to bridge relations between white settlers and the Mohawk nation. She and her family were forced into exile to Kingston in Canada, where she became a founding member of St. George's, a local parish.

Liturgical Prayers

Note: For eucharistic prayers written in expansive language and approved for trial use by the 1997 General Convention of the Episcopal Church, see Enriching Our Worship *(New York: Church Publishing Incorporated, 1997), 57–68.*

Gloria Patri

Glory to the Holy and Undivided Trinity; God who is Three in One and One in Three; who is beyond us, among us, within us; who was, and is, and is to come, world without end. *Amen.*

—*The Rt. Reverend Catherine M. Waynick*

Trisagion: Nine Times Holy

Holy God,
Holy and Mighty,
Holy Immortal one,
Have mercy upon us.

Holy God,
Holy Compassion,
Holy Abundant One,
Have mercy upon us.

Holy God,
Holy and Gracious,
Holy Beautiful One,
Have mercy upon us.

—*The Reverend Judith P. Ain*

When I was on the first American-Soviet Peace Walk between Leningrad and Moscow, I became particularly aware of the Trisagion as a part of our liturgy borrowed from the Orthodox tradition. I was struck by the traditionally masculine images, so I wrote several extra verses to expand and balance it.

Affirmation of Faith

We believe in the God of Life,
    who creates and loves people,
    who acts in history
    and who promises never to leave us alone.
We believe in Jesus of Nazareth,
    who is our brother,
    who wants not to be idolized but to be followed.
We believe that we dwell in the presence of the Holy Spirit;
    without her we are nothing;
    filled with her we are able to become creative,
    lively, and free.
We believe in the Church of Jesus Christ,
    a community where we find companions and
    courage for the struggles of life,
    where we grow in our understanding of the faith,
    through worship, prayer, nurture, and service.
We believe that God has a use for us in this time and
    place, that though we walk through the valley of
    the shadow of death, we are called to be
    instruments of God's peace.
We believe in living, hoping, laughing, and enjoying
    the good of the earth;
We believe that people can change, and God keeps
    pulling us to life and to a new world of joy
    and peace.

—The Reverend Dr. Constance M. Baugh

I am a Presbyterian minister who wrote this affirmation for a prison ministry. It was used in the service of Holy Communion to celebrate the Twenty-Fifth Anniversary of the Ordination of Women to the Priesthood in the Episcopal Church.

Absolution

God love you and have mercy upon you; through the cross of Christ, pardon you and set you free. God forgives you. Forgive others. Forgive yourself; in the name of the Source, the Word, and the Spirit. *Amen.*

Adapted from A New Zealand Prayer Book *by the editors*

Post Communion Prayer 1

Eternal Light, shine in our hearts.
Eternal Power, be our strength.
Eternal Wisdom, guide us as we serve you.
Eternal Goodness, you have drawn us to your heart
And united us in the Sacrament of Christ's Body and Blood.
Now grant that with all our heart, and mind, and strength,
We may evermore seek your face.
And finally, by your infinitive love
Keep us in your holy presence,
Through Jesus Christ, our Redeemer. *Amen.*

—*The Reverend Elizabeth Rankin Geitz*

Post Communion Prayer 2

You, gracious God, remembering your mercy, have helped your people in all generations, as you promised Abraham, Sarah, and Hagar; now stand with us, blessing those who have shared this feast of love, that we may go forth from this place, empowered to join with you in your ongoing creation, liberation, and blessing of the world. All this we ask in the name of Jesus Christ. Feed us daily, hold us fast, send us forth boldly, joyfully, and ever faithful in your Spirit. *Amen.*

—*The Reverend Dr. Carter Heyward*

This prayer has been published as part of a service of Holy Eucharist in Equal Rites *and* Saving Jesus.

Blessings

May the Wisdom of God lead you in her marvelous way,
Be your shelter by day and a blaze of stars by night.
May she stir your inmost being always to seek her,
And the Wisdom, Love, and Grace of God
Be upon you and remain with you always. *Amen.*

—*The Reverend Lynne A. Grifo*

May you call upon Sophia and find her in all your thoughts.
May her radiance enfold you and her laughter embolden you.
May she lead you in the paths of peace today and evermore. *Amen.*

—*The Reverend Dr. Alison M. Cheek*

In the name of the true and living Holy One,
Who made us for love,
Who saved us by love,
And who loves us still. *Amen.*

—*The Reverend Jean Dalby Clift*

Prayers of the People

For Women

During the silence following each bidding, the People may offer their own prayers.

Holy and gracious God, you created us in your image. Help us to recognize and honor your image in ourselves and in one another.

Silence

O God of creation,
Hear our prayer.

Holy and life-giving God, look with compassion on all those in this world suffering from violence and the broken relationships that destroy your image: Especially we pray for women and children living in poverty and those living in fear of abuse.

Silence

O God of hope,
Hear our prayer.

Holy and faithful God, you have called us into a goodly company of women. Hear our prayers for our sisters who are silent because of oppression, those who feel that their voices are not heard, and those who bear the brunt of war, that they may live in justice and peace.

Silence

O God of peace,
Hear our prayer.

Holy and unifying God, you have made us one with you. Calm the anxiety of women and men who are fearful of the changes in the church and in the world. Grant that your Holy Spirit may bind us together in your love.

Silence

O God of love,
Hear our prayer.

Holy and gift-giving God, you have promised to hear what we ask in Jesus' name. Grant to all women the opportunity to serve and lead in your Church; give them courage and hope so that they will be called to places where they will flourish and experience expanding possibilities. Give to all women and men in positions of leadership, spiritual, emotional, and physical wholeness.

Silence

O God of infinite possibility,
Hear our prayer.

Holy and creator God, you have filled the earth with beauty. Look graciously upon the women of the Anglican Communion; give us grace to rejoice in our diversity and the freedom to pursue our aspirations with respect for those whose cultures and journeys are different from our own.

Silence

O God of grace,
Hear our prayer.

Holy and ever-living God, we give you thanks for the love and wisdom of our foremothers, and we rejoice in the communion of our sister saints. We give thanks especially for the women pioneers—for the deaconesses, missionaries, and church workers who ministered in your Name.

Silence

O God of wisdom,
Accept our thanksgiving.

Holy and loving God, we give you thanks for the blessings and wisdom we have received from those we love who have died, and for the blessings and joy of children. Grant that we may always honor the child in each of us.

Silence

O God of abundant life,
Accept our thanksgiving.

Holy and reconciling God, we give you thanks for our own faith communities and all those who have supported us. We pray also for those who have stood in our way.

Silence

O God of strength,
Accept our thanksgiving.

The Leader may conclude with this Collect:
We give you thanks and praise, O God, for the spirit, wisdom, and insight of women throughout the ages and those gathered here today. Grant that we may always be supported by this community of love and prayer. *Amen.*

These prayers were composed by twenty graduates of the Church Divinity School of the Pacific and St. Margaret's House, Berkeley, California. The Reverend Caryl Marsh of Salt Lake City, Utah, was the editor.

For Those Who Are Abused

Deacon or other leader
O Lord, our Creator and Deliverer, you heard the cries of your people in Egypt and sent your servant Moses to lead them out of oppression. Hear our prayers for all your people who suffer from abuse and oppression, that we too might be a means to free them from their pain.

O Lord, our Deliverer,
Hear our prayer.

Bring to an end the divisions in your Church throughout the world, that unified in purpose, the Body of Christ may always remember and serve those men, women, and children whose suffering is hidden from our sight or painful for us to acknowledge.

O Lord, our Deliverer,
Hear our prayer.

Bestow your grace on all persons in positions of leadership throughout the Church, especially our Presiding Bishop, our bishop, and the laity and clergy in our parishes, that your Church may be holy ground where all your people can gather in safety and peace.

O Lord, our Deliverer,
Hear our prayer.

Guide the leaders of all the nations, that your justice may be brought to all who have been wronged and that every country might be a promised land for its people.

O Lord, our Deliverer,
Hear our prayer.

Open our eyes to those in our midst who suffer abuse, that we may also open our hearts to share their pain and bring them relief from their sorrow.

O Lord, our Deliverer,
Hear our prayer.

Lift up all your people whose suffering is beyond their strength to endure, that they may feel the healing of your compassionate love.

O Lord, our Deliverer,
Hear our prayer.

Strengthen all who care for the abused and who speak to the world of their pain, that they may find renewal for their labor in your healing presence.

O Lord, our Deliverer,
Hear our prayer.

Remind us always that as you pardon all wrongdoings and heal all ills, we may also forgive those who inflict pain on others and pray for their restoration to wholeness.

O Lord, our Deliverer,
Hear our prayer.

Hold in your loving care those who have died at the hands of others, and comfort those who mourn them with the knowledge that you will bring justice and healing to all who have been wronged.

O Lord, our Deliverer,
Hear our prayer.

The Leader may conclude with this Collect:
O Lord, our Creator and Deliverer, you enlightened and strengthened Moses to be a prophet and guide to your people when they cried out for help. Open our hearts, our ears, and our eyes, that we might also work for justice and comfort for all who suffer abuse. This we ask in the name of your Son, our Savior Jesus Christ, who came to set at liberty those who are oppressed. *Amen.*

—*The Reverend Nancy Casey Fulton*

For All God's People

The Leader and People pray responsively

Deacon or other leader
In peace we pray to you, O God.
We pray today with special intention for all people who struggle for survival, for visibility, for a voice, for equality, and for quality of life in a patriarchal world and church.

For all people in countries and cultures impacted by global capitalism. For the world's poor, destitute, and homeless, most of whom are women and children. Let not the needy be forgotten, or the hope of the poor be taken away.
We pray to you, O God.

For women here in this *city* and throughout our land who are beaten and abused physically, emotionally, or spiritually. For those who are exploited and enslaved as sexual objects, especially victims of sexual tourism in Asia. For people in other cultures torn by war who, because of their powerlessness, have been subjected to rape and other forms of torture.
We pray to you, O God.

For all people of minority cultures and ethnic groups in the United States who continue to be trivialized and endangered by the pervasiveness of racism. For all people, especially women, in this country who are economically exploited. For the health and welfare of every person in every circumstance.
We pray to you, O God.

With all people resisting their fundamentalist religious cultures. For lesbian, gay, bisexual, transgendered, divorced, and single people who suffer special forms of oppression and hatred within and beyond the Church. With men and women in Episcopal and other communities who care enough to struggle for the transformation of the Church and the world.
Sweet, sweet Spirit, empower your sisters and brothers.

With those women and men who will not make peace with imperialism, racism, or class elitism.
Inspire us, brother Jesus.

With those who do not fear diverse spiritualities or the wondrous variety of creatures on the earth.
Increase our wisdom, our Father.

With those who refuse to give in to despair or cynicism and who continue to dream, envision, and struggle for a more fully just world and a more courageous Church.
Encourage us, our Mother.

For the courageous witness of the first women ordained priests in this country: Merrill Bittner, Alla Bozarth, Alison Cheek, Emily Hewitt, Carter Heyward, Suzanne Hiatt, Jacqueline Means, Marie Moorefield Fleisher, Jeannette Piccard, Betty Bone Schiess, Katrina Martha Swanson, Nancy Hatch Wittig, Eleanor Lee McGee, Alison Palmer, Betty Powell, and Diane Tickell.
We give you thanks, O God.

For the empowering witness of the bishops who ordained them: Daniel Corrigan, Robert DeWitt, Edward Welles, George Barrett—and for the supportive presence of Antonio Ramos.
We give you thanks, O God.

For the faith and witness of the countless laywomen, deaconesses, and women religious throughout the Anglican Communion who have paved the way for all women, lay and ordained, in our ministries; especially for the lives and work of Li Tim Oi, Jane Hwang, Joyce Bennett, and Phyllis Edwards.
We give you thanks, O God.

For the contributions of women in all walks of life, in all churches, throughout all generations, especially today for the creative, liberating ministries of laywomen, women deacons, women priests, and women bishops throughout the Anglican Communion.
We give you thanks, O God.

For our sisters and brothers throughout the world who have yet to have their priestly vocations tested or acknowledged, but who continue their faithful work for Christ's gospel. For their support of our struggle over the years and their courage in remaining faithful ministers.
We give you thanks, O God.

We pray for all who have died, remembering their courage and faithful witness, especially for Li Tim Oi, Jane Hwang, Jeannette Piccard, Pauli Murray, Daniel Corrigan, Elizabeth Corrigan, Charles Lawrence II, Edward Welles, Catharine Welles, and William Stringfellow, with those we remember now. Sophia God, let your loving kindness be upon them.
Who put their trust in you.

The Leader may conclude with this Collect:
Merciful God, accept the fervent prayers of your people; in the multitude of your mercies look with compassion upon us and all who turn to you for help, for you are gracious, O lover of your creation, and to you we give glory, Creator, Christ, and Holy Spirit. *Amen.*

These prayers were used on the occasion of the Twenty-fifth Anniversary of the Ordination of Women to the Priesthood in the Episcopal Church. They reflect the combined efforts of the Reverend Dr. Suzanne Hiatt, the Reverend Dr. Carter Heyward, the Reverend Dr. Alison Cheek, the Reverend Canon Nancy Wittig, and the Reverend Carol Renée Anthony.

For Unity in the Church

Deacon or other leader
Gracious God, who knit our inmost parts before we were born, and who shelters us with a strong hand, in our gratitude receive the prayers we offer as we respond to each petition by saying, "Kyrie eleison."

In thanksgiving for the unity we share through our death and resurrection in Jesus Christ, that we who have been entrusted with the gift of new life, may bring life to the world and renewed hope to our church; for this we pray.
Kyrie eleison.

For the courage to hold fast to the high ideals of our calling, bringing the lamp of charity to those who live in despair and desperation, and through their cries receive the saving grace that enlightens our ministry; for this we pray.
Kyrie eleison.

For a renewed sense of the Body of Christ, the Church, that together with our Presiding Bishop, our bishop(s), and all other ministers, we may rededicate ourselves in the unity of the Triune God; for this we pray.
Kyrie eleison.

For the urgency to seek peace before the battle breaks, and economic justice before the weight of poverty fractures the will of nations; for this we pray.
Kyrie eleison.

For the forgiveness of our sins, that the wounds that we inflict on one another in the name of righteousness may be healed by the Divine Life that overcomes human frailty; for this we pray.
Kyrie eleison.

For those whose lives are approaching death, and for those who have died, remembering especially _____, that they and their loved ones may receive the comfort of the Holy Spirit; for this we pray.
Kyrie eleison.

In Christ, who baptized us with fire and water and called us to be a baptizing community, we continue our prayers either silently or aloud.

—*The Rt. Reverend Geralyn Wolf*

"Kyrie eleison" *means "Lord have mercy" in Greek. These prayers were written for the House of Bishops Conference in San Diego, California, September 1999.*

For Stewardship

The Leader and People pray responsively

Deacon or other leader
Nurturing God, your love is free, your compassion unconditional, and your mercy infinite. You shower upon us gifts abundant. Grant that we may know and trust these gifts, that we may discover the joy they bring, and inspire us to serve and to love out of that joy. Open our lips, O Spirit, that we may proclaim your benevolent truth and your call for justice in our communities, in our congregations, and in the world.
Spirit, open our lips.

Open our minds, O Creator, that we might dream a Church reconciled, a Church that knows only your love so abundantly that it bursts with a passion for ministry, a desire to give completely, and a sense of stewardship that seeks only to give back.
Creator, open our minds.

Open our hearts, O Giver of Gifts, to be transformed by the mighty outpouring of your compassion, so that our will to serve others with humility, integrity, and urgency is your desired will for us, your servants.
Giver of Gifts, open our hearts.

Open our eyes, O Sanctifier of Life, to the hurts and needs of others that challenge us to ministry. Teach us to see where our own abilities and resources—and the world's deep hunger—meet.
Sanctifier of Life, open our eyes.

Open our hands, O Spirit, to be your instruments of witness. Help us to work without caution, serve without recognition, to do justice, to love kindness, and to serve humbly with you, our God.
Spirit, open our hands.

Open our memories, O Redeemer of All, as we tenderly remember those who have died. (*Please add your petitions, silently or aloud.*) Help us honor the wisdom of those who devoted their earthly lives to your service, and who generously gave of their time and treasure.
Redeemer of All, open our memories.

The Leader may conclude with this Collect:
Nurturing God, your love is free, your compassion unconditional, and your mercy infinite. You shower upon us gifts abundant. Grant that we may know and trust these gifts, that we may discover the joy they bring, and inspire us to serve and love out of that joy. In the name of the Risen Christ we pray. *Amen.*

—*The Reverend Devon Anderson*

These prayers were composed for the Diocese of Michigan 1999 convention in honor of women's ministries of stewardship.

Litanies

Four Directions: A Native American Litany

The ceremony begins in darkness. Four readers are needed for this ritual. All stand in a circle around the altar or the cross. Each reads one of the "directions" prayers. Four candles are lighted as the four directional words are spoken. When the prayer begins, all face east, then turn to the south, west, and north. All face the center of the circle for the concluding prayer.

The Leader and People pray responsively

We look to the east and give honor
and thanks to the Creator for all gifts given
Place of rising sun comes red color
our time of infancy, time of emotional growth
receive love for all that is to come
We give honor and thanks to the Creator

We look to the south and give honor
and thanks to the Creator for all gifts given
Place of warmth comes golden color
our time of childhood, time of physical growth
receive strength for our visit upon Mother Earth
We give honor and thanks to the Creator

We look to the west and give honor
and thanks to the Creator for all gifts given
Place of setting sun comes black color
our time of adulthood, time to seek knowledge
bear fruit for the generations to come
We give honor and thanks to the Creator

We look to the north and give honor
and thanks to the Creator for all gifts given
Place of the Ancient Ones comes color white
Our time of being an Elder, time of Wisdom
spirituality lives to go forth
We look to the center of our being and give
honor and thanks to the Creator for all gifts given

In the center of this sacredness
we honor all we have become
to live with the Good Mind

It is done now, we are complete with the Creator
and now we can go forth to see what we must make
to take us where we need to be
that place where love and peace surround
We go with the Creator with us

—Ms. Ginny Doctor

Oración por las Mujeres que se Atreven a Crecer
(Prayer for Women Who Have Dared to Grow)

The Leader and People pray responsively

Por todas aquellas que hemos dejado atrás lo conocido
para arriesgarnos a entrar en lo desconocido
Te damos gracias, Dios del universo

Por todas aquellas que hemos venido con esperanza
Para arriesgarnos a entrar en lo desconocido
Te damos gracias, Dios del mundo

Por todas aquellas que hemos escogido venir
A pesar de nuestros temores y dudas
Te damos gracias, Dios de las naciones

Por todas aquellas que traemos nuestro entusiasmo,
energía, y visión
Te damos gracias, Dios de nuestra comunidad

Pos todas aquellas que hemos venido aquí en busca
De respuestas para nuestras preguntas
Te damos gracias, Dios de nuestra reunión

Por todas aquellas que no están seguras por que
Han venido a estas reuniones
O no están seguras adonde van
Te damos gracias, Dios de nuestra vida

Dios, te traemos nuestras dudas, nuestros temores, nuestras esperanzas
Nuestras habilidades, y nuestro entusiasmo, con la seguridad de que
Tu estas obrando en nuestro medio
Amen.

—*The Reverend Carmen B. Guerrero*

If you do not read Spanish, please find a Hispanic friend to translate this moving litany for you.

Blessing the Bread: A Litany for Many Voices

In the beginning was God,
In the beginning
    The source of all that is,
In the beginning
    God yearning,
    God moaning,
    God laboring,
    God giving birth,
    God rejoicing.

And God loved what she had made.
And God said,
    "It is good!"
And God, knowing that all good is shared,
Held the earth tenderly in her arms.
God yearned for relationship,
God longed to share the good earth,
And humanity was born in the yearning of God—
We were born to share the earth.

In the earth was the seed,
In the seed was the grain,
In the grain was the harvest,
In the harvest was the bread,
In the bread was the power,

And God said,
    "All shall eat of the earth,
    All shall eat of the seed,

All shall eat of the grain,
All shall eat of the harvest,
All shall eat of the bread,
All shall eat of the power!"

God said,
    "You are my people—
My friends,
My lovers,
My sisters,
And brothers,
All of you shall eat
Of the bread
And the power.
All shall eat!"

Then God, gathering up her courage in love, said,
    "Let there be bread!"
And God's sisters,
Her friends and lovers,
Knelt on the earth,
Planted the seeds,
Prayed for the rain,
Sang for the grain,
Made the harvest,
Cracked the wheat,
Pounded the corn,
Kneaded the dough,
Kindled the fire,
Filled the air,
With the smell of fresh bread.
And there was bread—
And it was good!

We the sisters of God say today,
    "All shall eat of the bread
And the power."
We say today,
"All shall have power
And bread."
Today we say,
"Let there be bread!

Let there be power!
Let us eat of the bread
And the power!
And all will be filled
For the bread is rising!"

By the power of God,
Women are blessed.
By the women of God,
The bread is blessed.
By the bread of God,
The power is blessed.
By the power of bread,
The power of women,
The power of God,
The people are blessed,
The earth is blessed,
And the bread is rising!

—*The Reverend Dr. Carter Heyward*

This litany was written to commemorate International Women's Year, Lafayette Park, Washington, D.C., 1978, and published in Our Passion for Justice.

Litany of Remembrance

The Leader and People pray responsively

Let us remember and give thanks for faithful women of God,
that their lives may inspire ours.
For Miriam, prophet who led the women of Israel in rejoicing at
their deliverance from Egypt;
For the unnamed woman who acted as prophet and anointed
Jesus before his burial;
God of abundant life,
We give you thanks.

That we may claim our gifts of leadership and have courage to
announce your truth by our words and actions,
God of graceful power,
We offer our prayer.

For Joanna and Susanna, disciples who followed Jesus and
supported him in his ministry;
For Mary Magdalene, disciple and first witness to the Resurrection,
who proclaimed the Good News;
For women leaders in the early Church: for Phoebe, Prisca, and Junia;
God of abundant life,
We give you thanks.

That we and all your Church may follow Christ faithfully and
bear witness to the good news of God in Christ Jesus,
God of graceful power,
We offer our prayer.

For the woman who had hemorrhaged for twelve years and
dared to touch the hem of your garment;
For the woman who had been bent over for eighteen years
and came to you for healing;
God of abundant life,
We give you thanks.

That we may recognize your healing grace and
be healed from all that weakens or cripples us;
That your healing grace may be with any who are sick or suffering;
God of graceful power,
We offer our prayer.

For women mystics of the Middle Ages: for Hildegard of Bingen,
Teresa of Avila, and Julian of Norwich, who used many names and
images to praise you and tell of your goodness and love;
God of abundant life,
We give you thanks.

That we may know you ever more deeply and praise you
as one God with many names;
God of graceful power,
We offer our prayer.

For the women of this country who fought against slavery and
worked for justice for all people: for Sojourner Truth, Harriet Tubman,
Eleanor Roosevelt, Rosa Parks;
For the women who struggled for women's rights: for Elizabeth Cady
Stanton and Susan B. Anthony;
God of abundant life,
We give you thanks.

That we may be empowered to strive for justice and
peace among all people;
God of graceful power,
We offer our prayer.

For women of the Episcopal Church who were leaders in mission
and ministry: for Mary Abbott Emery Twing, first national secretary
of the Women's Auxiliary; for Julia Chester Emery, leader of the Women's
Auxiliary for forty years; for Susan Knapp, deaconess and Dean of the New
York Training School for Deaconesses;
For the work of the Council for Women's Ministries and
for the member organizations of the Council;
God of abundant life,
We give you thanks.

That we may be faithful to the ministries to which you call us,
God of graceful power,
We offer our prayer.

Life-giving God, you have healed and empowered women
throughout all ages,
Grant that we may follow their examples and live faithfully as
your people in the world, in the name of Jesus Christ. Amen.

—*The Reverend Dr. Ruth A. Meyers*

Litany of Thanksgiving
Breaking Open the Jar: Remembrance and Hope—Mark 14:3–9

The Leader and the People pray responsively
We rejoice in the perseverance of women who, with Sarah, trust in God's
power to bring new life.
Truly I tell you, wherever the Good News is proclaimed in the whole world,
what she has done will be told in remembrance of her.

We rejoice in the prophetic words of women who, with Anna, announce
the Christ-child to all who are looking for the redemption of the world.
Truly I tell you, wherever the Good News is proclaimed in the whole world,
what she has done will be told in remembrance of her.

We rejoice in the faithfulness of women who, with Hannah, pray fervently,
exulting in the One who raises up the poor from the dust.

Truly I tell you, wherever the Good News is proclaimed in the whole world,
what she has done will be told in remembrance of her.

We rejoice in the strength and gifts of women who, with Prisca, lead the church in service to Christ Jesus.
Truly I tell you, wherever the Good News is proclaimed in the whole world,
what she has done will be told in remembrance of her.

We rejoice in the commitment of women who, with Ruth, devote themselves to relationships that bring wholeness and fulfillment.
Truly I tell you, wherever the Good News is proclaimed in the whole world,
what she has done will be told in remembrance of her.

We rejoice in the bold witness of women who, with the woman at Bethany, break open precious jars to bring glory to Jesus Christ.
Truly I tell you, wherever the Good News is proclaimed in the whole world,
what she has done will be told in remembrance of her.

—The Reverend Linda D. Anderson-Little
(Evangelical Lutheran Church in America)

Litany for Women Raising Special Children

The Leader and People pray responsively

When hope seems lost and doubt weakens faith,
O Lord, strengthen us.

In times of trouble when fear sets in,
O Lord, give us courage.

When desperation governs and judgment is clouded,
O Lord, forgive us.

That we may remember your promise and remain steadfast in our faith,
O Lord, strengthen us.

Give us grace that we may continue to do the work you have given us to do,
O Lord, strengthen us.

That we may become your instruments of peace and love to our families and friends,
Lord, hear our prayer.

That we may learn from the graciousness and generosity of Mary, the mother of our Lord Jesus.
Grant us wisdom.

Touch the hearts of all who dwell or work with us that they also may seek your love and deliverance.
Lord, hear our prayer.

The Leader may conclude with this Collect:
Lord, you have graciously entrusted us with the care of your special children. Grant us the courage to do your will to the best of our abilities, and the patience to wait for your grace and understanding. Give us strength to withstand the trying times, bearing in mind your promise to never put more on us than we can bear. Endow us, Lord, with the wisdom to make the right choices for those we love. All this we ask through Jesus Christ, our help and our redeemer. *Amen.*

—*Ms. Salome Chiduzie Nwosu*

I am a divorced mother of two. My son, who is eighteen now, has Asperger's Syndrome, similar to autism. My major source of relief has always been talking to my Lord and trying to help others in the same situation.

Litany for Healing

The Leader and People pray responsively

Healer God, we come before you paralyzed:
Paralyzed with fear for what tomorrow may bring;
Paralyzed with the pain of our friends, our loved ones, and ourselves;
Paralyzed by realities that seem to leave no room for hope.
God of action, help us to raise the roof over our heads:
Raise the roof and let light shine through;
Raise the roof and bring us closer to your presence;
Raise the roof and let hope into the rooms of our hearts.

God of love and compassion, we ask your forgiveness for our sins:
Sins of anger and fear;
Sins of hopelessness and despair;
Sins of indifference and denial;
Sins of accusation and judgment;
Sins that overpower hope, and faith, and miracles.

Miraculous God, help us to have faith in miracles:
Miracles that stop the flow of blood
Tears
Anger
Blame
Judgment;
Miracles that restore our bodies
Souls
Spirits
Relationships
Faith;
Miracles that enable us to love
Forgive
Act
Heal
Live.

Healing God, work mightily in our lives today,
Acting,
Loving,
Forgiving,
Making miracles,
That healing and being healed, we may walk again. Amen.

—*Ms. Shirin McArthur*

I wrote this litany for an AIDS healing service at Trinity Church in Boston. The gospel passage for that evening was the healing of the paralytic whose friends let him down through the roof (Mark 2).

Litany for Unsafe Neighborhoods

During the silence following each bidding, the People may offer their own prayers, either silently or aloud.

Let us begin by telling the truth about safety in our own lives.

We thank you for our families and friends, for laws and their enforcement, for our sense of well-being and security. We thank you especially for

Silence

God of grace,
Be with us.

We confess that we often feel uneasy, that there are people in our lives who are inappropriate and even violent, that the world and even our own dwellings can be frightening. We confess especially

Silence

God of protection,
Be with us.

O God, please touch us where we need comfort; push us to change patterns of living and thinking that are unsafe or harbor violence; place in our lives allies to stand with us when we are afraid; give us the words to speak when we are voiceless. We ask especially for

Silence

God of strength,
Be with us.

Let us now pray for others who are unsafe.

We pray for women, men, and children in countries that are at war from within and without. We pray especially for

Silence

God of justice,
Be with us.

We confess our complicity in the lack of safety in our neighborhoods by our own violations of laws and rights, by our own inaction on behalf of the safety of those we call "others," by our own place in the "way things are." We confess especially

Silence

God of mercy,
Be with us.

We hear your call to come closer to you by being with the poor, those in prison, those with no family or friends, and those who are sick. Yet we rarely venture beyond our own sphere. We hear especially your call to

Silence

God of the oppressed,
Be with us.

Collect
O God, you can make us whole by binding us one to the other. We are all one neighborhood. We ask you to open our eyes and ears; show us the way to safety in our own lives. Give us the courage and wisdom to join together to achieve safety for all; in the name of the Source, the Word, and the Spirit. *Amen.*

—*The Reverend Deborah W. Little*

Litany for Unity in a Congregation

Deacon or other leader
Most Gracious God, help us to respect and love those who do your work in our congregation. God in your mercy,
Hear our prayer.

Enable us to live in peace with all our sisters and brothers in this church. God in your mercy,
Hear our prayer.

Remind us to encourage the timid, help the weak, and uplift the dispirited. God in your mercy,
Hear our prayer.

Let us never repay wrong for wrong, but always forgive one another in your name. God in your mercy,
Hear our prayer.

Teach us to test our own actions in light of your Word. God in your mercy,
Hear our prayer.

Let us recognize the Holy Spirit at work in our church. God in your mercy,
Hear our prayer.

Give us the grace to be joyful and to give thanks in all circumstances. God in your mercy,
Hear our prayer.

Help us to pray without ceasing all the days of our lives. God in your mercy,
Hear our prayer.

Dear Father, sanctify us through and through. God in your mercy,
Hear our prayer.

All this we ask in the name of your Son Jesus Christ our Lord, who lives and reigns with you and the Holy Spirit, one God, for ever and ever. *Amen.*

—*Ms. Bonnie S. Bashor*

Pastoral Liturgies

Rite for Pregnancy Loss or Stillbirth

Opening Sentences and Prayers

Officiant	In the name of God, the giver of Life
	who creates and loves us all.
	The Lord be with you.
People	And also with you.
Officiant	Let us pray.

Loving God, source of Life and Love, we come before you this day with aching hearts. We had hoped to gather in the midst of your holy people to celebrate with *N.* and *N.* the birth of their child. Instead, we are here to mourn with them this unexpected and profound loss. O Lord, we cannot understand why this gift has been snatched away, and we pray that your Holy Spirit be present with us as we gather here this day. Bless *N.* and *N.* with the assurance of your love, and fill them with the knowledge that you are a companion to them in their grief. We ask this in the name of your own Child who died and rose again, Jesus Christ our Lord. *Amen.*

N. and *N.*, we are here with you today to acknowledge your loss, to be with you in your sorrow, and to be a sign of God's assurance that you are loved.

This segment should be included only if the family is comfortable with the idea of naming and representing the child. In the case of stillbirth, the parents may opt to have the child's body present, in which case the representation will not be necessary.

The psalmist and the prophets promise that God knew your child while *she* was still in *N.'s* womb, and called the child by name. What name have you given to your child?

N./N.: We have named our child *N.*

N. and *N.*, as you prepared your home to receive *N.*, you gathered those things that would keep *her* warm, happy, and healthy. You are invited to present now that which represents for you the child you have lost.

The parents may present a toy, a piece of clothing, a plant, or some other item that will be prominently displayed for the remainder of the service.

N./N.: We present this _____ as a symbol of our child, *N.*

Let us pray.

God, you have searched us out and known us, and we are yours. We dedicate to you the child, *N.*, beloved [though never seen] by *her* parents. We are limited, O God; we cannot see as you see. [Therefore we present to you this _____ as a symbol of the child, *N.*] We ask that you be present to us now as we listen to your Word, that we might hear in it the assurance of your love and companionship at this time. In Jesus' name we pray. *Amen.*

Readings

The parents, if able, or the officiant may choose two or three of the following readings.

Hebrew Scriptures
Isaiah 43:1–4a
Isaiah 49:15–16a
Jeremiah 29:11–13a

Psalm
23 or 91:1–4 or 121

New Testament
Romans 8:38–39

1 John 3:1–2a
Revelation 21:1–5

Gospel
Mark 4:35–39
Luke 9:46–48
John 6:37–39

Homily or Reflections

The officiant may here offer a brief homily or allow the parents to express their own feelings and thoughts.

Silence may be kept.

Prayers

Officiant
Let us pray.
Lord, you have blessed us with feeling and emotions, allowing us to love as you love, but also to grieve as you grieve. We bring before you the many conflicted emotions within us, and ask you to bless them to be a source of strength even among the sorrow. *Amen.*

If possible, the following litany will be read alternately by the parents, petition by one, response by the other.

We bring to you our anger, Lord, which keeps us from turning to you for comfort.
Bless us in our anger, O Lord.

We bring to you our confusion, Lord, as we try to make sense of this senseless loss.
Bless us in our confusion, O Lord.

We bring to you our pain, Lord, as we ache for the child we will never hold.
Bless us in our pain, O Lord.

We bring to you our sorrow, Lord, in the unfulfilled hopes and dreams for this child.
Bless us in our sorrow, O Lord.

We bring to you our emptiness, Lord, the hole left in our home and hearts.
Bless us in our emptiness, O Lord.

We bring to you our loneliness, Lord, where we feel exiled from consolation and comfort.
Bless us in our loneliness, O Lord.

Officiant
God of compassion and companionship, *N.* and *N.* now stand before you in the fragile beauty of their humanity. Bless them in their anger, confusion, pain, sorrow, emptiness, and loneliness. Grant them assurance that nothing can separate them from your love. Grant them peace of mind in their confusion and healing in their pain. Grant them consolation in their sorrow, fill them with your Holy Spirit in their emptiness, and grant them companionship in their journey. Assure them that as the world rushes by, unaware, Jesus will stop by the wayside and be with them.

Officiant [takes the item representing the child from the parents, and] joins the hands of the parents with one another.

God, we release to you this child, lost to the world but found in your presence. Enfold *N. (the child)* in the arms of your mercy. Renew the bond between *N.* and *N.*, that they do not find their hands empty. We ask your Holy Spirit to fill *N.* and *N.*, that they may be honest with each other in their sorrow and pain, patient with each other in their fragility, forgiving each other when their pain causes them to lash out. Let them be a source of strength and love for each other.

Bless their families and friends and all those whose hearts are filled with sadness at this loss. Grant them the assurance that comes with the hope of Resurrection. Grant to all those who sorrow the spirit of faith and courage, that they may have the strength to meet the days to come with steadfastness and patience, not sorrowing without hope, but trusting in your goodness; through the one who is the Resurrection and the life, Jesus Christ our Savior. *Amen.*

The Lord's Prayer may be recited here.

If the officiant is a priest, an appropriate benediction is said, then

Go forth in peace, in the knowledge and love of Christ.

People: Thanks be to God.

—*Ms. Nancy L. Moore*

The opening sentences and portions of the final prayer are from A New Zealand Prayer Book.

Liturgy for Divorce

The Gathering of the People

Dearly beloved: We have come together in the presence of God to witness and bless the separation of this man and this woman who have been bonded in the covenant of marriage. The courts have acknowledged their divorce and we, this day, gather to support them as they give their blessing to one another as each seeks a new life.

In creation, God made the cycle of life to be birth, life, and death; and God has given us the hope of new life through the Resurrection of Jesus Christ, our Savior. The Church recognizes that relationships follow this pattern. While the couple have promised in good faith to love until parted by death, in some marriages the love between a wife and a husband comes to an end sooner. Love dies, and when that happens we recognize that the bonds of marriage, based on love, also may be ended.

God calls us to right relationships based on love, compassion, mutuality, and justice. Whenever any of these elements is absent from a marital relationship, then that partnership no longer reflects the intentionality of God.

The Good News of the Gospel of Jesus Christ is that we are forgiven our sins and our failures, we are raised from the dead and restored to a new life. The death of love, like the death of the grave, has no power to rob us of the life that is intended for the people of God.

Thus we gather this day to support and bless *N.* and *N.* as they confess their brokenness, forgive each other for their transgressions, receive God's blessing, celebrate the new growth that has occurred in each of them, and make commitments for a new life.

The Declaration of Consent

Celebrant: *(to the man)*
N., do you enter into this parting of your own free will; do you confess before God, N., and the Church that you repent your brokenness that kept you in a destructive relationship? Do you seek forgiveness for the mutual respect and justice that you have failed to give and set your spouse free of this relationship, that you and she may receive from God and from each other the gift of new life and move toward health and wholeness once again?

Man: I do.

Celebrant: *(to the woman)*
N., do you enter into this parting of your own free will; do you confess before God, N., and the Church that you repent your brokenness that kept you in a destructive relationship? Do you seek forgiveness for the mutual respect and justice that you have failed to give and set your spouse free of this relationship, that you and he may receive from God and from each other the gift of new life and move toward health and wholeness once again?

Woman: I do.

The Ministry of the Word

Celebrant: The Lord be with you.

People: And also with you.

Celebrant: Let us pray.
O gracious and ever-living God, you have created us male and female in your image. Look mercifully upon N. and N., who come to you seeking your blessing. Forgive them for forsaking their vows and for the pain that they have caused each other. Restore each of them by your grace to a new life of hope, renewal, and growth, and keep them ever in the love of your mercy, through Jesus Christ our Savior. *Amen.*

A Reading from Scripture

Luke 15:1–7 *(Repentance and forgiveness.)*
Luke 9:42b–48 *(Your faith has made you well.)*
Psalm 55:12–23 *(Women who feel rejected.)*

The choice of a reading depends upon the individuals' need, whether for forgiveness or wholeness, or both.

The Undoing of the Vows

The MAN faces the woman, takes her right hand, and says:

In the name of God, I, *N.*, release you, *N.*, from your vow to be my wife. I thank you for the love and support you have given me. I ask your forgiveness for my part in the failure of our marriage.

The WOMAN faces the man, takes his right hand, and says:

In the name of God, I, *N.*, release you, *N.*, from your vow to be my husband. I thank you for the love and support you have given me. I ask your forgiveness for my part in the failure of our marriage.

The CELEBRANT asks each in turn to return their rings:

N., I give you this ring, which you gave me as a symbol of our marriage. In returning it, I set you free. I pray you will find peace and joy in your new life.

The rings are given to the celebrant, who places them upon the altar, or the man and woman may place the rings there themselves.

The CELEBRANT says:

I place these rings upon the altar to symbolize that your lives are lived in the mercy and love of God.

Or, if the couple choose to place their own rings on the altar, the CELEBRANT may say:

These rings are placed upon the altar to symbolize that your lives are lived in the mercy and love of God.

The Prayers

The Lord's Prayer

O God in heaven,
You who are Mother and Father
to us all,
Holy is your name.
Your reign has come.
Your will be done,
on earth as it is in heaven.
Give us today our daily bread.
Forgive us our sin
as we forgive those
who sin against us.
Deliver us from evil.
Save us from the time of trial.
For all time and all space,
all power and all glory are yours;
now and forever. *Amen.*

Let us pray.

Eternal God, creator and preserver of all life, author of salvation and giver of grace: Look with favor upon the world you have made and for which your Son gave his life, and especially upon *N.* and *N.*, who come to you seeking your blessing. Grant unto them grace in moving from the old ways and wisdom in the ordering of their new lives. *Amen.*

Grant that each may know the power of your love to transform death into life and to bring forth the discovery of new identity out of pain. Teach them to trust once again and restore their hope, that once more they may view the world through love-filled eyes. *Amen.*

Bestow on them your Spirit, that *N.* and *N.* may be guided and sustained by you in the choices they individually make. Inspire the service they offer to the world that it may be distinguished by compassion for all. By your grace, may each become a witness to your forgiving and healing love as they reach out to care for the needs of others. *Amen.*

Make their individual lives a sign of Christ's love to this sinful and broken world, that forgiveness may heal guilt, joy conquer despair, and trust be forever placed in you. *Amen.*

The man and woman kneel.

Most gracious God, we give you thanks for your tender love in sending Jesus Christ to come among us, to be born of a human mother, and to make the way of the cross to be the way of life. Defend *N.* and *N.* from every enemy. Lead them both into all peace, to a renewal of life, and the hope of wholeness and love. Bless them in their separate lives, in their work, in their rest, and in their play, in their joys and in their sorrows, in their life and in their death. Finally, in your mercy, bring each to that table where your saints feast forever in the blessing of your presence and love, through Jesus Christ, who with you and the Holy Spirit, lives and reigns, One God, for ever and ever. *Amen.*

Benediction

The blessing of God whose breath gives life
be with you always.

The blessing of God whose
love is forgiving
set you free from guilt and despair.

The blessing of God
who sanctifies your living
be with you this day,
to lead you to a new life
of hope, peace, love, and service.

May God be praised and glorified through your lives,
now and forever. *Amen.*

—The Reverend Dr. Vienna Cobb Anderson

The preceding prayer contains, by design, some familiar words from the wedding service of the Episcopal Church. They are to be found in "The Celebration and Blessing of a Marriage," The Book of Common Prayer, © *Church Pension Fund.*

Litany after Suicide

Most Gracious God, be with the friends and family of *N.* in their shock and grief over the sudden loss of their loved one.
We pray to you, O God.

Comfort them with the knowledge that you were with *N.* in *her* despair, and you knew the depth of *her* pain.
We pray to you, O God.

Sustain them with your limitless love when feelings of self-doubt, guilt, anger, or blame threaten to overcome them.
We pray to you, O God.

Hold them close to your heart in their dark night of endless questions and endless tears.
We pray to you, O God.

Remove from them all feelings of shame, for they and *N.* are all beloved children, created in your glorious image.
Hear our prayer, O God.

Help them to forgive themselves as they remember the last days and moments of *N.'s* life, that they may be healed of the wounds inflicted to their own body, mind, spirit.
Hear our prayer, O God.

Guide them in midst of their confusion and bewilderment as they seek to come to terms with the choice *N.* made.
Hear our prayer, O God.

Surround them today and always with the love of their family, friends, and church communities in the aftermath of this tragic death.
Hear our prayer, O God.

Collect
Most Gracious and Loving God, comfort us in the sure and certain knowledge that you can do more for *N.* now than we can even ask or imagine. Receive *her* into the arms of your everlasting mercy. Protect us as a mother bear protects her cubs; lead us as a tender shepherd leads his flock; in the name of your Child Jesus Christ, who lived, and died, and rose again that we might know the joy of your Resurrection. *Amen.*

—The Reverend Elizabeth Rankin Geitz

Pastoral Prayers

For the Oppressed

May God who sets the prisoner free and gives sight to the blind come to us who seek the Divine Presence in our daily lives through the prayers we offer. In recognition of our personal suffering, may we join with all oppressed people: those suffering with incurable diseases; the elderly who lack security; women and men caught in the spiral of success; the mentally ill who have no place to turn for help; the hungry and homeless whose life is tenuous; children who are abused; those who are dependent upon alcohol or drugs; parents under financial stress and the strain of raising children in today's world; single parents with constant demands; women who have been abused or ignored; those who are victims of classism and greed; men who feel imprisoned by their roles; young people who are abandoned and alienated from society; nations who struggle under the burden of debt; and all the people of God in every condition of life; that together we may pass from the bondage of Egypt into the wilderness of our formation, and to the land where all God's promises are realized; for this we pray. *Amen.*

—The Rt. Reverend Geralyn Wolf

For Women

Eternal Spirit, Earth-maker, Pain-bearer, Life-giver, Source of all that is and that shall be, Father and Mother of us all, Loving God, in whom is heaven:*
Awaken us with your Holy Spirit,
  and preserve us from the temptation to stay comfortably asleep;
encourage us to proclaim our authenticity,
  and preserve us from a false accommodation to the world;
breathe into us your breath of life,
  stir us up into activity,
  and preserve us from the inertia that leads to complicity in our own
    oppression;
open our eyes to the promises in creation,
open our hearts to the love and example of Jesus,
open our ears to the persistent whisperings of the Holy Spirit,
  and preserve us from a sense-deadened existence;
give us the confidence to engage technology
  and preserve us from regarding it with fear or with too much trust;

remind us that we are made in your image,
 that we, too, are creators, lovers, decision makers;
instill in us the pride of our heritage,
 and preserve us from excessive, crippling humility.
Above all, gracious God,
 give us the grace to hear your word to us
 and the courage to claim and act on that inner authority;
 preserve us from the tyranny of the external authority that comes from
  the world. *Amen.*

—*The Reverend Margaret Cunningham*

*From A New Zealand Prayer Book.

For Healing from Abuse

Jesus, by your gentle touch and encouraging word, you raised up the woman who had been bent over: Lift up the heads and hearts of those who have been bowed down by the shame and pain of (sexual) abuse. Heal them so that they may stand up with dignity and may praise you through the living of their lives in fullness and in hope. *Amen.*

—*The Reverend Canon Lorna H. Williams*

For Compulsive Overeaters

Gracious God, you spread a table of true nourishment in the wilderness and invite us all to feast: Let your loving presence fill the yearning hearts of all who run to excess food for solace or escape. Relieve our shame, heal our self-hatred and remorse, and wrap us in the cloak of your compassion. Give us courage to reach out for help and the grace to accept it. Uphold us daily with your power as we learn to care for our bodies and to listen to their needs. Strengthen us to seek the food that really satisfies and to discover that in the sweetness of your presence whoever comes to you will never hunger and whoever believes in you will never thirst. *Amen.*

—*The Reverend Margaret Bullitt-Jonas*

For Recovery

Healing Lord, God of our understanding, whose grace has given us a program of recovery: Keep us mindful that sobriety is not of our own doing but comes solely from you. Grant that we may continually seek to do your will and make us ever aware that you are always with us on this perilous journey; through Jesus Christ, our Lord. *Amen.*

—*Mrs. Katherine Johnson*

For Children

O God, we thank you for the treasure of children in our midst: Watch over them as they learn and play; keep them safe from harm; imbue them with wisdom; defend them from all evil; help us to meet their needs, and hold all of us in the palm of your hand; through Jesus Christ, your beloved Son, who lives and reigns with you and the Holy Spirit, now and forever. *Amen.*

—*Robin Antonia Hendrich, Esq.*

For a Child Who Has Been Molested

Most loving God,
she has been severely wounded,
hurt beyond words
with the betrayal of trust,
physical violence and abuse,
and the absence of love.
Bless *her*
with the abundance of your love
and with the support of loving people
who will help heal the wounds,
restore confidence and trust,
and teach *her*
to love again;
in the name of Jesus Christ
we pray. *Amen.*

—*The Reverend Dr. Vienna Cobb Anderson*

For Those in Nursing Homes

Bless, O God, with your Holy Wisdom, these daughters and sons whom you love. Even as we honor them for your gift of human wisdom—cherished and nourished through all their years—so now endow them, we pray, with wisdom and insight to know you ever more closely, to feel the motherly arms of your Holy Wisdom holding them, comforting, whispering "Courage," singing old songs of "God loves you, God loves you, now and forever be blessed." In the name of our God: Loving Parent, Healer, and Comforter. *Amen.*

—The Reverend Sharon K. Dunn

For People in the Midst of War

O God, you have loved each of us since before we were born, and you love each of us in equal and abundant measure. Yet we sometimes choose not to see ourselves in one another. We sometimes choose to live as though we were not the brothers and sisters we know ourselves to be. Pour your blessing upon all your people in every nation (*especially in N., for whom we pray today*), whatever their faith or ethnicity. Preserve their lives, deliver them from the terror of war, and, when this is over, guide them in the way of reconciliation and peace. Bring them a deepening sense of their oneness in the human family, that those things that unite your people may be seen and felt as greater than anything that can ever divide us. *Amen.*

—The Reverend Barbara Cawthorne Crafton

Prayers for the Church

For the Anglican Communion

Holy and gracious God, you cast your net of love so wide and gather us from the ends of the earth: So bless and guide our Anglican Communion that we may be held fast in the bonds of our affection for one another and in our love and service of you, through our Savior, Jesus Christ, who with you and the Holy Spirit reigns now and for ever. *Amen.*

—The Rt. Reverend Catherine S. Roskam

For Reconciliation

O God, in you all things are reconciled and no estrangement is found: Give us hope, even when we can see no way beyond the present conflict. You are the one who acts with power when human action fails. Forgive and heal our failure to find the way by ourselves, our human inability even to imagine forgiveness, our human preference for victory over reconciliation, and our perverse suspicion that even to see another point of view besides our own is to capitulate and lose face. Help us to seek our worth in your love for us, and not in any imagined superiority of one over another. You, O God, who bring good even from great evil, are one God for all people, and so we pray to you in hope. *Amen.*

—*The Reverend Barbara Cawthorne Crafton*

For Times of Change

Assist us, Lord, in living hopefully into the future. In the face of change, help us to set unnecessary fears aside and to recognize our potential for creative response. Help us to develop a reasonable optimism when confronted by "the new" and to guard against our own defensiveness. Be with us as we remember and celebrate former times, and keep us from unreasonable yearning for them, which takes us from the work you have set before us in our time. All this we ask in the name of your Child, our Savior, Jesus Christ. *Amen.*

—*The Reverend Linda C. Smith-Criddle*

For Welcoming

Holy Spirit living within us, guide our hearts and minds as we welcome today all those who worship with us at *N.* Give us discerning hearts so that every one who crosses our threshold feels welcomed in the spirit of your love. Help us to recognize each person as an individual sent by you who will enrich our lives. And most of all, O God, let this be a place of love and acceptance of all your children; in the name of your Child, our Savior, Jesus Christ. *Amen.*

—*Ms. Valecia Harriman*

For Stewards

Thank you, God, for making us your stewards. Stewards are the servants whose task it is to see that this earth and all of your Creation are used according to your purpose. We are those entrusted with the care of the members of your family. We are to see that the meal is prepared and set before them at your table. It is with joy that we assume this place of honor and responsibility in your household. As stewards, we acknowledge that all things come from you. All that we have is your own. Please accept our gifts of time, skill, money, and possessions. These are expressions of our love for you, a love like no other, as it has its origin in the love you first lavished upon us. Help us to do our work, according to your will and pleasure, that all may know the wonder and magnificent abundance of a life in your service. Accept this prayer in the name of Jesus, the Christ. *Amen.*

—*Ms. Terese A. (Terry) Parsons*

For Leaders

Almighty God, you have given us responsibility for the leadership of the Church for a season. Grant us patience, courage, and wisdom to discern your will amidst the many competing claims and conflicts of this present time. Give us an appreciative memory for all who have gone before, and a strong clear vision of the Church of the future. Let us exercise our stewardship with energy and enthusiasm, so that, when the time comes, we may joyfully relinquish our tasks to those who will come after. We ask this in the name of our redeemer, Jesus Christ, who calls us into fellowship and sends the Holy Spirit to guide and inspire us, generation after generation, that we may do all to your greater glory. *Amen.*

—*Dr. Pamela P. Chinnis*

A Seminarian's Prayer

Gracious God, you formed me in my mother's womb and called me to service in your Church: Enlighten my mind with your wisdom and truth, deliver me from pretension, pride, and preoccupation with self, and conform me daily to the image of your Son, that my ministry among your people may be an offering of prayer and praise to you, for the upbuilding of your Church and the in-breaking of your kingdom; through our Savior Jesus Christ, who with you and the Holy Spirit lives and reigns, now and for ever. *Amen.*

—*The Very Reverend Martha J. Horne*

Prayers for Special Occasions

For Families During Holidays

O Gracious God, as our families gather for this holiday season, let us help each other erase the barriers that can become shields at these seasonal meetings. As the blood flows through our veins from one generation to another, let us dwell on the goodness and dismiss the errors, the hurts, and the memories of misdeeds. Let us all become as children of all innocence, full of the excitement of the year ahead and full of the wonders of new discoveries about ourselves and about the good in others and in our world; in the name of your Child, our Savior, Jesus Christ. *Amen.*

—*Ms. Esther H. Moon*

For Mother's Day

On this Mother's Day, we give thanks to God for the divine gift of motherhood in all its diverse forms. Let us pray for all the mothers among us today; for our own mothers, those living and those who have passed away; for the mothers who loved us and for those who fell short of loving us fully; for all who hope to be mothers someday and for those whose hope to have children has been frustrated; for all mothers who have lost children; for all women and men who have mothered others in any way—those who have been our substitute mothers and we who have done so for those in need; and for the earth that bore us and provides us with our sustenance. We pray this all in the name of God, our great and loving Mother. *Amen.*

—*The Reverend Leslie Nipps*

For Dreamers

Gracious and Austere God,
Grant us, we pray, the will to declare ourselves
Hearers,
Bearers,
And Dreamers,
Of your life-giving word.
Amen.

—*Fredrica Harris Thompsett, Ph.D.*

Women and other mystics have often come to know God in dreams as well as in the Word. This prayer unites these sources of knowing.

Contributors

Italics indicate a published work by the contributor.